CONSCIOUSNESS
AND CULTURE

Consciousness and Culture

Emerson and Thoreau Reviewed

Joel Porte

YALE UNIVERSITY PRESS/NEW HAVEN & LONDON

Designed by Mary Valencia.
Set in Caslon type by Achorn Graphic Services.
Printed in the United States of America by Sheridan Books.

Library of Congress Cataloging-in-Publication Data
Porte, Joel.
Consciousness and culture : Emerson and Thoreau reviewed / Joel Porte.
p. cm.
Includes bibliographical references (p.) and index.
ISBN 0-300-10446-4 (alk. paper)
1. Emerson, Ralph Waldo, 1803-1882—Criticism and interpretation. 2. Thoreau, Henry
David, 1817–1862—Criticism and interpretation. 3. National characteristics,
American, in literature. 4. New England—Intellectual life—19th century.
5. Consciousness in literature. 6. Culture in literature. I. Title.
PS1638.P665 2004
810.9′003—dc22
2004043842

A catalogue record for this book is available from the British Library.

The paper in this book meets the guidelines for permanence and durability
of the Committee on Production Guidelines for Book Longevity of the Council
on Library Resources.

10 9 8 7 6 5 4 3 2 1

TO THE MEMORY OF EMILIE A. DIXON

CONTENTS

CONTENTS

PREFACE

Some years ago, Perry Miller, publishing a volume of Thoreau's "lost" journal, entitled his book *Consciousness in Concord*, suggesting that Thoreau confronted his townsmen with a "rustic caricature of the Byronic egotist." Thoreau's exquisite nurturing of his "consciousness," in the high Romantic mode, led Miller to believe that Thoreau's exploitation of the natural resources of his native village was as "self-centered, as profit-seeking, as that of any railroad-builder or lumber-baron, as that of any John Jacob Astor."[1]

Miller's use of an aggressively mercantile figure here is an example of a hyperbolic rhetoric that brought down imprecations on his head from the pens of less flamboyant scholars. Miller's point—that Thoreau believed "that pure consciousness solved all riddles"—is probably over the mark in its insistence that Thoreau was interested only in himself, that he was engaged in a perpetual process of intellectual, emotional, and spiritual pulse-taking that tended to put nature underfoot: "This lover of Nature was not a lover of nature itself" but rather of the "raw materials of tropes and figures" that he could draw from the natural world. I argue that such a gimlet-eyed view of Thoreau as a naturalist scants a crucial aspect of his work. Thoreau conceived of himself as "a mystic—a transcendentalist—& a natural philosopher to boot." It is accordingly a mistake, I believe, to privilege one of these terms over the other two. If "transcendentalist" means a sublime egotist, that may indeed be one Thoreau mood—but only one. Thoreau in fact tells us on the first page of *Walden* that he will indulge himself, in his narrative, by using the "I" throughout though it is usually supressed "in most books." That, he insists, employing a very Thoreauvian pun, is "the main difference" between his book and others—at least "with respect to egotism." A form of address that appears to be self-regarding does indeed represent a kind of "egotism"; but it is always, he goes on to say, "the first person that is speaking." We are the inevitable center of our perceptions and discourse; but the "eye," as Emerson tells us, is only the "first circle": from there we move out.[2]

The "I"—consciousness—as Emerson also tells us, is "double," living in two worlds at the same time: the mundane world of the "understanding" and the more exalted world of "the soul." (W. E. B. DuBois would give his own twist to Emerson's "double consciousness" later in *The Souls of Black Folk*.) So the term "consciousness" itself contains both a "high" and a "low" component. From one point of view, the nurturing of "consciousness" is a sacred duty enjoined on all of us by the requirement of developing what we now call "self-esteem." In the transcendentalist period this duty was frequently referred to under the rubric of "self-culture" and associated with the name of William Ellery Channing (though as I point out later, Frederic Henry Hedge also wrote on the subject in a *Dial* essay that Emerson and Thoreau both read). In a lecture delivered in September 1838, Channing insisted that "he who possesses the divine powers of the soul is a great being." Self-culture, defined as "the care which every man owes to himself, to the unfolding and perfecting of his nature," is egotistical in only a very narrow sense. It represents consciousness—a "self-searching" and "self-comprehending power"—employed to the end of developing a "self-forming power." If the locus of this work is initially personal, its use is finally social: the nurturing and elevating of the individual soul for the purpose of improving the condition of all humanity. There can be little doubt that both Emerson and Thoreau thought of the nurturing of "consciousness" in this context. If Emerson, for example, has been viewed by some as a reluctant participant in reform movements it is probably owing to his constant return to the question of self-reform or self-culture; as we shall note, his tendency to critique and even lampoon the foibles of actual reform movements can be seen as a necessary prolegomenon to all future efforts at reform. Both Emerson and Thoreau were critical by nature; but their critical impulses were constructive by intent. They were both concerned to represent the best aspects of the American spirit (to "brag for humanity," as Thoreau puts it in *Walden*).[3]

Finally, as provincial and even parochial as the transcendentalist movement appeared in its time, its main thrust was always "cultural" in the fullest sense of that term. *The Dial* may have published its share of self-indulgent maunderings—an example often given is Bronson Alcott's "Orphic Sayings"—but it also attempted to move at least New England into a wider range of reference. It reported at length on European and other foreign thought, art, and music; it was also catholic and comparative in its treatment of religious questions. Its range of reference was broad. Thoreau's work as a translator was especially notable in the journal. But the "translation" in a larger sense of other cultural languages was a deep purpose of *The Dial*.

PREFACE

I have been working on Emerson, Thoreau, and Transcendentalism since my graduate school days, which is to say for more than forty years. Naturally, notoriously, over this long stretch of time modes of critical discourse have changed and I have adjusted my own focus and critical vocabulary not so much to keep up with the times as to reflect my immersion, willy-nilly, in the mutating intellectual fields of force that have had an impact on how literary study is done. In 1960, for example, few scholars were talking about "cultural work" or the status of the "text" as a made object shaped not just by authors but also by the material conditions—social, economic—under which books get written (an exception: the still indispensible work of William Charvat). "Literary Theory," mainly relegated to departments of comparative literature, was not the subject of anxious concern generally (though we did have Wellek and Warren's *Theory of Literature,* and such influential work as Renato Poggioli's *The Theory of the Avant-Garde* and Northrop Frye's *Anatomy of Criticism*). Apart from the myth and symbol school that was fashionable for a while in American studies—and I wondered why Perry Miller used to fulminate ungenerously about R. W. B. Lewis's *The American Adam;* I loved it!—the reigning methodology that shaped my thinking was that of "intellectual history," as practiced by such figures as Arthur Lovejoy and Miller himself. Miller's commanding obsession was "the mind of America" (which often appeared to mean just the mind of New England)—a sweeping hypostatization that had a strong appeal, although like Emerson's "Oversoul" it seemed to exist in a realm apart that floated over the less exalted and frequently messy particulars that struck me as an important part of the cultural mix.

My doctoral dissertation, begun in 1960 under the direction of Perry Miller, became my first book, *Emerson and Thoreau: Transcendentalists in Conflict.* In it I tried to document an intellectual debate that seemed to me central to "transcendentalism" in its various strains; but the book suffered, under Miller's influence, from an exaggerated polemical stance that led me, essentially, to take Thoreau's part and underestimate the subtleties of Emerson's writing. I would try to make up for that failing by writing *Representative Man: Ralph Waldo Emerson in His Time* (1979). The second part of that title was intended to register not only an essentially historical point of view but also my desire to take the measure of Emerson's "time" in a different sense—charting the rhythms and seasons of his life story. But I actually began to modify my polemical approach to these linked figures in an essay published in 1968, "Emerson, Thoreau, and the Double Consciousness," which viewed them as working more cooperatively on a question that joined them as much as separated them. Perhaps without entirely realizing it, I was moving away from the static definitions of transcendentalism I had inherited from the previous work of others and toward a more fluid approach to this troubling rubric that could accommodate shifting positions and fruitful deconstructions (as accomplished later in the "detranscendentalizing" of Emerson by such critics as Lawrence Buell, Michael Lopez, and Richard Poirier). As we know, the word "transcendental"—especially in the phrase "transcendental signified"—would come into bad odor as a result of the relentless demystifying process to which Derrida and his followers were subjecting the Western "logocentric" tradition. But we remember that Kant wanted nothing to do with the "transcendent," which he took to be little more than linguistic hocus-pocus. And even Emerson himself could be a little wry on his signature term, as when he reported that "the view taken of Transcendentalism in State Street is that it threatens to invalidate contracts," or that it was reported it had something to do with teeth. Still, the belief that there is a higher law than "contracts," or that there exists a kind of meta-dentistry that might enable us to digest the divine, is hard to put down entirely. And certainly Emerson continued to experience moods in which the transcendental—"the pledge & the herald of all that is dear to the human heart, grand and inspiring to human faith"—lifted his spirit and drove his pen.[4] The same is true of Thoreau, though he might sometimes arrive at his higher laws through the modalities of ordinary experience. Yet Stanley Cavell was in the process of teaching us that the "quest of the ordinary" was also crucial to Emerson's work. The truth is that both Emerson and Thoreau could feel transcendental or descendental by turns and write accordingly.

Attempting to track their varying moods, I would over the years find myself working both sides of the street as I explored this endless dialectic of "high" and "low," the "prudential" and the "heroic," the common and the uncommon, the canny and the uncanny, in the work of Emerson, Thoreau, and their fellow travelers. Thus another piece I undertook after completing my dissertation, "Transcendental Antics," first delivered at a University of Houston symposium in 1967 and then published in *Veins of Humor* (edited by Harry Levin, 1972), played with the comic aspects of a movement that could at times seem insufferably high-minded.

"The Problem of Emerson," published in *Uses of Literature* (edited by Monroe Engel, 1973), has a special place in this series of essays, for it proposed a reading of Emerson favoring the actual texture of his writing more than his transcendental "ideas." Some students and friends have suggested that this is one of my better efforts and that it helped to initiate the Emerson "revival" that has been so conspicuous a feature of American literary studies over the past thirty years. If that is true, the virtue of the essay is mainly its injunction that no author, no matter how important his or her place in the ongoing "cultural work" of a nation, can continue to live without the detailed attention to texts that forms the basis of literary study.

The next three pieces are linked to specific occasions. "Representing America" was read at the Boston Public Library in April 1982 as one of a series of events to commemorate the centennial of Emerson's death. It was composed as a response to Quentin Anderson's notion (to me wrong-headed) that Emerson represented little more than an "imperial self" refusing to engage in the common life of his time. (And, indeed, the most recent turn in Emerson studies has concerned itself with the extent and nature of Emerson's involvement in the movement for social justice and reform—especially as regards slavery.) The seed to the talk was actually sown the previous year, when I participated, along with Conrad Wright, in a symposium at the Unitarian Church in Harvard Square, Cambridge, organized to discuss A. Bartlett Giamatti's attack on Emerson in his address at the Yale commencement in 1981. "Emerson as Journalist" was read at an MLA panel in 1984 put together by J. A. Leo Lemay to celebrate the publication of Emerson's *Journals and Miscellaneous Notebooks*. That symposium underlined how important for the new Emerson scholarship has been the recovery of Emerson's texts in their fullest and most accurate form. And finally, I read "Emerson at Harvard" in September 1986 as part of a panel I organized to help commemorate the 350th anniversary of the founding of Harvard College. The panel was called "American Literature: The View from Harvard," and also included talks by Alan Heimert, Daniel Aaron, and Warner Berthoff. "Holmes's Emerson" was written to introduce a new edition of Oliver Wendell Holmes's spirited and quirky *Ralph Waldo Emerson* (1885) and gave me a chance to explore the relations of these two near-contemporary Boston Brahmins whose careers and literary universes appear, on the face of things, to have had little in common. Thus I have continued to participate in the strong current interest in rehistoricizing and recontextualizing an Emerson who, for a long time, was viewed largely as a "wisdom" writer not linked to specific historic circumstance.

My next chapter, on "Emerson's French Connection," was written at the invitation of Bertrand Rougé, editor of the journal *Q/W/E/R/T/Y*, published at the University of Pau. It appeared in the fall of 2002 in anticipation of the Agrégation (French national examination) administered in the spring of 2003 and including an oral question on Emerson. But I chose the subject not only because I thought it would appeal to a French audience. In line with the ongoing publication of Emerson's texts, Ronald Bosco and Joel Myerson brought out an edition of *The Later Lectures of Ralph Waldo Emerson* (2001) containing a piece, "France, or Urbanity" (January

1854), not known previously even to many Emerson scholars. The timing of the lecture—just two months before Emerson delivered his second speech on the Fugitive Slave Law and not long before he began drafting *English Traits*—suggests something I had not thought much about previously: following his return from a trip to England and France in 1848, Emerson understood that he was developing an international reputation with the obligations attendant on his role as a public intellectual both in America and abroad. Accordingly, in Ralph Rusk's phrase, he was definitively coming down "from his ivory tower" and becoming truly cosmopolitan. This, then, is the period of Emerson's greatest involvement in what I have called above the work of cultural "translation." I think it rather significant that in his address of 7 March 1854 Emerson universalizes the issue of slavery in distinctly transnational terms: "What is useful will last; whilst that which is hurtful to the world will sink beneath all the opposing forces which it must exasperate. The terror which the *Marseillaise* thunders against oppression, thunders today,—*Tout est soldat pour vous combattre:* 'Everything that can walk turns soldier to fight you down.'" As Perry Miller once suggested, European ideas were "catalytic" in Emerson's formation; and France was an important part of the equation.[5]

In the following three essays I turn back to Thoreau, an early favorite of mine (the first paperback edition of *Walden* I owned is dated 1949). "Henry Thoreau and the Reverend Poluphloisboios Thalassa" was written for Matthew Bruccoli's 1973 collection, *The Chief Glory of Every People,* and represents, I suppose, the most unpronounceable title I ever devised for an essay (a formidable stumbling-block for copy editors and typesetters). But the joke— based on Homer—was Thoreau's and still seems to me a good one. In the piece, which was written under the influence of Gaston Bachelard and focuses mainly on *Cape Cod,* I explored Thoreau's anxieties about fathoming things, with a particular look at his interest in bottoms, an issue later revisited by other critics. "Society and Solitude," originally read at the University of Houston in 1967, was included in a special number of *ESQ* devoted to Thoreau and edited by Joseph McElroy (1973). In it I examine the claim that Thoreau's Walden experiment was prompted by antisocial tendencies—exemplified later on, perhaps, in Greta Garbo's famous remark, "I want to be alone." My conclusion is that wanting to be alone was not simply and totally the substance of Thoreau's desire (I think the same was true of Garbo), but that is the reputation that has stuck to him and one, I argue, that performs a certain kind of cultural work. The third Thoreau piece, "'God Himself Culminates in the Present Moment': Thoughts on Thoreau's Faith," was read at the Thoreau Society annual meeting in Concord in July 1978 and published later that year in the *Thoreau Society Bulletin*. When I delivered the talk I'm afraid I offended the religious sensibilities of some members of the audience by suggesting that their hero was not a Christian. I am sorry about that, but I still stand by what I said. Readers who want an author principally to buttress their religious beliefs should stay away from this dangerous heretic.

The next piece in this section, "'In Wildness is the Preservation of the World': The Natural History of Henry David Thoreau," delivered at the Cornell Plantations in September 1997 as the inaugural lecture in a new series, endowed by the Harder family, devoted to the conjoining of literary study and the vigorous current concern for the environment, participates in the recrudescence of interest in Thoreau as a naturalist that has attracted such leading Thoreauvians as Lawrence Buell and Laura Dassow Walls. "Writing and Reading New Englandly," published in *The New England Quarterly* in 1993 as an "essay-review," takes as its jumping-off point Richard Poirier's *Poetry and Pragmatism*, which links Emerson and William James as "pragmatists" motivated by a particular kind of linguistic skepticism. That view seems to me a distortion, itself motivated by a distinct ideological bent evident in certain pedagogical circles that began to be visible after World War II, and I used this occasion to set out the issues involved and put them in both theoretical and historical context. The essay seems to me an apposite way to end a book devoted to these advocates of self-reliance and sublime egotism who have become commanding figures in a cultural debate that has carried us far beyond the confines of New England.

I have already mentioned the organizations that provided the occasions when some of these chapters were first delivered as talks and the journals that published revised versions of the talks or that accepted those chapters written as essays. All of the chapters, in any case, have been recast—some several times—to allow for corrections and, I hope, to remove infelicities. I am grateful to Dianne Ferriss, of the Cornell University Department of English, who over a period of some years worked as my editorial assistant and keyed most of the chapters onto computer disk. Her skills and advice were invaluable. John Kulka, of Yale University Press, was enthusiastic about this collection when I first told him about it and guided me at every step of the way. Joyce Ippolito expertly copyedited the manuscript. Two anonymous readers for the Press deserve thanks for their positive reactions to my work and their suggestions for improvement. I also thank Elizabeth Hall Witherell, editor-in-chief of the Princeton Thoreau Edition, for copying a page of Thoreau's manuscript journal, and the Pierpont Morgan Library for permission to reproduce it in chapter 12. My wife, Helene, has provided companionship, encouragement, and a sharp critical judgment that has repeatedly rescued me from making blunders. Undoubtedly some faults remain, but there would be many more without her intervention.

Finally, I need to say something about the dedication of this book. When, in the early 1950s, I was an impecunious student in New York City, I was lucky enough to find part-time employment at Atlas Corporation, an investment trust located at 33 Pine Street (40 Wall Street). Eventually, the president of the company, Floyd Odlum (then well-known, now remembered if at all because he was married to the celebrated aviator and entrepreneur Jacqueline Cochran), would become my direct benefactor; but as I moved from the mailroom on the 57th floor, where I was a "runner," to the 58th floor and a better job as "office-boy" to the executives, I encountered the woman who became, effectively, my surrogate mother and a benefactress in more profound ways.

Emilie Dixon, née McMillan, a graduate of Smith College circa 1920, was in charge of the executive offices—and especially of running the kitchen and private dining room where Floyd Odlum and his vice-presidents were elegantly fed, along with their rich and (mostly) famous guests. Under her tutelage I learned to copy pertinent quotes from the ticker-tape and grocery-shop at Gristede's; but that was the least of it. Emilie had a passionate love for English language and literature. Graduating from Smith, she moved to New York and became an editorial assistant at *The Freeman*—a fledgling journal founded by Francis Neilson, Albert Jay Nock, and Van Wyck Brooks.[6] Emilie worshipped Nock and Brooks—but especially Brooks. She collected everything he published, plus reviews, and was far more interested in teaching me about his work than in instructing me about stocks and bonds. (After her death in 1969 her whole Brooks collection, plus a bound set of *The Freeman*, were shipped to me at Harvard.)

Emilie also gave me expensive books that I could not afford to buy for myself: the Oxford *Companions* to English and American literature, the *Oxford Bible*, a deluxe edition of Francis James Child's *English and Scottish Popular Ballads*, works on English language by the Fowler brothers (another passion), Greenough and Kittredge, Jespersen, Ivor Brown, and Frederick Bodmer—and much, much more. But it was her faith in me and her firm belief that I *could* go to Harvard and become an English professor that sustained and inspired me. The dedication of this book to her represents only a slight measure of my gratitude. And, in a small way, it brings the name of this wonderful woman, without direct descendants of her own, into public view.

EMERSON, THOREAU,
AND THE DOUBLE CONSCIOUSNESS

It was Thomas Carlyle who in 1834 advised his readers to close their Byron and open their Goethe, thereby suggesting that Goethe— "the keenest star in a new constellation," to use Margaret Fuller's phrase—was pre-eminently the man of his age. By 1850 Emerson was only summarizing cultivated opinion when he called Goethe, in *Representative Men*, "the soul of his century."[1]

But to many outraged critics that soul was irreparably corrupt. As early as 1817, somewhat distressed by much "which needs must be called stuff" in *Faust*, Edward Everett pronounced it a masterpiece only "with some hesitation." And Emerson himself, reviewing with distaste what he considered to be the skepticism and lack of affirmation of modern thought, noted in 1863 that "the great poem of the age is the disagreeable poem of 'Faust.'" The post–Civil War generation, determined, perhaps desperately, to look on the positive side of things, might, like Henry James's Olive Chancellor, read Goethe's message as being unequivocally in praise of renunciation and discipline. But Emerson could not overlook what was "painful" and "destructive" in Goethe's poem. He believed it stood "unhappily related to the whole modern world."[2]

Like Carlyle, Arnold, Clough, and many others, Emerson unhesitatingly identified the dangerous symptoms of modernity: subjectiveness and inner division. Looking back with a cool eye on the Transcendental movement in "Historic Notes of Life and Letters in New England," Emerson remarked repeatedly that it was a time of potentially destructive reflectiveness and self-consciousness. It was "the age of severance, of dissociation" and tended to solitude. "The young men," he wrote in a famous sentence, "were born with knives in their brain, a tendency to introversion, self-dissection, anatomizing of motives."[3]

In this context, Emerson's brief comment on *Faust* in "Historic Notes" is particularly suggestive: "The most remarkable literary work of the age has for its hero and subject precisely this introversion." Painful as he might find it (and late in life he would astonish his friends Norton and Lewes by remarking, "I hate 'Faust'; it is a bad book"), Emerson was forced to admit that in drawing the portrait of a radically divided soul, Goethe had created the central imaginative document of his time. Thus, if we wish to cite the lines from Goethe's poem that Emerson would undoubtedly have considered most relevant, it is Faust's celebrated anatomy of his problem that comes to mind:

> *Zwei Seelen wohnen, ach! in meiner Brust,*
> *Die eine will sich von der andern trennen;*

Die eine hält, in derber Liebeslust,
Sich an die Welt mit klammernden Organen;
Die andre hebt gewaltsam sich vom Dust
Zu den Gefilden hoher Ahnen.

[Two souls, alas! reside within my breast,
and each withdraws from, and repels, its brother:
one to the world is bound in clinging lust,
the other soars, all earthly ties unheeded,
to join ancestral gods, far from this dust.⁴]

If justification is needed for assuming that Faust's description of the inner conflict between his sensual and spiritual selves embodied one of the major meanings of the poem for Emerson, we have only to look at "The Transcendentalist," Emerson's earlier, less detached and somewhat apologetic description of the vital movement that he helped to start. There, he began by dividing mankind into Materialists and Idealists—those who believe in the senses and those who trust to consciousness—and unhesitatingly awarded the palm to the latter. But as he progressed, Emerson had to admit that there were no pure idealists, that even the best of the Transcendentalists were forced to recognize their dual natures, divided between Reason and Understanding. "These two states of thought," he conceded, "diverge every moment, and stand in wild contrast." Then Emerson restated the Faustian problem of the "zwei Seelen" in terms more suited to his own mild discourse than were the wild ravings of a Romantic hero: "The worst feature of this double consciousness is, that the two lives, of the understanding and of the soul, which we lead, really show very little relation to each other, never meet and measure each other: one prevails now, all buzz and din; and the other prevails then, all infinitude and paradise; and, with the progress of life, the two discover no greater disposition to reconcile themselves."⁵

Insofar as the young Transcendentalists suffered from this "double consciousness" (and they mostly did), they were all New England Fausts, with Nature, as Perry Miller aptly suggests, their Gretchen—

the pure maiden whom they wished to possess. For it was precisely the problem of reconciling the Soul with Nature, the "Not Me" (which, as Emerson was at pains to point out in *Nature*, includes "both nature . . . and my own body"), that plagued the Transcendentalists. Like Faust, torn between his earthly lusts and his spiritual strivings, they were dualists; yet they yearned for unity. Man should own "the dignity of the life which throbs around him," Emerson insisted, "in chemistry, and tree, and animal, and in the involuntary functions of his own body; yet he is balked when he tries to fling himself into this enchanted circle, where all is done without degradation." Man's self-consciousness, at once his glory and his anguish, keeps him from accepting wholeheartedly his animal body and the spontaneous life of nature. As the more chastened Emerson of "Experience" would say, "the discovery we have made, that we exist . . . is called the Fall of Man." And in such a mood, Emerson would want to "relax this despotism of the senses, which binds us to nature as if we were a part of it," even though becoming an innocent part of nature was possibly one way of attempting to solve the problem of the double consciousness.[6]

But perhaps it was not so much a solution as a clear awareness of the difficulty that was wanted. Most Transcendentalists believed that the true hero of the age was less the person capable of healing the division in human nature than the one who could manage to live nobly in a kind of sublime Faustian tension between hell and paradise. Reporting to his countrymen in 1834 on the life of Schiller, Frederic Henry Hedge suggested that the secret glory of Schiller's career lay in his "double nature." And Hedge unhesitatingly sketched the portrait of a great man: "He who is called to be a prophet in his generation,—whose office it is to unfold new forms of truth and beauty,—enjoys, among other prerogatives peculiar to his calling, the privilege of a two-fold life. He is at once a dweller in the dust, and a denizen of that land where all truth and beauty spring."[7]

Emerson's view was the same. He concluded his essay on Goethe, the last of his *Representative Men*, by suggesting that all should follow the example of the great poetic genius of the age: "We too must write Bibles, to unite again the heavenly and the earthly world." Goethe's weary Doctor Faust yearned for such a new revelation: "Wir sehnen uns nach Offenbarung"; and Melville's anguished dualist, Pierre, caught between his sexual appetites and his spiritual strivings, would respond: "I will gospelize the world anew, and show them deeper secrets than the Apocalypse!"[8]

If Henry Thoreau was impressed by *Faust,* he unfortunately left no record of his enthusiasm. The work of Goethe's that he mentions most frequently is the *Italiänische Reise.* But the Faustian problem of doubleness that we have been reviewing, whether suggested by Goethe or not, was of central—almost obsessive—concern to Thoreau. His "different selves," as Sherman Paul has remarked, "genius and talent . . . head and feet . . . soul and body, had to be harmonized; the tension of his life was in their resolution." Thoreau's "battle for unity . . . was the chronicle of his spiritual life."[9]

As we might expect, Thoreau's first impulse is to dissipate the problem in a pun. His linguistic joke in *A Week on the Concord and Merrimack Rivers* advised anyone who fears he is lost to "conclude that after all he is not lost, he is not beside himself, but standing in his own old shoes on the very spot where he is." A man, Thoreau insists, certainly has no business being "beside" himself if he is *integer vitae*—a unified soul. Furthermore, even the fear of spiritual division can be turned into a strength, if only through a play on words: "I am not alone if I stand by myself." The duplex soul can keep himself company, thereby proving doubly self-reliant.[10]

But Thoreau was clearly not satisfied with his own humorous treatment of the difficulty and returned to the subject in *Walden.* The chapter on "Solitude" is the proper place for such meditation, and Thoreau admits there, perhaps surprisingly, that he was once oppressed by the sense of being alone. He was also, to be sure, "conscious of a slight insanity" in his mood and knew that it would pass, but the very admission of such an "insanity"—the awareness of an unhealthy "other" contained within and potentially threatening the integrity of the soul—suggests a problem to be solved. Thoreau's initial attempt at a solution is similar to what we have seen in *A Week*, a kind of therapeutic schizophrenia: "With thinking we may be beside ourselves in a sane sense. By a conscious effort of the mind we can stand aloof from actions and their consequences." Once again, duplexity becomes a virtue: Thoreau can dissociate his sane self from the unhealthy self that is affected by loneliness and thus maintain his equanimity.[11]

But in the rest of this key passage Thoreau went beyond merely attempting to work out a cure for the evils of solitude and allowed himself to give full expression to the problem of the age, an awareness of the double consciousness:

> We are not wholly involved in Nature. I may be either the drift-wood in the stream, or Indra in the sky looking down on it. . . . I only know myself as a human entity; the scene, so to speak, of thoughts and affections; and am sensible of a certain doubleness by which I can stand as remote from myself as from another. However intense my experience, I am conscious of the presence and criticism of a part of me, which, as it were, is not a part of me, but spectator, sharing no experience, but taking note of it; and that is no more I than it is you. When the play, it may be the tragedy, of life is over, the spectator goes his way. It was a kind of fiction, a work of the imagination only, so far as he was concerned.[12]

Thoreau's admission here of a sense of Faustian doubleness, of a split between experiencing body and judging spirit, carries with it, especially in the searching tentativeness of its rhetoric, a deep note of personal concern, as if what he is saying were cause not only for congratulation but also for alarm. It was all very well for Thoreau to insist that "we are not wholly involved in Nature"; but a major reason for his experiment at Walden was specifically to seek total involvement in the natural world, to "have intelligence with the earth," so that he might come fully to terms with the part of himself that was "leaves and vegetable mould."[13] Of course, to be no more than "the driftwood in the stream" would hardly have been more satisfactory than to be totally "Indra in the sky." Both consciousness *and* the animal body were there to be dealt with; and Walden is largely an attempt to come to clarity about the relationship between the two—or rather, to achieve a dramatic resolution of the problem.

Thoreau ingeniously embodied the problem of the "zwei Seelen" in his crucial confrontation with the "Paphlagonian man," Alek Therien. He is Thoreau's Doppelgänger (or perhaps Thoreau is his), the animal self whom Thoreau must come to terms with before he can hope to be a unified soul.[14] That Therien is meant to represent the animal in man is made abundantly clear throughout Thoreau's description of him: he is "a great consumer of meat" (woodchucks) and characterized by "animal spirits"; he is coarse and sluggish, and "the intellectual and what is called spiritual man in him were slumbering"; his thinking is "primitive and immersed in his animal life," and, as Thoreau says flatly, "in him the animal man chiefly was developed." But Thoreau had somewhat reconditely embodied this notion at the beginning of the episode, where he tells us that Therien (whose name was of course omitted from the final version of *Walden*) "had so suitable and poetic a name that I am sorry that I cannot print it here." Thoreau's point is clearly that this "Homeric" man has a name that signifies, in Greek, exactly what his character is—θηρίον, a beast.[15]

But Thoreau not only establishes Therien's animal nature; he also makes it plain that the woodchopper and he are, oddly enough, doubles. Though now English-speaking, they are both of French extraction and their names sound alike. Each is twenty-eight years old. Both have blue eyes (though Therien's, significantly, are dull and sleepy). Thoreau, although now largely vegetarian, is occasionally also a devourer of woodchucks (as we are told in "Higher Laws"!). Both men are solitary and both are "writers" (Therien writes "a remarkably good hand," employing it mainly to inscribe the name of his native parish in the snow). Both men are garrulous ("I dearly love to talk," Thoreau admits in "Where I Lived"; "How I love to talk! By George, I could talk all day!" exclaims Therien); and neither man has any love for reformers. Finally, when Thoreau meets Therien after many months and asks the Canadian if he has got a new idea, Therien replies that a man who has work to do, such as hoeing, must "think of weeds"—a lesson that Thoreau takes to heart in the next chapter, "The Bean-Field," where he learns to think extensively of beans.

Many of these parallels are, of course, humorous; but Thoreau's jokes are always serious. It was indeed funny for him to find that he had so much in common with the animal-like woodchopper. Therien was a puzzle to Thoreau, who did not know "whether to suspect him of a fine poetic consciousness or of stupidity." Thoreau, it would seem, had still to come to terms with the ultimate value and meaning of the animal self. Or had he already decided how to do so? Thoreau's next sentence suggests a striking solution to the problem of relating soul and body: "A townsman told me that when he met him [Therien] sauntering through the village in his small close-fitting cap, and whistling to himself, he reminded him of a prince in disguise."

Thoreau surely intends us at this point to remember, and connect Therien with, a "parable" (very likely of Thoreau's own invention) previously presented in the book:

> . . . "there was a king's son, who, being expelled in infancy from his native city, was brought up by a forester, and, growing up to maturity in that state, imagined himself to belong to the barbarous race with which he lived. One of his father's ministers having discovered him, revealed to him what he was, and the misconception of his character was removed, and he knew himself to be a prince. So soul . . . from the circumstances in which it is placed, mistakes its own character, until the truth is revealed to it by some holy teacher, and then it knows itself to be *Brahme*."[16]

Therien, of course, is the "king's son" ("a prince in disguise") who has been raised in the forest and appears to be little more than an animal. But the "holy teacher," Thoreau, has set himself the task of demonstrating that the body is only the soul in disguise. "I perceive," Thoreau continues, "that we inhabitants of New England live this mean life that we do because our vision does not penetrate the surface of things."[17]

Thoreau, the true seer, thinks he can perceive that body and soul are continuous forms of one divine energy. But before he can convince others of this truth, Thoreau must be fully convinced himself; and he accordingly devotes the "Higher Laws" chapter to arguing out with himself, through a series of startling paradoxes, the hard proposition that body and spirit can and must exist together. By turns he is certain that the spirit can "transmute what *in form* [italics supplied] is the grossest sensuality into purity and devotion" yet afraid that the animal in us can "never change its nature." And at his lowest point (reminiscent of Emerson when he says that the awareness of existence is the fall of man), Thoreau seems willing to concede that "our very life is our disgrace," and that we are hopelessly dualistic— "the divine allied to beasts." But he is still determined to prove that we can elevate what is mean and learn "to eat, drink, cohabit, void excrement and urine" in a spiritual fashion. Thoreau ends the chapter, like Orpheus enchanting the beasts, trying with his flute to awake John Farmer to a higher life.[18]

The real proof, however, that metamorphosis is the true law of creation—that body and soul are interchangeable forms of life—comes in the "Spring" chapter, where many "princes" lose their disguises and are transformed: Walden, famously, casts off its death mask of winter ice and comes alive; the alligator (in Thoreau's imagination) comes out of the mud; buds become leaves and flowers; grubs turn into butterflies; and, most miraculously, "man" is born from the sand of the railroad cut, where—in Thoreau's etymological fantasy—the moist animal body within becomes a leaf without, finally to be translated into the graceful and noble hawk that Thoreau deftly uses at the end of the chapter as a figure for his own soaring spirit. And it is clearly no accident that the description of the hawk is followed by the sharply paradoxical image of a vulture, feeding on carrion, which Thoreau insists should at once cheer and disgust us. He intends that we see the hawk and the vulture as one continuous expression of life, for nature "continually transcends and translates itself," earth becoming spirit and spirit returning to earth without end.

Such is Thoreau's method of trying to prove that Thoreau and Therien are one, that the prince and his disguise—soul and body— are cognate forms. "We are enabled to apprehend at all what is sublime and noble," he insists, "only by the perpetual instilling and drenching of the reality which surrounds us."[19] But Emerson, it seems, among others, was not entirely convinced. In a notebook entry made apparently some two years after Thoreau's death, he complained that "Henry pitched his tone very low in his love of nature,—not on stars & suns . . . but tortoises, crickets, muskrats, suckers, toads & frogs. It was impossible to go lower."[20] Yet Thoreau was determined to show that it was precisely this split between "lower" and "higher" that prolonged the anguish of "doubleness"— the Faustian double consciousness. He had attempted, in *Walden*, to write an "apocalypse" designed to reveal the vital energy at work beneath the scurf of earth—to create a "Bible" that tried to unite heaven and earth by demonstrating the interdependency of spiritual aspiration and physical energy.

TWO

TRANSCENDENTAL ANTICS

Henry Thoreau notes in his essay on Carlyle that "the tran-scendental philosophy needs the leaven of humor to render it light and digestible." The hint is worth pursuing, for I would insist that the comic impulse is a significant component of Transcendentalism. Its abundant presence within the movement itself testifies to a self-awareness, a self-criticism, an ability to see oneself in the round, a fundamental balance and sanity, which are important characteristics of the great burgeoning of American consciousness we know as Transcendentalism. And one should add that the susceptibility of Transcendentalism to comic criticism from the outside is equally important as a reminder that the beliefs and postures of members of the group were frequently perceived as extravagant; and extravagance—that quality Thoreau prayed for (and praised in Carlyle)—easily lends itself to exaggeration and caricature. But it is also a sign of passion and commitment, of fervent searching and a need to express oneself hyperbolically, and these things, one need hardly say, lie at the heart of the Transcendental ferment. In addition the ease with which Transcendentalism lent itself to critical lampooning brings many of the salient characteristics of the movement into high relief. But enough of prelude. "To use too many circumstances ere one come to the matter," as Bacon observes, "is wearisome." Let us turn directly to a light-hearted portrait of what James Joyce refers to as "Concord on the Merrimake."[1]

I shall begin with the retrospective glance of a contemporary—a portrait etched in acid from the pen of James Russell Lowell in 1865. Casting his thoughts back some thirty years, Lowell was reminded of the Boston publication of *Sartor Resartus*, and he asserted that Carlyle's "sermon on Falstaff's text of the miserable forked radish gave the signal for a sudden mental and moral mutiny. . . . On all hands with every variety of emphasis, and by voices of every conceivable pitch, representing the three sexes of men, women, and Lady Mary Wortley Montagues," Lowell continued—with a slighting allusion to the birth of the American bluestocking—on all hands the cry went out that the time of the Newness had come.

The nameless eagle of the tree Ygdrasil was about to sit at last, and wild-eyed enthusiasts rushed from all sides, each eager to thrust under the mystic bird that chalk egg from which the new and fairer Creation was to be hatched in due time. . . . Every possible form of intellectual and physical dyspepsia brought forth its gospel. Bran had its prophets, and the presartorial simplicity of Adam its martyrs. . . . Everybody had a mission (with a capital M) to attend to everybody else's business. No brain but had its private maggot, which must have found pitiably short commons sometimes. Not a few impecunious zealots abjured the use of money (unless earned by other people), professing to live on the internal revenues of the spirit. Some had an assurance of instant millennium so soon as hooks and eyes should be substituted for buttons. Communities were established where everything was to be common but common sense. Men renounced their old gods, and hesitated only whether to bestow their furloughed allegiance on Thor or Budh. Conventions were held for every hitherto inconceivable purpose. . . . All stood ready at a moment's notice to reform everything but themselves.[2]

Lowell's description, despite its personal animus and precisely because of its splenetic sense of comedy, brings clearly before us some of the major impulses, as well as some of the important problems, involved in the ferment of the 1830s and forties. Crusaders burning to remake the world pinned their hopes on dietary reform or the removal of restrictions in dress; others saw the crass commercialism of the State Street bankers as the chief evil of the time. "The Americans have no faith," Emerson told his audience in 1841; "they rely on the power of a dollar"[3]—and five years later this lament was expanded into Theodore Parker's thundering jeremiad, "A Sermon of Merchants." Lowell also reminds us of the strength of the communitarian impulse, the hungry search for meaningful society; and his facetious mention of Thor and Budh only underlines the fact that the Transcendental movement had its birth in a profound religious upheaval.

On this point one might draw a parallel probably too often overlooked by historians of Transcendentalism: namely, that there is a connection between the seriocomic religious fervor of Transcendental reform and that passionate wave of religious revival which characterized American religion at large during the first half of the nineteenth century. I believe that both impulses were radically allied, equally expressive of forces deeply rooted in the American character, and equal sources of native American humor. "The dominant theme in America from 1800 to 1860," writes Perry Miller in *The Life of the Mind in America*, "is the invincible persistence of the revival technique. . . . We can hardly understand Emerson, Thoreau, Whitman, Melville, unless we comprehend that for them this was the one clearly given truth of their society." The "revolution" of 1800–1801, writes Alan Heimert—referring to the Second Great Awakening—"reawakened the evangelical hope of the great community . . . a nineteenth century in which humanity's social arrangements would be perfected."[4]

This hope, of course, was also that of the Transcendental reformers and their community of aspiration and attitude with the Awakening—the connection between revival and reform—is nowhere better illustrated than in Constance Rourke's classic study, *American Humor*. The movement of revivalism, she writes, "was away from creeds and close formulas, toward improvisation, rapturous climaxes, happy assurances, and a choral strain. In the revivals of Methodism and the other free new faiths all was generic, large, and of the crowd; in the end all was wildly hopeful. Rhapsody was common; the monologue in the experience meeting unfolded those inner fantasies toward which the native mind was tending in other, quite different aspects of expression, not in the analytic forms of Calvinism, but as pure unbridled fantasy and exuberant overflow." And she continues:

> The pattern of comedy appeared again in the innumerable cults which sprang up in the '30's and '40's as from some rich and fertile seeding-ground. Religious and social traditions were flung to the four winds. The perfectionists declared that the bondage of sin was non-existent and that the Millennium had already begun. At Oneida the bonds of earthly marriage

were broken. Spiritualism proposed to break the bonds of death. The theme of death, which had been a deep preoccupation in the life of the pioneer, was repeated by these cults, with a fresh and happy outcome. Life was to be prolonged, the Millennium had arrived; in the state of perfection death might never come at all. Most of the new religious communities created almost overnight in the '30's and '40's agreed to release mankind from sin, poverty, or mortal care. They all possessed formulas, religious, economic, or social; and they all anticipated conclusions such as the world had never known. Triumph was their note. . . . Hysterical, wrapped in a double sense of national feeling and religious conviction, the believers passed into moods of wildest exaltation. "New, new . . . make all things new." The enchanting cry resounded through all this ecstasy of faith.[5]

Here we might juxtapose with Rourke's formulation some sentences from Emerson. Explaining in his lecture "The Transcendentalist" what were called "new views" in New England, Emerson said that "Transcendentalism is the Saturnalia or excess of Faith" and announced that newness was to be the order of the day: "I do not wish to do one thing but once. I do not love routine."[6] These mingled themes of newness and ecstasy had already been iterated and reiterated gaily by Emerson and Margaret Fuller in their high-spirited introduction to the first number of *The Dial*. Announcing a "new design" in their opening sentence, they called theirs "a Journal in a new spirit," the voice of those making "new demands on literature," eager to express "new views." Drawing on "the conversation of fervid and mystical pietists," on a faith "earnest and profound," *The Dial* would express "a new hope," open "a new scope for literature and art," and ultimately through its perpetually innovational criticism cast "a new light on the whole world."[7]

Thus does the cry of the cults described by Miss Rourke—"New,

new . . . make all things new"—echo through Transcendental writing. And she continues:

> Among all these cults a latent humor broke out; this was clear in the names which they chose or accepted, such as the placidly humorous variations on Harmony and the grotesque nomenclature of the Shakers, Groaners, Come Outers, New Lights, Hard Shell Baptists, and Muggletonians. . . . A wide level of comic feeling had been established, sometimes infused with pliant hope, most often with exuberance. Frequently it was hard to tell when burlesque was involved, when fakery, when a serious intention. The basic feeling was romantic, but it crested into a conscious gaiety which raced beyond the romantic. Even in the most ponderous of these assertions there was something lighthearted.[8]

Now this comic extravagance inherent in and common to American revivalism, religious cultism, and Transcendentalism clearly assumes in Miss Rourke's discussion the character of a perennial national habit or mood, the expression of something fundamental in the American spirit. First, of course, there is the idea of how necessary has been the cultivation—indeed, the exaggeration—of hope in a land where almost everything had to be done from scratch, whether because of the actual thinness of American culture and tradition or because of the programmatic assertion that life in the new world had to be purely self-defined and self-generating. Great hope was needed to sustain a perpetually unrealized and perhaps unrealizable dream of social and religious perfectability; and perhaps just such a great and constantly renewed hope was the almost conscious counterweight to a gnawing fear that the needful energy or spirit might flag or disappear. Secondly, the humor associated with religious and spiritual movements in America since the declension of the true Bible commonwealth—since the loss, that is, of the Calvinistic ideal—suggests an anxiety that is being shuffled off in nervous, if not hysterical, laughter: an anxiety about losing the true faith and traducing one's forefathers, one's traditions, those institutions and beliefs that one still half believes in. The American genius for creating new religions and cults and for throwing oneself into them with exaggerated intensity is matched by a characteristic comic awareness that incessant newness, the perpetual casting off of yesterday's ideas and institutions, is a near-relation to faddism and folly. The impassioned American cry is for something ever new and better, and the American comic response to that answered prayer represents an awareness that the promised perfection is and must always be short of its promise. But the possibility that foolishness or even fakery may crown the irrepressible American effort to regenerate or reform must not be taken as a sign of failure or loss of heart. On the contrary, as Miss Rourke suggests in her statement about how the comic exuberance of American revivalism and cultism "crested into a conscious gaiety which raced beyond the romantic," the very consciousness of gaiety is a final mark of sanity—a guarantee that wild improvisation and romantic delusion are always being counterbalanced and corrected by amused self-awareness. Thus, the ultimate value of American spiritual experimentation may lie in precisely the kind of sharpened perspective and insight that its comedy foments.

There is probably no better example of this sort of fruitful interplay between extravagant action or thought to which one is committed and a simultaneous awareness of comedy than that provided by the Transcendental ferment. Here, finally, American religious fervor broke the mold of formalized religion, and the passion for reform exhausted the available channels of reformation. The result, at its best, was a literature of witty observation and reflection that still carries its force today. And having said that, I must return to Emerson, one of the great American masters of combining participation with ironic detachment. A good place to begin is his own *Dial* essay, "The Comic":

> If the essence of the comic be the contrast in the intellect between the idea and the false performance, there is good

reason why we should be affected by the exposure. We have no deeper interest than our integrity, and that we should be made aware by joke and by stroke, of any lie that we entertain. Besides, a perception of the comic seems to be a balance-wheel in our metaphysical structure. It appears to be an essential element in a fine character. Wherever the intellect is constructive, it will be found. We feel the absence of it as a defect in the noblest and most oracular soul. . . . The perception of the comic is a tie of sympathy with other men, is a pledge of sanity, and is a protection from those perverse tendencies and gloomy insanities into which fine intellects sometimes lose themselves.[9]

Emerson himself offers us many pledges of his own sanity, examples of how he attempted to enforce the integrity of his being by dissociating himself—now slightly, now pointedly—through gentle humor or mild satire, from some of the more egregious follies of the Transcendental brotherhood. But what is to be noticed is the sharp distinction between Lowell's ill-tempered lampoon of what he considered to be little more than a spiritual disease, and Emerson's delicately managed comic portraits. For Emerson, the perception of the comic side of Transcendentalism was indeed a way of reasserting his ties of sympathy with other, non-Transcendental people; but he clearly had no intention thereby of denying the bonds of mutual affection and concern that allied him to those fine, though occasionally extreme, intellects among whom he would always be numbered. Leaving the Transcendental club, Emerson could sometimes hear, as others of the group perhaps could not, the voice of nature whispering, "So hot? my little Sir."[10] But this perception of the disparity between the placid calm of nature and the fret and fume of Transcendental disputation, and the comic statement to which such perception gave rise, would not usually cause Emerson to forget or disparage the moral, artistic, or spiritual fervor that produced the heat.

A good example of Emersonian comedy playing ambivalently over the vagaries of Transcendental reform may be found in his report for *The Dial*, in July 1842, on "a Convention of Friends of Universal Reform" (otherwise known as the Chardon Street and Bible Conventions), Emerson noted the presence of "men of every shade of opinion, from the straitest orthodoxy to the wildest heresy, and many persons whose church was a church of one member only" and then allowed himself to sketch a consciously humorous portrait of the gathering: "A great variety of dialect and of costume was noticed; a great deal of confusion, eccentricity, and freak appeared, as well as of zeal and enthusiasm. If the assembly was disorderly, it was picturesque. Madmen, madwomen, men with beards, Dunkers, Muggletonians, Come-Outers, Groaners, Agrarians, Seventh-day-Baptists, Quakers, Abolitionists, Calvinists, Unitarians, and Philosophers,—all came successively to the top, and seized their moment, if not their *hour*, wherein to chide, or pray, or preach, or protest."[11]

Carrying the idea of Democratic equality (one person one vote) to its comic conclusion, Emerson has Calvinists and madmen rubbing shoulders—through subtle inference and comic juxtaposition reducing them all, as it were, to one level. In this miscellaneous gathering tradition and eccentricity have equal rights, but neither has any special privilege. All have the same opportunity to rise momentarily out of the disorderly assembly and try to be heard, but does this—Emerson's comic voice seems finally to say to us—constitute an example of the great American community to be? Or of any community at all? A few well-known sentences from *Moby Dick* are especially apposite here: "They were nearly all Islanders in the Pequod, *Isolatoes* too, I call such, not acknowledging the common continent of men, but each *Isolato* living on a separate continent of his own. Yet now, federated along one keel, what a set these *Isolatoes* were!" What a set indeed is Emerson's nineteenth-century American circus of opinion, and his humor quietly expresses the same uneasiness that laces Melville's sentences. Is this unstable federation really an ecumenical council, or simply a grotesque collection of isolated individuals—"persons whose church was a church of one member only"—who have come to speak but not truly to listen, and who will depart as separate and alone as they have come? Emerson's description of the Chardon Street Convention continues, it must be admitted, in a generally optimistic fashion, but it is surely no exaggeration to see in his humor here a clear sign of that growing distrust of Transcendental reform and ebullient hope that was increasingly to characterize the writing of Thoreau and that of such demi-Transcendentalists as Hawthorne and Melville. For all of these men, the humor of Transcendentalism became a judgment on the extravagance of its promises—and, perhaps, on the promise of American life generally.

The growth of Emerson's own distrust, at all events, is not hard to document. Scarcely two years after reporting on the Chardon Street Convention, he delivered a lecture on "New England Reformers" in which his humor, now sharpened into mild satire, was butressed by a pervasive mood of bemused detachment. Speaking of those who had attended the many reform meetings and conventions, he wrote: "They defied each other, like a congress of kings, each of whom had a realm to rule, and a way of his own that made concert unprofitable." The democratic picturesqueness of Chardon Street has become the despotic determination of each to have his own way; and Emerson now views the zeal and enthusiasm of New England reformers as almost pure folly. He continues:

What a fertility of projects for the salvation of the world! One apostle thought all men should go to farming, and another that no man should buy or sell, that the use of money was the cardinal evil; another that the mischief was in our diet, that we eat and drink damnation. These made unleavened bread, and were foes to the death to fermentation. It was in vain urged by the housewife that God made yeast, as well as dough, and loves fermentation just as dearly as he loves vegetation; that fermentation develops the saccharine element in the grain, and makes it more palatable and more digestible. No; they wish the pure wheat, and will die but it shall not ferment. Stop, dear Nature, these incessant advances of thine; let us scotch these ever-rolling wheels! Others attacked the system of agriculture, the use of animal manures in farming, and the tyranny of man over brute nature; these abuses polluted his food. The ox must be taken from the plough and the horse from the cart, the hundred acres of the farm must be spaded, and the man must walk, wherever boats and locomotives will not carry him. Even the insect world was to be defended—that had been too long neglected, and a society for the protection of ground-worms, slugs and mosquitos was to be incorporated without delay. With these appeared the adepts of homeopathy, of hydropathy, of mesmerism, of phrenology.

On and on goes Emerson's list of the things that were attacked as being the source of all evil—law, trade, manufacturing, the clergy, academia, marriage—but the conclusion of his witty thrust is surprising indeed: the result of this "din of opinion and debate" which he has so wonderfully made sport of he claims to be good, for it asserts "the sufficiency of the private man." The reader, it seems to me, has more justification for feeling that Emerson's treatment of this din of opinion and debate insists rather on the sufficient foolishness of private idiosyncrasy and group hobbyhorses. And so it turns out to be, for the body of his lecture expresses a deep disillusionment with most methods of reform and a belief only in individual character. Not the excesses he has pilloried, but rather the humorous detachment—exemplified by his own handling of these things—which sees the world in perspective truly asserts "the sufficiency of the private man." "They are partial," Emerson argues of reformers further on in the lecture; "they are not equal to the work they pretend. They lose their way; in the assault on the kingdom of darkness they expend all their energy on some accidental evil, and lose their sanity and power of benefit. It is of little moment that one or two or twenty errors of our social system be corrected, but of much that the man be in his senses."

Clearly, the only method of reform that Emerson believes in, the only way of forcing people back into their senses, is the use of his own special brand of literary drollery—that Emersonian voice of near-comic exhortation: "Do not be so vain of your one objection. Do you think there is only one? Alas! my good friend, there is no part of society or of life better than any other part. All our things are right and wrong together. The wave of evil washes all our institutions alike. Do you complain of our Marriage? Our marriage is no worse than our education, our diet, our trade, our social customs. Do you complain of the laws of Property? It is a pedantry to give such importance to them. Can we not play the game of life with these counters, as well as with those?"

I suppose there is no denying that Emerson's posture of comic detachment here verges on something close to terminal discouragement or even despair. It seems that the habitual perception of humor had itself become Emerson's major defense and the only method of Transcendental reform he still believed in: a conscious gaiety that transformed Transcendental crotchets into whimsical insights and Transcendental querulousness into valuable, if painful, satiric thrusts. "What is it we heartily wish of each other?" Emerson continues. "Is it to be pleased and flattered? No, but to be convicted and exposed, to be shamed out of our nonsense of all kinds, and made men of, instead of ghosts and phantoms. We are weary of gliding ghostlike throughout the world, which is itself so slight and unreal. We crave a sense of reality, though it comes in strokes of pain."[12] Emerson's comic unmasking of folly is his ultimate Transcendental weapon—painful to the point of existential anguish—as it is the major weapon of other great Transcendental writers. This passage from "New England Reformers" clearly looks forward to another satiric thrust, that almost morbid twist of Thoreau's knife in *Walden*, which is meant to impart life though its antic maneuvers toy with death: "If you stand right fronting and face to face to a fact, you will see the sun glimmer on both its surfaces, as if it were a cimeter, and feel its sweet edge dividing you through the heart and marrow, and so you will happily conclude your mortal career. Be it life or death, we crave only reality. If we are really dying, let us hear the rattle in our throats and feel cold in the extremities; if we are alive, let us go about our business."[13]

The chief business of much Transcendental writing and of the criticism which it directly—indeed, defiantly—inspired was precisely that of convicting and exposing folly, of shaming the world out of its nonsense. And such reform had of course to begin at home. Time and time again, the Transcendentalists, and those who remained warily on the fringes of the group, lampooned the extravagances that they mostly all shared—as if to demonstrate that imaginative excess coupled with the ability comically to deflate one's own excesses were the twin characteristics which, precisely through their inseparability, defined the special quality of the intellectual spirit of the times. Melville, for example, alternately attracted and repelled by Transcendentalism, embodied his ambivalent attitude toward the movement in the wide spectrum of his comic response to the Newness—broadly humorous in *Mardi, Moby Dick,* and *Pierre,* but poignantly funny in "Bartleby the Scrivener" and savagely satiric in *The Confidence-Man.* Melville chided these "new-light" Apostles, with their "Pythagorean and Shelleyan dietings on apple-parings [and] dried prunes," who "went about huskily muttering the Kantian Categories through teeth and lips dry and dusty as any miller's, with the crumbs of Graham crackers"; but his humor was explicitly meant as a tribute. "Let me here offer up three locks of my hair," Melville exclaimed with gently mocking praise in *Pierre,* "to the memory of all such glorious paupers who have lived and died in this world. Surely, and truly I honor them—noble men often at bottom—and for that very reason I make bold to be gamesome about them; for where fundamental nobleness is, and fundamental honor is due, merriment is never accounted irreverent. The fools and pretenders of humanity, and the imposters and baboons among the gods, these only are offended with raillery."[14] Despite his decidedly irreverent pun on "bottom," Melville had no fear of offending the true Transcendental masters because he knew that what was valuable and noble in them was finally beyond the reach of raillery. Besides, their comic self-awareness of folly often easily overmatched his own efforts at friendly satire.

What, in fact, was Transcendentalism at its best, if not a willingness to risk hyperbolic foolishness in the service of truth? Hawthorne could complain good-naturedly of Concord that "never was a poor little country village infested with such a variety of queer, strangely dressed, oddly behaved mortals," but he asserted equally: "It was the very spot in which to utter the extremest nonsense, or the profoundest wisdom—or that ethereal product of the mind which partakes of both, and may become one or the other, in correspondence with the faith and insight of the auditor."[15] Emerson must have known, when he published that first, momentous book in 1836, that his description of himself as a transparent eyeball was comically overdone; but the risk of self-mockery was the price—indeed, the guarantee—of making a serious point with sufficient emphasis. Emerson's object was to convince his audience that spiritual rebirth was contingent on their opening their eyes, literally, to the great new world which was their birthright. Needing more than anything else to behold God and nature face to face, they had—like Emerson—to become transparent eyeballs and see all. Then, and only then, would their true prospects (the title of the last section of *Nature*) come into focus. "So shall we come to look at the world with new eyes," he concluded headily, insisting that unclouded perception—both sight and insight—could perform the miracle of turning visions into reality.[16]

Because Emerson's major purpose was to force the sluggard intellect of America to "look from under its iron lids," he had to enact the meaning of his essay by becoming a metaphoric eyeball, even at the risk of seeming silly. Or perhaps becoming metaphorically foolish was the only way of underscoring—indeed, publicizing—his point.

Christopher Cranch's now well-known caricature of Emerson as a wide-eyed visual organ on legs takes the author up on his own implicit offer to seem ridiculous. But in this case, to Emerson's ultimate advantage, exaggeration and truth enforce one another, and Emerson's meaning is made certain. Indeed, he would later, in his *Poems* of 1846, reiterate and make further use of this comic self-portrait, ironically allegorizing himself as Uriel, the archangel of the sun, whose "piercing eye" with its "look that solved the sphere" made the stern old Unitarian war gods shudder and helped destroy their bland and complacent Paradise.[17]

Few readers may have noted and truly appreciated the significant comedy of Emerson's eyeball humor, but it was not lost on Henry Thoreau, who continued the jocular tradition in his first book. James Russell Lowell must have been in a particularly dour mood when he wrote, with surprising imperceptivity, that "Thoreau had no humor."[18] But I wonder how many readers of *A Week on the Concord and Merrimack Rivers* have noticed that Thoreau turned Emerson's own favorite literary device against his master when he waggishly "attacked" Emerson in the "Sunday" section of the book:

> What earth or sea, mountain or stream, or Muses' spring or grove, is safe from his all-searching ardent eye, who drives off Phoebus' beaten track, visits unwonted zones, makes the gelid Hyperboreans glow, and the old polar serpent writhe, and many a Nile flow back and hide his head! [Then Thoreau broke into a mock-heroic paean.]

> *That Phaeton of our day,*
> *Who'd make another milky way,*
> *And burn the world up with his ray;*

> *By us an undisputed seer,—*
> *Who'd drive his flaming car so near*
> *Unto our shuddering mortal sphere,*

Disgracing all our slender worth,
And scorching up the living earth,
To prove his heavenly birth.

The silver spokes, the golden tire,
Are glowing with unwonted fire,
And ever nigher roll and nigher;

The pins and axle melted are,
The silver radii fly afar,
Ah, he will spoil his Father's car!

Who let him have the steeds he cannot steer?
Henceforth the sun will not shine for a year.
And we shall Ethiops all appear.

From his [quoting Emerson's poem "The Problem"]

—"lips of cunning fell
The thrilling Delphic oracle."

And yet, sometimes,

We should not mind if on our ear there fell
Some less of cunning, more of oracle.

"It is Apollo shining in your face," Thoreau concluded. "O rare Contemporary, let us have far-off heats. Give us the subtler, the heavenlier though fleeting beauty. . . . Let epic trade-winds blow, and cease this waltz of inspirations."[19]

It is hard to know where to begin unraveling the complications of Thoreau's wit here. He starts, of course, by hyperbolically verifying the justice of Emerson's metaphoric representation of himself as an "ardent eye," but then Thoreau's humor turns into an expression of anxiety over the danger that this "undisputed seer" may permanently outshine all other Concord literary lights; whence Thoreau accuses the local Apollo of being too clever and smooth in his inspirational music. "Let epic trade-winds blow," exclaims the younger man with over-inflated metaphoric grandeur, commencing to aim his wit against himself as his attack on Emerson turns into a comic advertisement for Ulysses D. Thoreau on the way up—since, naturally, an excellent example of the kind of rough heroic literature being advocated is Thoreau's book itself, an oracular chronicle of Henry the Navigator's brave voyage up these mysterious inland rivers. But, of course, the joke is quite obviously and consciously on Thoreau himself, for his epic journey is no more than a gentle jaunt from Concord to Concord; and the joke will once again be on this self-styled great adventurer when his next contribution to the world's heroic literature documents an errand into the wilderness of Walden Pond—otherwise identifiable as neighbor Emerson's woodlot. Thus, in the very act of lampooning Emerson's own comic literary tactics, Thoreau continues the Transcendental tradition of shrewd and effective self-parody learned from his mentor.

Examples could be multiplied, but I trust my point is sufficiently clear. The Transcendental persuasion, as I see it, was very largely an antic persuasion—an American Renaissance and Reformation of the spirit that owed much of its force to humor. It was a romantic movement endowed with a conscious gaiety that raced beyond the romantic into that supernal realm where the silly and the solemn meet and merge. Although the comedy of Transcendentalism has often been represented as little more than a merely parochial humorous outburst—Henry James called it "a kind of Puritan carnival" that "produced no fruit"[20]—it was the kind of inevitable comedy that arises from the tensions of a deeply serious human debate. In this case, the debate itself was carried on largely in the spirit of revel. And to judge by the continuing interest of general readers and scholars alike, the Transcendental revels have not yet ended.

THREE

The Problem of Emerson

"The more we know him, the less we know him." Stephen Whicher's wistfully encomiastic remark epitomizes the not entirely unhappy perplexity of a highly influential group of scholars and critics, beginning perhaps with F. O. Matthiessen, who, returning to Emerson's writings with enormous sympathy, intelligence, and sensitivity, attempted to discover a real human figure beneath the bland (or pompous, or smug) official portrait. Predictably, in view of the compensatory biases of modernist criticism, they found a "new" Emerson whose complexities belied that older optimistic

all-American aphorist once dear to captains of industry, genteel professors of literature, and hopeful preachers in search of suitably
uplifting remarks. Like the other great figures of the American
Renaissance, Emerson was now found to be one of us—as richly
evasive and enigmatic a figure, almost, as Hawthorne, or Melville, or
Dickinson. Not only is Emerson incapable of being "summed up in
a formula," Whicher insisted, "he is, finally, impenetrable, for all his
forty-odd volumes."[1]

What is instructive in Whicher's remark is its insistence on penetrating to the heart of Emerson the *man* (since, surely, one of the
most astute Emersonians of the twentieth century was not admit-
ting that he could make no sense of the master's works). Although I
shall myself concentrate here on the problem of getting to the heart
of Emerson's *writing*, I think there is something to be learned from
Whicher's interest in Emerson's character, since it focuses attention
on an important aspect of the Emerson problem. For one thing, the
meaning and value of Emerson's work have typically been overshad-
owed, and frequently undermined, by an emphasis on his example
and personal force. Two of his most distinguished critics offer representative remarks in this regard. Henry James, Jr., speaking for
those who had known Emerson, properly emphasized the manner
in which he made his impression, "by word of mouth, face to face,
with a rare, irresistible voice and a beautiful mild, modest authority."
This is an appealing portrait, suggesting an ethereal attractiveness
that clearly made Emerson humanly persuasive. Santayana roughly
seconds James's point, but his description of Emerson's authority
sharpens the issue somewhat:

> Those who knew Emerson, or who stood so near to his time
> and to his circle that they caught some echo of his personal
> influence, did not judge him merely as a poet or philosopher,
> nor identify his efficacy with that of his writings. His friends
> and neighbors, the congregations he preached to in his younger
> days, the audiences that afterward listened to his lectures, all

agreed in a veneration for his person which had nothing to do with their understanding or acceptance of his opinions. They flocked to him and listened to his word, not so much for the sake of its absolute meaning as for the atmosphere of candor, purity, and serenity that hung about it, as about a sort of sacred music. They felt themselves in the presence of a rare and beautiful spirit, who was in communion with a higher world.[2]

Santayana's clear impatience here with that atmosphere of high-minded religiosity that always vitiated the New England air for him is not intended, I think, to imply a disparagement of Emerson, to whom he was fundamentally sympathetic. Certain difficulties, nevertheless, are suggested in this description of Emerson's virtual canonization as one of the leading saints in the select American hagiology. ("He is a shining figure as on some Mount of Transfiguration," wrote George Woodberry in 1907.) What would be the fate of Emerson's writings when that "fine adumbration," as James called him, should himself be translated to the higher world? Would his literary reputation endure the dissipation of his rare personal emphasis? Worse, could his writings weather the inevitable iconoclasm that tumbles every American idol from his pedestal? "I was never patient with the faults of the good," Emerson's own Aunt Mary Moody is quoted as saying. And the mild saint seems to have written his own epitaph when he noted, in *Representative Men,* that "every hero becomes a bore at last."[3]

As we know, Emerson's fate, somewhat like Shakespeare's, was that he came to be treated as an almost purely allegorical personage whose real character and work got submerged in his role as a touchstone of critical opinion. More and more, the figure of Emerson merged with current perceptions of the meaning and drift of American high culture, and the emblem overwhelmed his substance. To the younger generation of the nineties, for example, notably John Jay Chapman and Santayana, certain aspects of Emerson represented the pale summation of that attenuated genteel tradition with which they had lost patience. As the debate sharpened and positions hardened over the next quarter-century or so, Emerson functioned as a kind of polemical football in the ongoing culture wars. To the Puritan-baiting intellectuals of the twenties, he stood for little more than the final weak dilution in the New England teapot; but for the conservative New Humanists, who—like Fitzgerald's Nick Carraway—"wanted the world to be in uniform and at a sort of moral attention forever," Emerson was the pre-eminent voice of the American conscience and the patron saint, accordingly, of their rear-guard action.[4] Even T. S. Eliot, though he sympathized with the general position of the school of Babbitt and More, wrote in 1919, while praising Hawthorne, that "the essays of Emerson are already an encumbrance"; and Eliot's key word suggests not so much a literary burden as a *monumental* physical weight—the Lares and Penates of Victorian culture which the brave new Aeneases of the twenties were determined to jettison:

> *Matthew and Waldo, guardians of the faith,*
> *The army of unalterable law.*[5]

The American master seemed to keep watch over outmoded standards of conduct, not the new canons of poetry. As a result, "in those days [the twenties]," asserts Malcolm Cowley, "hardly anyone read Emerson." Such a quirky exception as D. H. Lawrence only proved the general rule, for this self-admitted "spiritual drug-fiend," despite his odd personal taste for Emerson, summarized the temper of the times when he argued, in 1923, that "all those gorgeous inrushes of exaltation and spiritual energy which made Emerson a great man now make us sick. . . . When Professor [Stuart] Sherman urges us in Ralph Waldo's footsteps, he is really driving us nauseously astray." With a *"Sic transeunt Dei hominorum,"* Lawrence reluctantly ushered the tarnished deity from his niche. The devils—Melville and Poe— were in, and the leading saint went marching out.[6]

The "recovery" of Emerson that began with Matthiessen in the 40's and picked up speed later is based on the sympathetic perception that beneath the seemingly ageless smiling public mask there lies a finite consciousness troubled with a tragic sense of contingency and loss—a little-known Emerson, as James said in 1887, with "his inner reserves and scepticisms, his secret ennuis and ironies." Indeed, the erstwhile saint has been turned not only inside out but upside down and shown to have a demonic bottom nature. In an improbable context of Siberian shamans become Thracian bards, Harold Bloom argues for a Bacchicly wild and primitivistic Emerson: "The spirit that speaks in and through him has the true Pythagorean and Orphic stink. . . . The ministerial Emerson . . . is full brother to the Dionysiac adept who may have torn living flesh with his inspired teeth."[7]

The trouble with these strategies for redeeming Emerson is that they, too, like the Victorian apotheoses, are rooted in the character of the man (though in this case it is a presumably more appealing, because more complex, figure) and therefore depend for their force on our assenting to a particular reconstruction of Emerson's personality which may have little to do with the common reader's literary experience of Emerson. While praising Stephen Whicher's *Freedom and Fate: An Inner Life of Ralph Waldo Emerson*, Jonathan Bishop notes that "in the midst of one's appreciation for the achievement of this book, and the other works whose assumptions are comparable, one can still feel that the point of view adopted involves a certain neglect of the literary particulars."[8]

Though many literary particulars are brilliantly illuminated in Bishop's own book, which is undoubtedly one of the best modern readings of Emerson, it unfortunately does not escape some of the typical difficulties of Emerson criticism. Predicated, like Whicher's work, on the notion that there is a "true, secret Emerson" who is the real and really interesting man we are after, *Emerson on the Soul* tells us that the reader's job is "to distinguish the excellent moments," which scarcely ever "exceed a page or two of sustained utterance" (though Bishop is uneasy with the old commonplace which argues that Emerson was little more than a sentence maker or at best a paragraph maker, he, too, sees little organic form in whole essays or books). This authentic Emerson—sometimes, indeed, by a kind of typographical mystification, identified as "Emerson"—predictably exhibits himself most freely in the private journals or letters. To arrive at these "interesting moments" in the public utterances, "one makes a drastic selection," avoiding "the dull tones, the preacherly commonplaces, the high-minded vapid identity" which obviously do not express the genuine Emerson we are seeking. The ability to recognize this profounder, more complex, more valuable tone may also serve as a kind of moral test of honesty in the reader, for "a coward soul is always free to interpret what Emerson says in a way that does not allow it to reach through to the places in him where matters are genuinely in a tangle." Thus, Bishop claims finally that the authentic Emerson discoverable to our best selves can still serve as a hero and prophet for the American scholar. Relying on a carefully controlled close reading of Emerson, Bishop reaches back fundamentally to join hands with the traditional notion that Emerson's highest value lies in the moral authority with which he utters permanent truths and thereby remains, as Arnold said, "the friend and aider of those who would live in the spirit."[9]

It was usual for Perry Miller, when initiating his survey of American authors, to insist on the notion that "writing is written by writers." This innocent tautology was intended to convey the idea that the great figures being studied were not primarily to be considered as landmarks in the growth of American culture nor as so many statues in an imaginary pantheon whom it was our patriotic duty to revere, but rather as *writers* whose continuing claim on our attention resides in their exhaustless *literary* vitality. Writing is not necessarily written by famous authors, with beards and visitable houses; it is the fruit of patient labor by men and women fundamentally, and often fanatically, devoted to their craft. Books, as Thoreau says in the "Reading" chapter of *Walden,* "must be read as deliberately and reservedly as they were written." And such a reading is encouraged by thinking of authors primarily as writers, and only secondarily as famous hermits, spinsters, he-men, statesmen, spiritual leaders, madmen, madwomen, or the like.

Now, it is a curious fact that Emerson, who is often acknowledged to be the greatest, or at least most important, author of the American Renaissance and even of American literary history altogether, was—before the Emerson revival of the late twentieth century—not accorded that careful scrutiny of his work as *writing* which Poe, Hawthorne, Melville, Thoreau, Dickinson, Whitman, and other more minor figures, began to receive early on. The heart of the problem seems to have lain, as I have already suggested, in the overwhelming, indeed intimidating, emphasis on Emerson's personal authority, his example, his wisdom, his high role as the spiritual father and Plato of America. Even so sharp a critic as Henry James, with his exquisitely developed sense of writing as a craft, was blinded from seeing any pervasive formal excellence in Emerson's work by the "firmness" and "purity," the "singular power," of Emerson's moral force—his "particular faculty, which has not been surpassed, for speaking to the soul in a voice of direction and authority." Though James assumed Emerson's "importance and continuance" and insisted "that he serves and will not wear out, and that indeed we cannot afford to drop him," he did so only as a special tribute to this great man, allowing him to be "a striking exception to the general rule that writings live in the last resort by their form; that they owe a large part of their fortune to the art with which they have been composed." Despite occasional "felicities, inspirations, unforgettable phrases," James felt it was "hardly too much, or too little, to say of Emerson's writings in general that they were not composed at all." He never truly achieved "a fashion and a manner" and finally "differs from most men of letters of the same degree of credit in failing to strike us as having achieved a style." James concluded his survey of Emerson's career by positing a large and significant *if:* "if Emerson goes his way, as he clearly appears to be doing, on the strength of his message alone, the case will be rare, the exception striking, and the honour great."

It is a matter of some interest, and no little amusement, that Henry's scientific brother was moved to make precisely the claim for Emerson, at the centenary celebration, which the distinguished novelist and critic had withheld. "The form of the garment was so vital with Emerson that it is impossible to separate it from the matter. They form a chemical combination—thoughts which would be trivial expressed otherwise, are important through the nouns and verbs to which he married them. The style is the man, it has been said; the man Emerson's mission culminated in his style, and if we must define him in one word, we have to call him Artist. He was an artist whose medium was verbal and who wrought in spiritual material." Perhaps it was the unsatisfied artist in William James himself who was enabled to make these observations about Emerson which, though for a long time almost universally ignored, still carry weight: his "thoughts . . . would be trivial expressed otherwise"; his "mission culminated in his style." William James's valuable hints were not picked up, and Henry's prescient *if* progressively exerted its force.[10]

Emerson, as any candid teacher of American literature in the 50's and 60's could have reported, manifestly did not make his way "on the strength of his message." He in fact, became the least appreciated, least enjoyed, least understood—indeed, least read—of America's unarguably major writers. Even many intelligent and willing students, dropped in the usual way into the great *mare tenebrum* of Emerson's weightier works, gratefully returned to shore, dragging behind them only out of a sense of duty a précis of Emerson's "message," which, they usually admitted, contained little meaning and less pleasure for them. Nor did students of Emerson's writing receive much practical help from well-intentioned critics who, while praising Emerson as a prophet of romanticism, or symbolism, or existentialism, or pragmatism, or organicism, sadly conceded that the master's reach exceeded his grasp so far as exemplifying the particular *-ism* in successful works of literary art was concerned. Seen from this perspective as a flawed genius whose theory and practice were always disjunct, Emerson may actually have exasperated his readers by seeming to promise more than he could perform. As Charles Feidelson noted, "what he gives with one hand he takes away with the other."[11]

I myself, to echo the conclusion of *Nature*, came in the 1970's to look at the world of Emerson with new eyes and was greatly gratified and exhilarated to discover a kind of verification of my views in the—surprisingly—delighted reactions of students. The Emerson we now see, I am convinced, has always existed; indeed it is the same Emerson whom William James was moved to praise as an artist. This Emerson's interest and appeal reside in the imaginative materials and structures of his writing—in his tropes and *topoi*, his metaphors and verbal wit, in the remarkable consistencies of his conceiving mind and executing hand. What I am prepared to state categorically is that the familiar rubrics of Emersonian thought, the stock in trade of much Emerson criticism, though undeniably there, can be a positive hindrance to the enjoyment of Emerson's writing. Though some Emersonians will undoubtedly continue until the end of time to chew over such concepts as Compensation, the Over-Soul, Correspondence, Self-Reliance, Spiritual Laws, *et id genus omne*, the trouble with such things is that they are not very interesting. They make Emerson seem awfully remote, abstract, and—yes—academic. My experience has been that when these topics are mentioned the mind closes, one's attention wanders. Similarly, the now standard debate over Emerson's presumed inability, or refusal, to confront evil (usually capitalized) has had the unfortunate effect first of making him seem shallow compared, say, to a Hawthorne or a Melville; and, second and more importantly, it has frequently shifted discussions of Emerson to a high plane of theological or metaphysical argument where one's ordinary sense of reality, and the powers of practical criticism, falter in pursuit. Evil with a capital has a way of teasing the imagination into silence.

My thesis then is simple: Emerson, as he himself frequently insisted, is fundamentally a poet whose meaning lies in his manipulations of language and figure. The best guide to change, or growth, or consistency in Emerson's thought, is his poetic imagination and not his philosophic arguments or discursive logic. The alert reader can discover, and take much pleasure in discovering, remarkable verbal strategies, metaphoric patterns, repetitions and developments of sound, sense, and image throughout Emerson's writing. One finds an impressively unified consciousness everywhere in control of its fertile imaginings.[12]

As an initial illustration of what I am claiming for Emerson's work, I would momentarily leave aside the juiciest plums—*Nature*, the "Divinity School Address," the great essays—and turn briefly to a book for which, probably, only the most modest assertions of imaginative structure can be made, hoping, nevertheless, that its example will prove instructive. Like most nineteenth-century travel books, *English Traits* cannot be expected to succeed entirely in transcending the episodic nature of its author's peregrinations and his own normal desire, with his varied audience in mind, to include something of interest to everyone. Typically, since such an omnium-gatherum will amiably avoid pushing toward overwhelming conclusions and let its appeal reside precisely in its miscellaneous character, any search for organic form seems defeated at the outset—perhaps.

In the preface to an edition of *English Traits*, Howard Mumford Jones confronts Emerson's difficulty in making a unified book of his heterogeneous materials and complains specifically that Emerson spoiled the natural form of his work by beginning with a chapter on his first, earlier visit to England and concluding, not logically with "Results," but anticlimactically with his "Speech at Manchester."[13] I believe, however, that the sympathetic reader of *English Traits* can supply some possible justifications for Emerson's procedure. The opening chapter is an expression of disappointment with England, and this is the keynote of the book. Here, the disappointment, though it has a personal basis, is emblematic of the young American's unfulfilled expectations of the Old World and prophetic of his developing hope for America. He goes abroad eager to meet certain great men—Landor, Coleridge, Carlyle, Wordsworth—and finds them sadly isolated, mutually repellent, and embittered, "prisoners . . . of their own thought" who cannot "bend to a new companion and think with him." They thus fail as poets in Emerson's own high sense (as "liberating gods," that is, who help man "to escape the custody of that body in which he is pent up, and of that jail-yard of individual relations in which he is enclosed"). Their vaunted originality somehow evaporates for the young seeker: Coleridge's talk falls "into certain commonplaces"; Wordsworth expiates his "departure from the common in one direction" by his "conformity in every other." Significantly, both Carlyle and Wordsworth talk much of America, turning Emerson's thoughts back whence he came and pointing us forward to Emerson's peroration in Manchester, where he will, as delicately as possible, summarize his negative reaction to this "aged England," this "mournful country," with its pathetically atomistic island mentality, its conformity to custom, its played-out spirit, and suggest that if England does not find new vigor to restore her decrepit old age (as the weight of his whole book tends to prove it cannot), "the elasticity and hope of mankind must henceforth remain on the Alleghany ranges, or nowhere."

The huge, virtually endless American continent is the mysterious force against which Emerson measures the fixed, finite, island prison, the "Gibraltar of propriety," which is England. Here we have the central imaginative structure of *English Traits*. Though initially England seems "a paradise of comfort and plenty," "a garden," we quickly learn that this miracle of rare device, like Spenser's Bower of Bliss, is a false paradise where "art conquers nature" and, "under an ash-colored sky," confounds night and day. Coal smoke and soot unnaturally make all times and seasons of one hue, "give white sheep the color of black sheep, discolor the human saliva, contaminate the air, poison many plants and corrode the monuments and buildings." This is the epitome of the fallen modern world of industry, where "a terrible machine has possessed itself of the ground, the air, the men and women, and hardly even thought is free." Everything, we are told, "is false and forged," "man is made as a Birmingham button," and "steam is almost an Englishman." The whole island has been transformed into the thoroughfare of trade where all things can be described, in Emerson's eyes, as either "artificial" or "factitious": the breeds of cattle, the fish-filled ponds and streams, the climate, illumination, heating, the English social system, the law, property, crimes, education, manners, customs—indeed, "the whole fabric." All is "Birminghamized, and we have a nation whose existence is a work of art—a cold, barren, almost arctic isle being made the most fruitful, luxurious and imperial land in the whole earth."

In this setting, we are not surprised to learn that the two most mysterious and imponderable of life's gifts, religion and art, are particularly vulnerable to the general fate. Since these two subjects touch the quick of Emerson's concern, it is especially fascinating to note in this regard how the fundamental paradigm of America (as revealed in and through its transcendental minister, Emerson) against which all is being tested palpitates within Emerson's language and metaphors. True religion is utterly missing from England, for it is an alien and frightful thing to the English: "it is passing, glancing, gesticular; it is a traveler, a newness, a surprise, a secret, which perplexes them and puts them out." We should keep this consciously orphic sentence in our ear as we glance at the next chapter, "Literature," on the way to Emerson's culminating vision of America. Speaking of English genius, Emerson notes: "It is retrospective. How can it discern and hail the new forms that are looming up on the horizon, new and gigantic thoughts which cannot dress themselves out of any old wardrobe of the past?" Now, the alert student of Emerson will recognize here an unmistakable echo of the opening paragraph of *Nature* ("Our age is retrospective . . . why should we grope among the dry bones of the past, or put the living generation into masquerade out of its faded wardrobe. . . . There are new lands, new men, new thoughts"). What this echo should tell us is that the very same living, prospective, titanic American nature which, Emerson insisted in 1836, would inspire a new poetry and philosophy and religion of "revelation," as opposed to the backward-looking, dead, limited British tradition—that "great apparition," as he terms it in *Nature*, is fully present to Emerson's imagination twenty years later in *English Traits* as he attempts to explain what the English spirit dares not face and isolates itself from. Walking the polished halls of English literary society, Emerson seems to find himself "on a marble floor, where nothing will grow," and he concludes that the English "fear the hostility of ideas, of poetry, of religion—ghosts which they cannot lay . . . they are tormented with fear that herein lurks a force that will sweep their system away. The artists say, 'Nature puts them out.'" Recalling the opening paragraph of *Nature* and hearing still that orphic sentence from the preceding chapter on religion, we may now feel confirmed in our intuition about Emerson's real point: that great force which threatens the English and "puts them out" is equivalent to the religio-poetic mystery of American nature.

Emerson's metaphoric confrontation between England and America, which represents the fundamental thrust of *English Traits*, culminates most forcefully and appropriately in the fourth chapter from the end, entitled "Stonehenge." Traveling with Carlyle, who argues that the English have much to teach the Americans, Emerson concedes the point but does not budge from his instinctive belief: "I surely know that as soon as I return to Massachusetts I shall lapse at once into the feeling, which the geography of America inevitably inspires, that we play the game with immense advantage; that there and not here is the seat and centre of the British race; and that no skill or activity can long compete with the prodigious natural advantages of that country, in the hands of the same race; and that England, an old and exhausted island, must one day be contented, like other parents, to be strong only in her children." Emerson's conviction that the English mind is simply rendered impotent by, and turns away self-defensively from, the enormously perplexing forces that embosom and nourish us seems strengthened by his visit to Stonehenge itself. "The chief mystery is, that any mystery should have been allowed to settle on so remarkable a monument, in a country on which all the muses have kept their eyes now for eighteen hundred years." Ignoring this strange and unsettling secret at the heart of its own island, the English mind leaves Stonehenge "to the rabbits, whilst it opens pyramids and uncovers Nineveh." Emerson completes this series of speculations and, in a very real sense, the point of his whole book in a fine paragraph toward the end of "Stonehenge" that at once expresses his own sense of America's ineffable power and his firm belief that the Englishman is unable to comprehend it:

> On the way to Winchester, whither our host accompanied us in the afternoon, my friends asked many questions respecting American landscapes, forests, houses,—my house, for example. It is not easy to answer these queries well. There, I thought, in America, lies nature sleeping, overgrowing, almost conscious, too much by half for man in the picture, and so giving a certain *tristesse,* like the rank vegetation of swamps and forests seen at night, steeped in dews and rains, which it loves; and on it man seems not able to make much impression. There, in that great sloven continent, in high Alleghany pastures, in the sea-wide sky-skirted prairie, still sleeps and murmurs and hides the great mother, long since driven away from the trim hedge-rows and over-cultivated garden of England. And, in England, I am quite too sensible of this. Every one is on his good behavior and must be dressed for dinner at six. So I put off my friends with very inadequate details, as best I could.

In the face of such a passage as this, the critic of Emerson may be commended most for appreciative silence.[14] I want only, with these lines in mind, to underline my previous point about this book and Emerson generally: namely, that the excellent moments in his writing are not, as has so often been said, incidental gems in a disjointed mosaic, but typically the shining nodal points in a carefully woven imaginative web.

Although some Emerson scholars in our own time have noticed that certain motifs or metaphors are central to Emerson's literary project, their perceptions have frequently been ignored in practical Emerson criticism. Three important examples, all from Emerson scholarship of an earlier time, will illustrate my point. In *Emerson's Angle of Vision*, Sherman Paul taught us that "for Emerson the primary agency of insight was seeing"; the eye "was his prominent faculty." Another valuable perception was offered by Vivian C. Hopkins in *Spires of Form*, where she asserted that "Emerson's own term of 'the spiral' admirably hits the combination of circular movement with upward progress which is the heart of his aesthetic. Optimism controls Emerson's idea of the circle becoming a spiral, ever rising as it revolves upon itself." Finally, Stephen Whicher, writing on "Emerson's Tragic Sense," noted that "something resembling the Fall of Man, which he had so ringingly denied, reappears in his pages."[15] I want to suggest, very briefly, how useful an awareness of three such motifs as these, often in combination with one another, can be, not only for the illumination of individual essays and books, but also for an understanding of change or development overall in Emerson's work.

Although most readers of *Nature* since 1836 have taken special notice of the famous eyeball passage, either to praise or to ridicule its extravagance, surprisingly few students, without prompting, notice that in this figure resides the compositional center of gravity of the essay.[16] Despite Emerson's insistence in this crucial paragraph that his purpose is to "see all," to become nothing more nor less than *vision*, readers of *Nature* seem generally not to see that in the magnificent opening sentence of the piece—"Our age is retrospective"— the key word means precisely what it says and is rhetorically balanced by the title of the last section—"Prospects." It is a question of seeing in a new way, a new direction. Emerson is inviting us to behold "God and nature face to face," with our own eyes, not darkly and obscurely through the lenses of history. *Nature* concerns the fall of humanity into perceptual division from the physical environment.

Salvation is nothing less than perceptual reunification—true *sight* externally and *insight* internally. The Poet, the *seer*, as Emerson was to suggest in the essay of that name, is a type of the savior "who reattaches things to nature and the Whole" through his vision:

> As the eyes of Lyncæus were said to see through the earth, so the poet turns the world to glass, and shows us all things in their right series and procession. For, through that better perception, he stands one step nearer to things, and sees the flowing or metamorphosis. . . . This insight, which expresses itself by what is called Imagination, is a very high sort of seeing, which does not come by study, but by the intellect being where and what it sees, by sharing the path, or circuit of things through forms, and so making them translucid to others.[17]

The echoes of *Nature* in this passage from "The Poet" tell us that we can all function as our own poet-saviors by becoming pellucid lenses, transparent eyeballs, and perfecting our vision. "The eye is the best of artists"; "the attentive eye" sees beauty everywhere; wise men pierce the "rotten diction" of a fallen world "and fasten words again to visible things," achieving a viable "picturesque language"; "a right action seems to fill the eye"; "insight refines" us: though "the animal eye" sees the actual world "with wonderful accuracy," it is "the eye of Reason" that stimulates us "to more earnest vision." Mounting to his splendid peroration in "Prospects," Emerson reminds us that "the ruin or the blank, that we see when we look at nature, is in our own eye. The axis of vision is not coincident with the axis of things, and so they appear not transparent but opake." A cleansing of our vision is all that is required for "the redemption of the soul." In such a case, Emerson says at the start of his last paragraph, we shall "come to look at the world with new eyes." Since "what we are, that only can we see," we must make ourselves whole again. Emerson culminates his quasi-religious vision with a ringing sentence that catches up the Christian undertone of the essay and assimilates it to the naturalistic promise of America's nascent literary hopes: "The kingdom of man over nature, which cometh not with observation,—a dominion such as now is beyond his dream of God,—he shall enter without more wonder than the blind man feels who is gradually restored to perfect sight." Emerson's last word, of course, underlines once again the point of the whole essay. And the important allusion here to Luke 17:20–21 tells us that the visionary perfection we seek has stolen upon us unawares and lies waiting within.[18]

This heady faith, expressed in the controlling trope of *Nature*, which believes that clarified sight can literally reform our world, for the most part governs the first series of Emerson's *Essays* and is embodied in the opening sentence of "Circles": "The eye is the first circle; the horizon which it forms is the second." Emerson's meaning, enforced here by a favorite pun and emphasized throughout "Circles" (when a man utters a truth, "his eye burns up the veil which shrouded all things"; when the poet breaks the chain of habitual thought, "I open my eye on my own possibilities"), is that the self, represented here by the creative eye, is primary and generative: it *forms* the horizon—goal, world view—that it sees. This is the "piercing eye" of Uriel which, in the poem of that name, is described as "a look that solved the sphere." But, as we know, by the time Emerson came to write "Uriel" in the mid-1840s his "lapse" had already taken place and his own reference to the "ardent eye" (as Thoreau was to term it) is consciously ironic. Indeed, and this is my central point, as we move into his second series of *Essays* and beyond, we may verify the fundamental shift in Emerson's optative mood brought about by his "sad self-knowledge" through simply observing the transformations that his visual metaphor undergoes. In the crucial "Experience," for example, Emerson accedes to the notion of the Fall of Man, redefining it as "the discovery we have made that we exist"—the discovery that the individual consciousness is limited and contingent. "Ever afterwards we suspect our instruments. We have learned that we do not see directly, but mediately, and that we have no means of correcting these colored and distorting lenses which we are." Emerson now has only a "perhaps" to offer concerning the "creative power" of our "subject-lenses," and he serves up his own optimistic perception from "Circles" in a new, markedly qualified, form: "People forget that it is the eye which makes the horizon." What we have created is no more than an optical illusion. Emerson further confirms his diminished sense of personal power later in the book, in the first paragraph of "Nominalist and Realist," when his trope reappears: "We have such exorbitant eyes, that on seeing the smallest arc, we complete the curve, and when the curtain is lifted from the diagram which it seemed to veil, we are vexed to find that no more was drawn than just that fragment of an arc which we first beheld. We are greatly too liberal in our construction of each other's faculty and promise." It is worth noticing, by the way, how the essentially figurative nature of Emerson's imagination unerringly guides him to the witty choice of "exorbitant" in this passage.

But an even more impressive example, in this regard, of the progressive metamorphosis of Emerson's metaphor as his perceptions changed may be found in "Fate." By 1852, when the essay was completed, Emerson had so qualified his views that Nature, which sixteen years before was the book of life and possibility, became now "the book of Fate." In 1836 Emerson asserted in "Prospects" that "nature is not fixed but fluid. Spirit alters, moulds, makes it. . . . Every spirit builds itself a house; and beyond its house a world; and beyond its world, a heaven." Now he was forced tragically to concede that "every spirit makes its house; but afterwards the house confines the spirit." Faced with this crushing sense of limitation, Emerson returned to his favorite metaphor in a new, notably ironic, mood:

The force with which we resist these torrents of tendency looks so ridiculously inadequate, that it amounts to little more than a criticism or a protest made by a minority of one, under compulsion of millions. I seemed, in the height of a tempest, to see men overboard struggling in the waves, and driven about here and there. They glanced intelligently at each other, but 'twas little they could do for one another; 'twas much if each could keep afloat alone. Well, they had a right to their eye-beams, and all the rest was Fate.

Here sight, as Jonathan Bishop has remarked well, "the sense especially associated with the intellectual freedom of the Soul, has dwindled until it can provide only a bare proof of impotence." The rhetorical procedure in "Fate," to be sure, is insistently dialectic, but this old Emersonian game of yin and yang is rather mechanically worked out, and a balance is not struck for the reader, I think, because we sense clearly where the weight of Emerson's own imagination leans. When, a few pages later, he argues for the power of individual will by saying, of the hero, that "the glance of his eye has the force of sunbeams,"[19] we can hardly fail to recall the convincing paragraph I have quoted. Intelligent glances may serve as a kind of spiritual consolation to drowning men, but eyebeams and sunbeams alike seem insubstantial as levers against the overwhelming force of Fate.

An analogous indication of discouragement in Emerson's optimistic philosophy may be seen in the fortunes of another central metaphor—that of the ascending spiral or upward-pointing staircase (or ladder). In this case, I believe we can actually pinpoint the shift in Emerson's attitude as occurring somewhere between the composition of "The Poet" and "Experience" (which is to say somewhere between late 1842 and early 1844). I think it is even possible to assert in this regard that although "The Poet" stands first in the second series of *Essays*, the ebulliently hopeful mood and metaphoric coordinates of that piece hark back to the first book of *Essays*, whereas "Experience," which is printed directly following "The Poet," actually marks a new departure in both tone and imagery.

Emerson's first collection of *Essays* is largely controlled by figures of ascension. In "Self-Reliance" we read that "the soul *becomes*," that power "resides in the moment of transition from a past to a new state, in the shooting of the gulf, in the darting to an aim." The inchoate metaphor develops in "Compensation," where Emerson affirms that "the soul refuses limits," for man's "life is a progress, and not a station." The law of nature "is growth," and "the voice of the Almighty saith, 'Up and onward for evermore!'" The method of man is "a progressive arrangement," we are told in "Spiritual Laws"; and this means, as regards the affections (in "Love"), that we must pass from lower attractions to higher ones: "the lover ascends to the highest beauty, to the love and knowledge of the Divinity, by steps on this ladder of created souls." Since, in "Friendship," we "descend to meet," we must make room for one another's merits—"let them mount and expand"—parting, if need be, so that we may "meet again on a higher platform." This is the "spiritual astronomy" of love, as it is the law of the soul's progress in "The Over-Soul" ("the soul's advances are not made by gradation, such as can be represented by motion in a straight line; but rather by ascension of state"). Emerson's figure develops further, in the first series of *Essays,* with "Circles," which is essentially devoted to working out a set of variations on the notion of man as "a self-evolving circle," a rising spiral, who scales the "mysterious ladder" of upwardly mobile life. In a very real sense, however, the figure culminates in "The Poet," for he is the Christ-like hero whose *logos* breaks our chains and allows us to "mount above these clouds and opaque airs" in which we normally dwell. Poets are "liberating gods" who preach "*ascension,* or, the passage of the soul into higher forms . . . into free space." Released by this extraordinary savior, we live the heavenly life of the redeemed imagination: "dream delivers us to dream, and, while the drunkenness lasts, we will sell our bed, our philosophy, our religion, in our opulence."[20]

This divine bubble is punctured sharply in "Experience" as Emerson, in typical fashion, picks up his own language and places it in a startling new context: "Dream delivers us to dream, and there is no end to illusion." The imagination is now seen as a kind of devil of deceit who provokes the fall of man into a "middle region" of uncertainty and confusion:

> Where do we find ourselves? In a series, of which we do not know the extremes, and believe that it has none. We wake and find ourselves on a stair; there are stairs below us, which we seem to have ascended; there are stairs above us, many a one, which go upward and out of sight. But the Genius which, according to the old belief, stands at the door by which we enter, and gives us the lethe to drink, that we may tell no tales, mixed the cup too strongly, and we cannot shake off the lethargy now at noonday. Sleep lingers all our lifetime about our eyes, as night hovers all day in the boughs of the fir-tree. All things swim and glimmer. Our life is not so much threatened as our perception. Ghostlike we glide through nature.

Vision is darkened here. Indeed, Emerson's mood is sinister, almost Poesque, as he, too, in a sort of "lonesome October," wanders "in the misty mid region of Weir" which we find in "Ulalume." Or, to use the terms of Wallace Stevens, Emerson is trapped in something like a "banal sojourn," a time of indifference, when man's depressed spirit dumbly mutters: "One has a malady, here, a malady. One feels a malady." That malady can perhaps best be described as loss of affect, a contemporary version of acedia; a dejected state in which Emerson cannot even feel that this terrible threat to perception is a threat to life because his very sense of self is "ghostlike." This is the form evil takes in Emerson's lapsarian mood. The optimistic spiral has collapsed upon itself and Emerson, having set his "heart on honesty in this chapter," finds himself forced down his ladder into what Yeats calls "the foul rag-and-bone shop of the heart." Though it would be more than mildly misleading to suggest that the Emerson of "Experience," and after, truly joins hands with Yeats in giving voice to a peculiarly modern sense of discouragement and dislocation, it is nevertheless fair to say that the Emerson who began to conceive of existence in such grayly tragic terms as these took a large step toward insuring that his writing could have a continuing life for twentieth-century readers.[21]

Most Emersonians would probably agree that to redeem Emerson by resorting to what Newton Arvin calls a "cant of pessimism" is to do him a disservice. This is not to say that the expression we find, in such an essay as "Experience," of a kind of existential *nausea,* a feeling that reality eludes us and that we are all, as Sartre says, "*super-fluous,* that is to say, amorphous, vague, and sad"—that the expression of such things in Emerson is not particularly valuable. This side of Emerson deepens our interest in him, making us feel that his sense of the way life can be sometimes corresponds more nearly to our own. But, if we resist the temptation to overemphasize Emerson's journals and letters and pay attention mainly to those published works by which the world has known him for more than a century, the fact remains that the "House of Pain" was not Emerson's dominant structure and should not constitute his major claim on us.[22]

My own intent has been to show that the problems which have perennially dogged Emerson's reputation and hindered a true appreciation of his work can largely be obviated if we focus our attention on his writing *as writing.* His work, I am saying, does have this kind of interest to a high degree; and a fundamentally literary approach to Emerson can yield surprising dividends of reading pleasure and a new understanding of what he was about. As a final short demonstration of my argument, I propose to examine a familiar—in some ways, too familiar—specimen brick from the Emerson edifice, the Divinity School "Address." Like most monuments of Emerson's prose, this piece has been so solidly in place for so long that we tend to overlook what is really in it. Though it is normally spoken of in terms of Emerson's evolving career, or the Unitarian-Transcendentalist controversy, or its doctrine (or the absence thereof), its real interest, it seems to me, lies in its exhibition of Emerson's skill as a literary strategist and of his mastery of organic form.

On the first of April preceding that momentous July evening when Emerson delivered his bombshell, he told a group of divinity students informally that "the preacher should be a poet."[23] That is precisely and totally the "doctrine" of his address, which is both an exposition and an enactment of that belief. The key concept, and word, in the address is *beauty*, for Emerson was determined to prove that "the institution of preaching—the speech of man to men" (which is also, we should note, the institution of literature) is utterly nugatory if moral truth is separated from the delight of living. The "new Teacher" whom Emerson called for in the last sentence of his speech was charged with showing "that the Ought, that Duty, is one thing with Science, with Beauty, and with Joy." Accordingly, those two final words, beauty and joy, govern Emerson's startlingly heretical portrait in the address of the archetypal preacher, Christ, who is offered to us as a kind of first-century aesthete, replete with "locks of beauty," who was "ravished" by the "supreme Beauty" of the soul's mystery and went out in a "jubilee of sublime emotion" to tell us all "that God incarnates himself in man, and evermore goes forth anew to take possession of his world." The man who is most enamored of the "beauty of the soul" and the world in which it is incarnated is called to serve as "its priest or poet," and Emerson urges such men to feel their call "in throbs of desire and hope."[24]

It is precisely the absence of any evidence of such emotions that characterizes the unnamed formalist preacher whom Emerson describes in a striking *exemplum* about halfway through the address:

I once heard a preacher who sorely tempted me to say, I would go to church no more. Men go, thought I, where they are wont to go, else had no soul entered the temple in the afternoon. A snow storm was falling around us. The snow storm was real; the preacher merely spectral; and the eye felt the sad contrast in looking at him, and then out of the window behind him, into the beautiful meteor of the snow. He had lived in vain. He had no one word intimating that he had laughed or wept, was

married or in love, had been commended, or cheated, or cha-
grined. If he had ever lived and acted, we were none the wiser
for it. The capital secret of his profession, namely, to convert
life into truth, he had not learned. Not one fact in all his experience, had he yet imported into his doctrine. This man had
ploughed, and planted, and talked, and bought, and sold; he
had read books; he had eaten and drunken; his head aches; his
heart throbs; he smiles and suffers; yet was there not a surmise,
a hint, in all the discourse, that he had ever lived at all. Not a
line did he draw out of real history. The true preacher can be
known by this, that he deals out to the people his life,—life
passed through the fire of thought.[25]

Emerson, the preacher, moves in thought down into the congregation and reminds himself of a typical parishioner's experience:
boredom.[26] If habit had not brought him to the church, he would
not have gone, for there is nothing to attract him, no promise of
reality, no pleasure. The true preacher, the true poet, bases his verbal
art on personal experience in the actual world that surrounds us all,
thus transmuting "life into truth." Otherwise, words are mere counters that leave us untouched. Emerson's real genius here, however,
lies in the business of the snowstorm. Playing the role of listener, he
allows his wandering attention to move outside the window and find
its sole available pleasure in the "beautiful meteor of the snow."
Perhaps only a New England consciousness could invent such a
phrase; but then Emerson is writing of what he knows and loves (as
in his poem "The Snow-Storm"). The fine irony of the passage is
that the preacher should seem *spectral* compared even to the frigid
and ghostly reality of snow. What Emerson has done himself is to
insist on some sort of interpenetration between that which goes
on inside the church and the beautiful world outside. His example
suggests that the skillful preacher will attempt to do the same.[27]

Now, in our backward movement through the address, let us
confront the magnificent strategies of the opening passage. On what

was apparently a splendid Sunday evening in July 1838, Emerson mounted the pulpit in Divinity Hall to speak, nominally, to the senior class in divinity; but they were a small group, and the room was packed with faculty members and friends. Emerson's intent, as I have noted, was to *demonstrate* that "the preacher should be a poet," that religious truth and human pleasure must coexist, and that the two worlds of chapel and physical universe are mutually enriching. Accordingly, in a prose that is consciously purple, Emerson began his address by inviting this sternly theological audience to allow its attention to wander, as his own had wandered on that boring Sunday in winter, beyond the chapel window to the ripe world of nature outside:

> In this refulgent summer, it has been a luxury to draw the breath of life. The grass grows, the buds burst, the meadow is spotted with fire and gold in the tint of flowers. The air is full of birds, and sweet with the breath of the pine, the balm-of-Gilead, and the new hay. Night brings no gloom to the heart with its welcome shade. Through the transparent darkness the stars pour their almost spiritual rays. Man under them seems a young child, and his huge globe a toy. The cool night bathes the world as with a river, and prepares his eyes again for the crimson dawn. The mystery of nature was never displayed more happily. The corn and the wine have been freely dealt to all creatures, and the never-broken silence with which the old bounty goes forward, has not yielded yet one word of explanation. One is constrained to respect the perfection of this world, in which our senses converse.

An example of how inattentive even some of the most devoted Emersonians have been to the master's art is provided by Stephen Whicher's comment: "the address itself was calculated to give no offense, on grounds of vocabulary at least, to a Unitarian audience." It is precisely in its vocabulary that the barefaced effrontery of Emerson's gambit resides. There is probably not another place in all his writings where Emerson is so consciously arch. The only astute comment I have found on this passage belongs to Jonathan Bishop: "the immediate rhetorical motive, evidently enough, is shock: an address to a small group of graduating divinity students is not supposed to begin by an appeal to the sensual man." Emerson's stance, as Bishop says, is that of a "voluptuary," and the word is well chosen. Following the "unusually aureate" (Bishop's term) *refulgent*—which suggests a kind of shining forth, or epiphany, in the summer's beauty—Emerson explodes his real charge in the sentence: *luxury*. We must remind ourselves that Emerson's audience, trained in theology, was not likely to overlook the implications of that red flag, for *luxuria*, one of the seven deadly sins, means lust. Although that technical meaning, of course, is not Emerson's, a calculated air of aesthetic indulgence permeates this opening remark.[28]

In the sentences that follow, Emerson measures out his language with extreme care to one end: the creation in words of an unfallen world of the senses where formal, traditional religion is unnecessary because nature provides its own sacraments. It is hard to see how Emerson's frank appropriation of religious terms and concepts could have failed to offend much of his audience. The rays of the stars are *almost spiritual*. (Is not heaven then *really* above our heads? Conversely, can a natural phenomenon *almost* approach spiritual truth?) Man, returned to the innocence of childhood, is bathed by the cool night as in baptismal waters, whereby his eyes are *prepared* for the dawn (a familiar type of the coming of Christ).[29] The technical term *mystery* is applied to nature; but unlike theological mysteries, this one is openly and happily "displayed." In the next sentence, Emerson announces that the central sacrament, the Eucharist (over which, of course, he had created a controversy when he left the Second Church of Boston six years earlier), is "freely dealt to all creatures" by nature—without condition or exclusion. Then, to a congregation still committed to the belief that the creation is fully expounded in the Bible, Emerson states that no "word of explanation" has been provided—and implies that none is needed. Finally, this Christian audience, all children of the Puritans, are told that they are "constrained to respect," not (as we should expect) the dogmas and duties of their faith, but rather the *perfection* of this world, a totally natural world, the one "in which our senses converse." Can we really doubt that to most of Emerson's listeners all of this seemed the sheerest effrontery (although to many others since it has seemed merely a flowery portal, the blandly poetic induction to a serious theological dissertation)? But it is clear that Emerson's aim was not fundamentally to offer an insult but to enact a meaning which would develop organically in the course of his address and to which he would "come full circle" at the end: namely, as we have noted, that Ought and Beauty, Duty and Joy, Science and Ecstasy, Divinity and the World, must merge in the new hypostatic unity of a living religion of the soul.

There is "a sort of drollery," Henry James remarks, in the spectacle of a society in which the author of the Divinity School address could be considered "profane." What they failed to see, James continues, is "that he only gave his plea for the spiritual life the advantage of a brilliant expression."[30] Emerson, of course, has long since ceased to be thought profane. The problem is exactly the reverse: it is Emerson's pieties that have damned him. What I have tried to argue here is simply that we can, in search of a living Emerson, make much better use of the advantage of which James speaks: Emerson's "brilliant expression."

FOUR

REPRESENTING AMERICA

It was Emerson, as a figure in literary culture, who really put America on the map; who created for himself the practically nonexistent role of man of letters, and for about a half-century— from the gritty age of Jackson to the gilded age of Grant—criticized, cajoled, sometimes confused, but mainly inspired audiences in America and abroad. When Emerson died in 1882 he was indisputably a *figure*—sometimes a figure of fun, but mainly one to be spoken of with reverence approaching awe. Matthew Arnold declared that Emerson's was the most important work done in prose in the nineteenth century. Nietzsche called him a "brother soul." One of his disciples, Moncure Conway, likened him to Buddha, and William James pronounced him divine.[1]

Somewhat more equivocal homage was also paid to Emerson in the fiction of the period. In the novels of Howells he is seen both as the prophet of pie-in-the-sky and the proponent of pie in the morning. In Kate Chopin's *The Awakening*, he helps both to raise and extinguish the consciousness of the restive heroine as she falls asleep over the *Essays* while plotting her escape from a stifling bourgeois marriage. Most notably, in Henry James's *The Bostonians* the master's spirit appears incarnated in the irrepressible though aged Miss Birdseye, the "frumpy little missionary" who represents a last link with the "heroic age of New England life—the age of plain living and high thinking, of pure ideals and earnest effort, of moral passion and noble experiment." She still burns with the "unquenched flame" of Transcendentalism, and, in the "simplicity of her vision," looks to a higher if slightly faded reality: "the only thing that was still actual for her," James avers, "was the elevation of the species by the reading of Emerson and the frequentation of Tremont Temple." He declares her to be "sublime," but gives us reason to wonder about that heroic reading of Emerson through what are memorably described as "displaced" and "undiscriminating" spectacles. Somehow, the Transcendental vision had gone askew, the transparent eyeball seemed to be clouding over. Soon Henry Adams would pronounce Emerson "naif," and T. S. Eliot would dismiss him as "an encumbrance."[2]

If Emerson seemed old hat to disconsolate intellectuals in the 20's because of his cosmic optimism, that did not keep ordinary readers from enjoying his aphorisms and apothegms. Bliss Perry's *The Heart of Emerson's Journals* was a best-seller in 1926. But even Perry had to admit by 1931 that Transcendentalism had long since gone out of fashion and that its epitaph was being written in doctoral dissertations.[3] Though Emerson himself was still holding his own among a readership as yet unbesieged by diet books and sex manuals, he was nevertheless steadily receding into an historical past that would soon be virtually nonexistent except to the specialist. Now, too, Emerson has largely been relegated to the doctoral dissertation and scholarly monograph—though Melville and Hawthorne are hardly household words. America's great literary figures and their books appear to be largely invisible to the distracted and impatient eyes of what, in some quarters, is described as a "post-literate" society.

Nevertheless, I intend to argue that Emerson continues to nag the American conscience even when its ears are filled with other things. Emerson did not simply write stirring lectures, addresses, essays, and poems; he was passionately concerned with cultural analysis and devoted to cultural growth—twin imperatives that informed his total career. Emerson sits at the crossroads in a crucial moment of American history and like his own sphinx asks the unanswered questions of our collective life—questions about the relative claims of conservatism and radicalism, the establishment and the movement, private property and communism; questions about slavery and freedom, the rights of women, the viability of institutions, the possibility of reform, the efficacy of protest, the exercise of power—indeed he asks perpetually about the meaning of America itself and its prospects among the nations. I offer this very abbreviated naming of topics only by way of suggesting that Emerson has strong claims to being considered an *American* thinker deeply involved in public culture and not only a Transcendental meditator on the infinitude of the private self. There is no other writer of America's so-called literary renaissance who was more soaked in culture. "Emerson's roots lay deep in the common soil," Bliss Perry notes; "he represented a significant generation of American endeavor, and . . . was a factor in the social and political as well as the intellectual history of his era."[4]

Why should it be necessary to rehearse what was a commonplace of Emerson criticism more than fifty years ago? Because the most persistent position taken in the 1960's and '70's by well-respected and much read commentators is that Emerson was all but totally abstracted from his place and time, from what is called "history" and "culture" and "the associated life." "The idea of community was dying in him and his fellows," writes Quentin Anderson. "He would not be involved in time, he was not a member of a generation." Along the same lines, Ann Douglas argues that Emerson, as opposed to Margaret Fuller, led a life of metaphor, substituted eloquence for experience, lived in literature and not in history. Somehow these critics, in Larzer Ziff's phrase, became convinced of Emerson's "turn away from history"—of his having conceived of himself as transcending time and circumstance so that he might, like Marie Antoinette, play at being a shepherd in some primitive Arcadia of the spirit.[5]

But Emerson believed no such thing—except perhaps in his youth when he allowed himself to parrot 4th of July rhetoric about the "uncontaminated innocence" of America versus the corruptions of the Old World. Even on this occasion—I am citing an 1821 journal entry when Emerson was 18—he complains that "it is the misfortune of America that her sudden maturity of national condition was accompanied with the knowledge of good and *evil* which would better belong to an older country." He was *hoping* for "reform and improvement," not making a unilateral declaration of independence from the collective experience of humankind. Boston thought of itself more as the Athens of the West than as the garden of Eden. When Emerson did cast himself in the role of primal man before the Fall, it was for the purpose of introducing a certain tone of feeling— a momentary sense of release from the malady of the quotidian— into his discourse, not for the purpose of deluding himself and others as to where they actually stood. "Adam in the garden," he wrote in 1839, "I am to new name all the beasts in the field & all the gods in the Sky. I am to invite men drenched in time to recover themselves & come out of time, & taste their native immortal air." Emerson was not thinking of casting off his clothes along with his intellectual baggage and fleeing into the virgin forest to start life over but rather of planning a winter lecture series that would give his audience a sense of refreshment and renewal. A few days after setting down his Adamic entry, Emerson admonished himself to trust his own time, and the lecture series he produced was entitled "The Present Age."[6]

Emerson in fact believed that the best use of history "is to enhance our estimate of the present hour." If he *was* coming out of history it was for the purpose of entering his own time more fully. What Emerson disliked was the notion of some Hegelian dialectic or logic of events that reduces individual experience to a mere moment in an unfolding drama. That was not his definition of freedom. What he rejected was the notion of history as an iron rule of cause and effect that necessarily determines present conduct—the notion, for example, that we are all controlled and circumscribed by descent or inheritance. Men and women *are*, Emerson might say, indubitably because their parents have been, but *what* they are is yet to be seen. Time will devour us unless we master it. Emerson internalized or subjectified history so as to be able to use it, to make it part of his own fiber. He did not step out of history but into it, deciding to make it rather than be made by it. "Every mind must know the whole lesson for itself," he writes, "must go over the whole ground. What it does not see, what it does not live, it will not know." Observing that all history was acted by human spirits and written by human minds like his own, Emerson declared himself competent to interpret all the texts that time had transmitted. The way to solve the riddle of the sphinx is to set yourself up on her pedestal. Thus Emerson insisted that "an autobiography should be a book of answers from one individual to the main questions of the time." Why should we pay attention to what does not concern us? "Shall he be a scholar?" he continues, "the infirmities & ridiculousness of the scholar being clearly seen. Shall he fight? Shall he seek to be rich? Shall he go for the ascetic or the conventional life?. . . Shall he value mathematics? Read Dante? or not? Aristophanes? Plato? Cosmogonies . . . What shall he say of Poetry? What of Astronomy? What of religion? Then let us hear his conclusions respecting government & politics. Does he pay taxes and record his title deeds? Does Goethe's Autobiography answer these questions?" The inference is that it does not, at least not for an American living in the 1840s.[7]

In dealing with Emerson, then, criticism is always in danger of neglecting the actual record in its density and richness and becoming infatuated with its own theses—viewing Emerson, for example, only as an endless seeker with no past at his back, a sort of Transcendental rocket racing into trackless space and attempting to drag American literature with it. To speak honestly, however, though we are all inextricably wedded to time and the "associated life," we nevertheless have moments, perhaps neither quite in time nor quite out of it, when another sort of experience seems possible. A fit of religious exaltation might be one example, sexual ecstasy another. In such moods, if we were Emerson, we might write *Nature* or "The Over-Soul" or "Bacchus" or "Merlin"; but such an expression could only be partial, never the whole of what we want to say. "I am always insincere," Emerson notes, "as always knowing there are other moods." We may wish to sell all we have and join this crusade against time and change, but Emerson will not allow us to hold him to it. We discover that he is not always the moonshiny man we took him for.[8]

James Joyce was no Transcendentalist but even he allowed Stephen Dedalus to exclaim that history was a nightmare from which he was trying to awaken. Of course, with a name like Dedalus it was easy to feel burdened by the past, and the same was true for Ralph Waldo Emerson. The Protestant Reformation was in his blood, even antedating the settlement of America, as was implied by a middle name derived from the Waldensian sect. (The site of Thoreau's hut on Emerson's property was thus an appropriate place for the man Emerson called "a protestant *à l'outrance*.")[9] Far from refusing to be "a member of a generation," as Anderson claimed, Emerson knew precisely which generation he belonged to—the seventh in a line directly descending from the settlers of the Bay Colony.

American history was family history for him. Peter Bulkeley, "one of Emerson's sixty-four grandfathers at the seventh remove," according to Oliver Wendell Holmes's calculation, was moderator, along with Thomas Hooker, at the famous Cambridge Synod of 1637, and resolved that "an assemblage of females, consisting of sixty or more, as is now every week formed, in which one of them, in the character of principal and prophetess, undertakes to expound the scriptures, resolve casuistical cases, and establish doctrines, is determined to be irregular and disorderly." That resolution was passed in order to deal with antinomian Anne Hutchinson, but Margaret Fuller's conversations, which Emerson and others attended with so much pleasure, might also have been labeled disorderly conduct if the authority of the theocrats had not been broken in the continuing Protestant Reformation in America. Emerson's other forebears had much to do with it. His father William noted with chagrin in his dutiful *Historical Sketch of the First Church in Boston* that his own great-grandfather and grandfathers were zealous supporters of George Whitefield. It was therefore natural for Emerson to continue the struggle when his own time came. He characterized his father's generation as belonging to an "early ignorant & transitional *Month-of-March,* in our New England culture," thereby clearly implying that his own Transcendental summertime was the inevitable next step. Although that all but insolent way of describing his father's own historical moment scarcely did justice to William Emerson's accomplishments as a liberal Congregationalist—he helped to advance the cause of the arts by joining in the founding of the *Monthly Anthology* and the Massachusetts Historical Society—it does suggest that the young Emerson's own identity consciously emerged from generational conflict. Like his father he had graduated from Harvard College and become pastor of an important Boston church; and again like his father he was elected to the Boston School Committee and named chaplain to the state senate. It was all easy, fatally easy, but the identity thus procured was false. It was precisely by stepping into his father's shoes that Emerson had avoided the responsibility of defining and being a member of his own generation, and it was only when he cast himself loose from the church and became a Transcendentalist that he was enabled to think of a generation—in the words of Eduard Spranger—as a "culture-renewing moment" and not as an "age-group movement."[10]

Nothing was more crucial to Emerson's development than his realization that his generation, his "culture-renewing moment," constituted a new and distinct age. Instead of binding him, time had presented him with an opportunity. He became virtually obsessed with defining his age. As early as 1827 he set down in his journal under the heading "Peculiarities of the present Age" almost a program for his own career: "It is said to be the age of the first person singular. . . . The reform of the Reformation . . . Transcendentalism. Metaphysics & ethics look inwards." By the following year at least he had read Hazlitt's *The Spirit of the Age* and found out more about his destiny. He learned there, for example, that Wordsworth and Coleridge, though members of his father's "age-group movement," were closer to him in their own impulses and aims. They—but especially Wordsworth—were for Hazlitt pure emanations of the spirit of the age, the *modern* spirit, ushered in and exemplified by the French Revolution. The specter of what Hazlitt called "legitimacy" and the spirit of liberty were locked in a life and death struggle. As early as 1801 the writer and reformer Hannah More suggested presciently that the spirit of the revolution had unlocked a force fomenting generational conflict that would inform the Zeitgeist for some time to come: "Not only sons but daughters," she wrote, "have adopted something of that spirit of independence and disdain of control, which characterizes the time." It was a time for protest and original action, and Emerson knew this well enough; but the grip of tradition was strong and this young Jacob found it difficult to wring a blessing from the patriarchal specter with whom he wrestled.[11]

Waldo had been educated to prize his pedigree, though it was his own humor to despise it. And there, close by his side, was his father's sister and surrogate, Aunt Mary, who frequently spoke of the virtues of Waldo's clergymen ancestors, renowned for their piety and elo-quence. He acknowledged all that but chafed under the weighty inheritance, insisting, bravely: "The dead sleep in their moonless night; my business is with the living." His father's spirit, however, both introjected and externalized in Aunt Mary, still walked rest-lessly abroad and asked to be remembered. Quentin Anderson writes of the "failure of the fathers," but Emerson was more concerned with the likelihood of his own failure in attempting to establish a new identity and vocation after he had cast off the well-established one of his father. On the title-page of *The Spirit of the Age* Hazlitt had invoked Hamlet, and that is precisely how Emerson felt. Later he would insist that "it was not until the 19th century, whose specula-tive genius is a sort of living Hamlet, that the tragedy of Hamlet could find such wondering readers." Hazlitt had begun his chapter on Coleridge by lamenting that "the present is an age of talkers, and not of doers; and the reason is, that the world is growing old. We are so far advanced in the Arts and Sciences, that we live in retrospect, and doat on past achievements." Troubled by such an allegation, Emerson would both echo it and strike out at it in the opening of his first book: "Our age is retrospective. It builds the sepulchres of the fathers. . . ." The burden of the past—America's religious history as personal imperative—was strong and debilitating for Emerson.[12]

The following year, 1837, in "The American Scholar," he whis-tled a brave tune as he walked past the old sepulchres, but the bones rattled again and his inner debate revived: "Our age is bewailed as the age of Introversion. Must that needs be evil? We, it seems, are critical; we are embarrassed with second thoughts; we cannot enjoy anything for hankering to know whereof the pleasure consists; we are lined with eyes; we see with our feet; the time is infected with Hamlet's unhappiness,—'Sicklied o'er with the pale cast of thought.'" He did not think that his own visionary gleam was a thing to be pitied. Should he, like Oedipus, put out his eyes because he had offended his father? One year later Emerson delivered his decisive blow against his father's church and profession in The Divinity

School Address and then, indeed, the bones rattled more strongly than ever. Even friends of his own age were troubled, complaining that though they approved intellectually of his doctrine, their feelings were still bound to the old ways. Emerson replied to one such that he "would write for his epitaph, 'Pity 'tis, 'tis true.'" What could this brave New World Hamlet do when surrounded by so many youthful Poloniuses? He would have to continue striking out even at the risk of wounding them. Emerson's fundamental criticism was that America—or New England at least—had devoted far too much energy to arid theological and ecclesiastical dispute. His patriotism consisted in saying simply this: that the American mind and spirit had better ways to occupy itself.[13]

There can be little doubt that Emerson's personal sense of paralysis and uncertainty during the crucial period when he was forging his new identity colored his thoughts and utterances for many years to come. In Ann Douglas's formulation, "as chief apostle of the emerging cult of self-confidence, Emerson would spend his life in a complex effort to shut out the voices of self-contempt." That is not wrong, but I would shift the emphasis a bit. Emerson's Hamlet-complex, so to speak, made him perennially concerned with questions of manliness and potency. As he would come to phrase it in the 1850s, "life is a search after power"; but under his breath one can hear Emerson saying, "our experience in life, though, is too often one of powerlessness." The exercise of power, especially in an American context, troubled Emerson, and this internal debate found its most cogent public expression in his last great book, *The Conduct of Life*. As a compendium of what is usually considered Emerson's most mature and worldly wisdom the book is worth returning to, and one such reconsideration was included in A. Bartlett Giamatti's baccalaureate to the Yale class of 1981.[14]

Still uneasy, I think, as was Quentin Anderson, about the student revolution of the late 60's and early 70s', Giamatti characterized Emerson's views as "those of a brazen adolescent" and recommended that they be jettisoned. Echoing Anderson, and others, Giamatti pronounced himself disturbed at what he took to be Emerson's desire "to sever America from Europe, and American culture and scholarship and politics from whatever humankind had fashioned before." He argued that Emerson stood for "self-generated, unaffiliated power." Emerson, he claimed, was a prophet "of the secular religion that was the new America" of his time, and Giamatti's key text was the essay "Power" in *The Conduct of Life*. Here is his commentary, in brief:

> In the dark pages of that powerful meditation on power, on the eve of the War, Emerson amply reflects a view of politics and politicians that is disdainful of the hurly-burly, the compromising and dirtiness of it all. But Emerson makes it clear that he does not share those fastidious views. Those views, he says, are only held by the "timid man"; by the "churchmen and men of refinement," implicitly effete and bookish. Emerson was not for them. He was for the man who is strong, healthy, unfettered, the man who knows that nothing is got for nothing and who will stop at nothing to put himself in touch with events and their force. . . . The "thinkers" Emerson really admires are those with "coarse energy,—the 'bruisers,' who have run the gauntlet of caucus and tavern through the county or the state," the politicians who despite their vices have "the good-nature of strength and courage."

Now *The Conduct of Life* is a manifestly and designedly dialectic exercise, chapter balancing and opposing chapter in the Emersonian mode, and should be read that way. But we may at least test the accuracy of Giamatti's paraphrase by listening to Emerson's words:

> Those who have most of this coarse energy,—the 'bruisers,' who have run the gauntlet of caucus and tavern through the county or the state, have their own vices, but they have the good nature of strength and courage. Fierce and unscrupulous, they are usually frank and direct, and above falsehood. Our politics fall into bad hands, and churchmen and men of refinement, it

seems agreed, are not fit persons to send to Congress. Politics is a deleterious profession, like some poisonous handicrafts. Men in power have no opinions, but may be had cheap for any opinion, for any purpose,—and if it be only a question between the most civil and the most forcible, I lean to the last. These Hoosiers and Suckers are really better than the snivelling opposition. Their wrath is at least of a bold and manly cast.[15]

We notice that Emerson is not really eulogizing the "bruisers"; indeed he says that "men in power have no opinions, but may be had cheap for any opinion." Though he admires their "strength and courage," he knows that they are "unscrupulous." What appeals to him is their candor and directness: whatever they are, they *are* that honestly. Emerson understands that "politics is a deleterious profession," that none come back quite clean from bathing in those murky waters. All high principles are finally compromised in the Washington miasma. The best we can hope for, says Emerson, is men of rough honesty who have no stomach for lying or truckling and will stand boldly for what they want, be it good or bad. They will use what power they can and not dissemble, and we are therefore enabled to meet them on their own grounds. Emerson simply had come to the realization that the exercise of power is the name of the game in politics. "Our people," he writes in his journal in 1844, "are slow to learn the wisdom of sending character instead of talent to Congress. Again & again they have sent a man of great acuteness, a fine scholar, a fine forensic orator, and some master of the brawls has crunched him up in his hand like a bit of paper."[16]

That is the obvious bearing of Emerson's remark in "Power" about "churchmen and men of refinement." Giamatti claims that Emerson is disdainful of them and "not for them." But I believe Emerson was simply articulating his *own* sense of powerlessness— and that of his class—when faced with raw and brutal force. He says, let us observe again, "our politics fall into bad hands, and churchmen and men of refinement, it seems agreed, are not fit persons to send to Congress." They may be fit for pulpits and lyceum halls and college classrooms, as Emerson himself was, but they are not fit for Congress, where the "strong, healthy, unfettered" are the ones who carry the day in the caucus room and senate chamber and must therefore be met by opponents who can deal with them on their own terms. But in the 1845 journal entry on which Emerson drew for this passage in "Power," he concludes by insisting: "Yet a bully cannot lead the age."[17]

It is worth adding, in connection with Giamatti's allegation that Emerson rejected "churchmen and men of refinement," that Emerson had reason enough, by the time he published *The Conduct of Life* in 1860, to feel betrayed by the presumed men of principle of his own class and background. Following Webster's infamous speech of the 7th of March 1850 in favor of the Fugitive Slave Law, almost 1,000 distinguished citizens of Boston, including Oliver Wendell Holmes Sr., published a letter in support of Webster's position and Emerson was outraged. As the crisis over the Fugitive Slave Law sharpened, Emerson filled his journal with angry denunciations of men of refinement and churchmen who supported what he called the "filthy law." "The fame of Webster ends in this nasty law," he wrote, "and as for the Andover & Boston preachers, Dr Dewey & Dr Sharpe who deduce kidnapping from their Bible, tell the poor dear doctor if this be Christianity, it is a religion of dead dogs, let it never pollute the ears & hearts of noble children again."[18]

After President Fillmore signed the Fugitive Slave Law, Sharp preached a sermon in which he argued that "free citizens of the United States, living under the protection, and enjoying the benefits of our blessed laws, with all the advantages of the national compact, [cannot] be justified in encouraging poor fugitive slaves to acts of resistance." Such was the climate in which Emerson was writing. "I met an episcopal clergyman," he notes, "& allusion being made to Mr Webster's treachery, he replied, 'Why, do you know I think that the great action of his life?' I am told"—Emerson goes on—"they are all involved in one hot haste of terror, presidents of colleges &

professors, saints & brokers, insurers, lawyers, importers, jobbers, there is not an unpleasing sentiment, a liberal recollection, not so much as a snatch of an old song for freedom dares intrude." It was at this time that James Russell Lowell's vernacular mouthpiece, Hosea Biglow, lamented: "Massachusetts,—God forgive her,/She's akneelin' with the rest!"[19]

"We have seen the great party of property and education in the country," Emerson was to write, "drivelling and huckstering away, for views of party fear or advantage, every principle of humanity and the dearest hopes of mankind; the trustees of power only energetic when mischief could be done, imbecile as corpses when evil was to be prevented." Emerson was worried in the long run less about the southern democrats and their doomed cause than he was about the propertied Whigs of the north with their material interests. They, and not the "bruisers," were the real "trustees of power." Can one actually believe, with Giamatti, that Emerson extolled "self-generated, unaffiliated power," when we hear him saying, "The American marches with a careless swagger to the height of power, very heedless of his own liberty or of other peoples', in his reckless confidence that he can have all he wants, risking all the prized charters of the human race, bought with battles and revolutions and religion, gambling them all away for a paltry selfish gain"?[20]

Emerson would have nothing to do with an American civilization, so-called, willing to cover its crimes with cries of manifest destiny and America first. "We have much to learn, much to correct," he writes, "a great deal of lying vanity. The spread eagle must fold his foolish wings and be less of a peacock." "I wish to see America," he continues, "not like the old powers of the earth, grasping, exclusive and narrow, but a benefactor such as no country ever was, hospitable to all nations, legislating for all nationalities. Nations were made to help each other as much as families were; and all advancement is by ideas, and not by brute force or mechanic force." That last clause is essential Emerson.[21]

Emerson was a severe critic of an America capable of invading Mexico, oppressing blacks, and denying women equal rights. He was outspoken on all these issues and had to suffer public obloquy for his positions. "Humanity asks," he writes, "that government shall not be ashamed to be tender and paternal, but that democratic institutions shall be more thoughtful for the interests of women, for the training of children, and for the welfare of sick and unable persons, and serious care of criminals, than was ever any the best government of the Old World." America in the New World represented for Emerson at least potentially the noblest hopes of humankind. "It is our part," he notes, "to carry out to the last the ends of liberty and justice." As against the degraded New England voice that would finally proclaim that "the business of America is business," Emerson argued for a different definition: "Trade and government will not alone be the favored aims of mankind, but every useful, every elegant art, every exercise of the imagination, the height of reason, the noblest affection, the purest religion will find their home in our institutions, and write our laws for the benefit of men."[22]

Emerson sat for better than forty years in his study in Concord experiencing what he calls the "tedious joys" of reading and writing in order to set his place, his people, himself down on paper. Far from indulging himself in an escape from history or a life of metaphor, Emerson was concerned to represent his experience as fully as possible from the peculiar angle of vision permitted by his inheritance and upbringing. With the blood of the Puritans in his veins and in his head the writings of Plato and Shakespeare and Milton and Goethe, and the Persians and the Indians, and Mme. De Stael, and Wordsworth, and Carlyle, and George Sand, and Thoreau, and Margaret Fuller . . . But why continue the list? Emerson was as well-versed in world culture as anyone in his time. He was provincial only in his habits and his residence. Like some immense Moby-Dick of the mind, he strained all this intellectual plankton through himself and it became—Emerson; in the process, true enough, taking on some of the white-tint and enigmatic quality of his New England–disciplined being. But who would care about an Emerson who was simply another carbon-copy of the more genial middle-brow commentators already proliferating in mid-nineteenth-century American letters? The America Emerson represented was a more difficult and rigorous proposition—one, as Melville recognized, that dived deep and sounded into the farthest reaches of heavenly space. Though Melville found himself unable to "oscillate in Emerson's rainbow," he nonetheless pronounced him a "great man."[23]

We may locate Emerson's greatness in the capaciousness of his thought. He could *imagine* anything—including an American republic capable of eating its own filth, politically speaking, and being nourished thereby. Emerson may have been fastidious for himself but he knew that America needed a comprehensive appetite and strong digestive system in order to survive. He was therefore prepared to accept the exercise of raw power not because it pleased him or accorded with his own standards but because it was the expression of something authentic and vital in the American experiment. It was—to use his own figure—the dirty water that sometimes fetched the pump when clean water was not to be had.[24] But it was no more than a way of priming the motor, of getting things in motion. Finally the means could be justified only by the ends they achieved.

The Emerson presented to us by many of his self-serving commentators has often been little more than a caricature of his complex spirit, and it is therefore not very reassuring to hear Giamatti claim that "you do not have to read the prophet to realize his ideas are all around us." Such a procedure will yield us nothing but a straw man conveniently set up and knocked down for polemical purposes. Emerson lives in the veracity of his words as they jump out from the page—words that continue to speak with authority on the difficult issues that beset both our personal and civic existence. The only fit celebration of Emerson's life is a pledge that we will not desert his pages. That was William James's belief, and I want to conclude by citing his own description of how he participated in the Emerson centenary in 1903: "I let R.W.E. speak for himself, and I find now, hearing so much from others of him, that there are only a few things that *can* be said of him; he was so squarely and simply himself as to impress every one in the same manner. Reading the whole of him over again continuously has made me feel his real greatness as I never did before. He's really a critter to be thankful for."[25]

———

FIVE

EMERSON AS JOURNALIST

A mong the many unexpected pleasures and rich tidbits to be found in Emerson's *Journals and Miscellaneous Notebooks* is a brief entry in the fall of 1849 that anticipates the publication of *Representative Men* with a Swiftian gesture of self-satire that deserves attention. Emerson, we recall, had once—famously—wished to write *whim* on the lintels of his doorpost; now he whimsically reinscribed the threshold of his forthcoming book as if implicitly to mock the provincial consciousness that felt obliged, as he would himself note, to "continue the parrot echoes of the names of literary notabilities & mediocrities" when more original material lay very close to hand:

BIGENDIANS	LITTLEENDIANS
Plato	Alcott
Swedenborg	Very
Shakspere	Newcomb
Montaigne	Channing
Goethe	RWE
Napoleon	Thoreau*

* The left-column list is that of the men whose biographies appear in *Representative Men.* Whether Emerson intended to set up parallels with the names in the right-hand column isn't clear, but either in interests or manner, there are demonstrable relationships between all pairs except Napoleon and Thoreau.[1]

Here, alas, is one of the few cases where the JMN annotator is caught napping, for Emerson's intent to parallel his great universal men with their lesser local avatars is clear enough, as is the obvious comedic relish with which he did so, and the pairing of Thoreau with Napoleon is the best of the lot—conjoining two feisty semi-French bantams, one a corporal the other captain of a huckleberry party, who introduced the spirit of the *sans culottes* equally into politics and literature.

Perhaps the one real mystery in the entry, however, is the linking of Charles Newcomb's name with that of Shakespeare. It is true enough that in the preceding pages of this journal Emerson attempted to flesh out the affiliation, noting that Newcomb was a soliloquizing genius given to "abridged stenographic wit & eloquence," but if Shakespeare—with his "subtlety & universality"—was "only just within the possibility of authorship," Newcomb—whom Emerson pronounced his "best key" to the Bard—was just beyond it, the very type of the inspired Transcendental non-author. He could indeed be seen as Shakespeare only satirically, through the wrong end of the telescope; and his chapter in the Concord edition of *Representative Men,* to paraphrase Hawthorne, would look exceedingly like a collection of blank pages. In fact, Newcomb, along with Jones Very, and Margaret Fuller, and Bronson Alcott, and Caroline Sturgis, and Ellery Channing—that crowd of eccentric local geniuses scornfully referred to by Theodore Parker as *id genus omne* and classified "not valuable"—was categorized by Emerson himself as "not impartable." He could therefore be most appropriately celebrated through an invisible sketch in an unpublished volume—or rather, in a rare volume of which only the table of contents is extant.[2]

Emerson's little joke, however, as I have already suggested, comically masks a serious impulse. As he awaited the appearance of *Representative Men,* Emerson pronounced himself dissatisfied with his new book for several reasons. First and foremost, like Carlyle, he had gone after the "literary notabilities" but left unexpressed the "greatness of the common farmer & labourer." Indeed with appropriate Transcendental logic Emerson allied himself not only with the unexpressed but with the unexpressible—in particular with the solid inarticulate life of an Alek Therien, the Canadian woodchopper whom Thoreau would puzzle over in *Walden,* saying, "I did not know whether he was as wise as Shakespeare or as simply ignorant as a child, whether to suspect him of a fine poetic consciousness or of stupidity." Therien was thus, apparently, as eligible for inclusion in an alternative *Representative Men* as Charles Newcomb, and perhaps in the same slot—the chapter occupied by the Bard. Emerson concluded his ruminations on his book, and on Therien, by acknowledging that "the whole human race agree to value a man precisely in proportion to his power of expression, & to the most expressive man that has existed, namely Shakspeare, they have awarded the highest place."[3] But the unanswered question remains: what about the mute inglorious Shakespeares of rural America? Newcomb was beyond authorship, Therien beneath it, but they were united as examples of unwritten lives—the *un*represented representative men of the New World. We are brought, accordingly, to the crucial issue that glares at us precisely through Emerson's refusal, or inability, to confront it directly while worrying around it obsessively: why did he not publish a book entitled *Representative Americans?*

Of course we cannot answer that question in any definitive fashion, though several things immediately come to mind. Emerson's book, like so much of his work, came to birth on the lecture platform, and lyceum audiences were hungry for "culture"—meaning normally information about the great world apart from provincial America. Moreover, Emerson's print-audience quickly came to extend far beyond the local—meaning that he soon found himself writing not only for an ever-expanding American market but for Great Britain as well. Who, outside of the Concord-Boston axis, would care about the likes of Charles Newcomb or Jones Very or Alek Therien—or even Henry Thoreau? Then, too, Emerson's posture by 1850 when he actually published *Representative Men* was that of a universal sage. He was expected to write for the Eternities, not for the Times. And so, with few exceptions, he did—*publicly,* not privately. For the Emerson I am considering here was—like Thoreau—for a long time reporter to a journal of no very wide circulation, one of the most splendid achievements of which was to be the creation of a veritable gallery of representative Americans—women as well as men. That such was Emerson's intent, at least by October 21, 1841, is clear from a journal entry that was to be used, with some interesting changes, in his "Lecture on the Times":

And why not draw for these times a portrait gallery? . . . A camera! A camera! cries the century, that is the only toy. Come let us paint the agitator and the dilettante and the member of Congress and the college professor, the Unitarian minister, the editor of the newspaper, the fair contemplative girl, the aspirant for fashion & opportunities, the woman of the world who has tried and knows better—let us examine how well she knows. Good fun it would be for a master who with delicate finger in the most decisive yet in the most parliamentary & unquestionable manner should indicate all the lions by traits not to be mistaken yet so that none should dare wag his finger whilst the shadow of each well known form flitted for a moment across the wall. So should we have at last if it were done well a series of sketches which would report to the next ages the color & quality of ours.[4]

When this passage was translated into Emerson's lecture two interrelated things happened: the refreshingly miscellaneous character of the catalog was tidied up into more logical shape ("the agitator and the dilettante," for example, becomes "the agitator" versus "the man of the old school"), and—predictably—a universalizing objective replaced the obvious satiric impulse in the journal entry. The lecture paragraph announced its desire to indicate "those who most accurately represent every good and evil tendency of the general mind" so that "all witnesses should recognize a spiritual law as each well-known form flitted for a moment across the wall"; but the journal entry focusses on the "good fun" of the "master" whose pen contains enough of the mordant to sketch "the lions" of the day accurately, "so that none should dare wag his finger."[5] Emerson's intent, publicly, is to represent, in the sense of *typify*, the opposing tendencies of his day. His private interest is in representing his contemporaries in a very different sense; that is, in setting them down *decisively*—if need be, pinning them wriggling to the pages of his journal. As a result, the actual "color & quality" of Emerson's age is reported most fully and critically and magnificiently, not so much in his published writings, as in the unexpurgated pages of his private diaries—in short, in his *Journals and Miscellaneous Notebooks*. That is where we find the representative Americans unfortunately excluded from his 1850 volume.

Good examples abound of how the relatively approbative monotone of the published portraits belies the rich complexity of Emerson's private sketches, but one of the best is that of Edward Everett, who—as Harvard professor, editor of the *North American Review*, member of Congress, and Unitarian minister—managed to spread himself across four of Emerson's categories. The single sustained description of Everett in Emerson's works—several quite glittering pages in "Historic Notes of Life and Letters in New England"—presents the golden-tongued orator, with only very muted criticism, as a kind of Boston and Cambridge Pericles capable of opening "a new morning" to the "rudest undergraduate . . . in the lecture-room of Harvard Hall," prompting Oliver Wendell Holmes to speak of "the glowing words of Emerson whenever he refers to Edward Everett."[6] But the fuller story, as revealed in the journals, is considerably more interesting. On April 30, 1846, for example, Emerson went to Cambridge to see Everett inaugurated as president of Harvard College and commented caustically the next day on this delivering "to the convent door" of the tarnished scholar by his "political brothers"—and especially by his "evil genius," Daniel Webster. Noting that the new president—characterized as a "mere dangler & ornamental person"—pleased Boston well because he was "so creditable, safe, & prudent," Emerson goes on, with surprising prescience, to link the academy with the establishment:

> It is so old a fault that we have now acquiesced in it, that the complexion of these Cambridge feasts is not literary, but some what bronzed by the colours of Washington & Boston. The aspect is political, the speakers are political, & Cambridge plays a very pale & permitted part in its own halls. A man of letters—who was purely that—would not feel attracted, & would be as much out of place there as at the Brokers' Board.

Emerson's conclusion mercilessly records his feeling that this erstwhile representative of "Grecian beauty" whose "power lay in the magic of form" had become the hollow shell of a frigid propriety:

> The close of Everett's Inaugural Discourse was chilling and melancholy. With a coolness indicating absolute skepticism & despair, he deliberately gave himself over to the corpse-cold Unitarianism & Immortality of Brattle street & Boston.[7]

In view of such a judgment, we observe without surprise Emerson's ferocious comments five years later on Everett's support of the Fugitive Slave Law:

Does he mean that we shall lay hands on a man who has escaped from slavery to the soil of Massachusetts & so has done more for freedom than ten thousand orations, & tie him up & call in the marshal, and say—I am an orator for freedom; a great many fine sentences have I turned—none has turned finer, except Mr Webster, in favour of plebeian strength against aristocracy; and, as my last & finest sentence of all, to show the young men of the land who have bought my book & clapped my sentences & copied them in their memory, how much I mean by them—Mr Marshal, here is a black man of my own age, & who does not know a great deal of Demosthenes, but who means what he says, whom we will now handcuff and commit to the custody of this very worthy gentleman who has come on from Georgia in search of him; I have no doubt he has much to say to him that is interesting & as the way is long I don't care if I give them a copy of my Concord & Lexington & Plymouth & Bunker Hill addresses to beguile their journey from Boston to the plantation whipping post?[8]

That exhibits an Emerson who is still insufficiently known: the ultimate patriot for whom the integrity of the law and the integrity of the word were one.

Emerson's aim, in his journal at least, was not only or even mainly to contemplate his navel but rather to represent his age and country comprehensively and without restraint—to draw that national "portrait gallery," from the man of the old school to the modern priest and reformer, which he called for in 1841. Though that program may sound like one for a more canny realist than Emerson is normally acknowledged to have been, it is literally true that all the portraits he projected, and more, are to be found in his writings—and particularly in his *Journals and Miscellaneous Notebooks*. Perhaps it is not without reason that Bliss Perry compares him to Balzac.[9]

In 1825, for example, the young Waldo and his brother Edward made a pilgrimage to Quincy, Massachusetts, for the express purpose of encountering a patriarch of the "old school," President Adams, and thereby experiencing history themselves. The portrait Emerson sketched in his journal of this vital link with America's eighteenth century deftly captures not only the prickly integrity of the grand old man but also his youthful enthusiasm for a great evangelist in a time of fervent religious revival:

> He talked of Whitefield and remembered when he was Freshman in College to have come in to the Old South (I think) to hear him, but could not get in; he however saw him thro' a window & distinctly heard all. "He had a voice such as I never heard before or since. He *cast* it out so that you might hear it at the meeting house (pointing towards Quincy Meeting house) and had the grace of a dancing master, of an actor of plays. His voice & his manner helped him more than his sermons. I went with Jonathan Sewall." And you were pleased with him, Sir? "Pleased, I was delighted beyond measure."[10]

Emerson's portraits of other men, and women, of the old school—Josiah Quincy, his step-grandfather Ezra Ripley, his Aunt Mary (whom he calls one of the "great men of the American past")—give us these representative figures from his national gallery as living moments in his own biography. His further portraits—of the member of Congress, Webster; of the woman of the world, Margaret Fuller; of the priest, Edward Thompson Taylor—are equally valuable for the way in which historical detail is first warmed by personal acquaintance and finally set aflame by the Emersonian imagination. Fourteen years before Melville translated Father Taylor to the pages of *Moby-Dick* as Father Mapple and described him "with truly sailor-like but still reverential dexterity, hand over hand," mounting the steps of his pulpit "as if ascending the main-top of his vessel," Emerson heard this pastor of the seamen's Bethel preach in Concord, invited him to spend the night in the Emerson house, and set down this impression in his journal: "I delight in his great personality, the way & sweep of the man which like a frigate's way takes for the time the centre of the ocean, paves it with a white street. . . . [H]is prayer is a winged ship in which all are floated forward."[11] That, too, could be the viewpoint and voice of Ishmael, but is in fact only the language of an ex-Unitarian minister turned chronicler of his age in a private journal now, fortunately, of wide circulation.

SIX

EMERSON AT HARVARD

The American literary record in the three or four decades following the Revolution is not very imposing, and the view from America's cultural capitol in the period—I mean Boston—was scarcely more sanguine than that from outside. Writing in the leading intellectual journal of the time, *The North American Review*, in 1818, William Cullen Bryant tried to assume a hopeful stance, observing that after "the few quaint and unskilful specimens of poetry" remaining from America's first century "a purer taste began . . . to prevail." But Bryant's catalog of promising contemporary talent strikes us now as mostly a giving of alms for oblivion. One item may stand for the funereal whole: "The posthumous works of St. John Honeywood, Esq. were published in the year 1801. These modest remains, the imperfect but vigorous productions of no common mind, have not been noticed as they deserved. They contain many polished and nervous lines." It would be otiose to add, Requiescant in pace, for posterity hears no further of Mr. Honeywood's "modest remains." Some fifteen years prior to Bryant's essay, the Rev. Samuel Miller, in his Brief Retrospect of the *Eighteenth Century*, attempted to award the poetic laureateship of 1801 to another minister, John B. Linn, D.D., of Philadelphia for his *Powers of Genius*—"a didactic and descriptive poem" displaying "imagination, taste, and reading." But even the Rev. Miller felt obliged to add, "the respectable *Poets* of America are not numerous." Perhaps it was only when a poet would aggressively turn away from being respectable—I am thinking of Whitman in 1855—that the literary scene could truly change.[1]

Beginning at least as early as 1815, and continuing on in a litany of Harvard Phi Beta Kappa orations culminating in Emerson's great utterance of 1837, "The American Scholar," wherein Emerson would accuse the intellectual class of being "timid, imitative, tame"—merely "decent, indolent, complaisant"—Harvard men demonstrated that they could be sharply critical of their own performance. "The truth is," admitted Walter Channing, class of 1808, "we have wanted literary enterprise and been sadly deficient in genuine intellectual courage."[2] Perhaps it was the weight of an increasingly deadly and deadening classical curriculum that forced the national muse to seek non-academic lovers. It is a matter of curious interest that many of the great names in the nineteenth-century American literary record have either scanty or no formal collegiate education—Whitman, finally, standing for the egregious extreme of autodidacticism. Washington Irving skipped college altogether; Bryant himself spent only seven months at Williams College; James Fenimore Cooper was expelled from Yale after two years devoted to pranks and running up debts; Poe, for the same reason, lasted only one year at the college in Charlottesville; and Emily Dickinson, repeating Bryant's experience, retired from Mary Lyon's Female Seminary at Mount Holyoke after seven months. Most extravagantly, Melville announced in 1851 that a whale-ship was his Yale and Harvard College. The appropriately acerbic one-liner is offered by Henry Thoreau, class of 1837, who observes that the Harvard of his time presented all the branches of learning but none of the roots.

I want, however, to focus on Emerson, not just because I know him best, but rather because—to paraphrase what he himself said about Goethe—he was the cow from whom all the others drew their milk. Emerson's obsessive concern with the state of American letters in the first half of the 19th century—his programmatic insistence that America's "long apprenticeship" to the learning and literature of other lands was drawing to a close—functioned as a perpetual prod to the major writers of his time, almost all of whom finally blossomed in response or reaction to his repeated appeals. I focus on Emerson also because in letters and journals and addresses and essays he provides the fullest and most trenchant documentation we have of the literary scene in his time and place. When Emerson, in 1850, insolently characterized his father's generation as belonging to an "early ignorant & transitional *Month-Of-March,* in our New England culture,"[3] he was effectively dismissing his Harvard seed-time as a chilly beginning for the burgeoning Transcendental summer, for his teachers and their curriculum were essentially of his father's generation. With the exception of George Ticknor's innovational lectures on French literature in his senior year, Emerson heard nothing in class about modern writing. Drill in Greek, Latin, mathematics, ethics, logic, grammar, rhetoric, and the like, was basically what Harvard College was all about. Of course the boys were not discouraged from reading the approved authors of England's great Augustan age (Addison, Steele, Pope, Dr. Johnson), and Scott's novels and poems were ok; but more recent and racy stuff, like Wordsworth and Byron, was definitely an extra-curricular activity—not to mention American authors.

And here we might pause for a moment to glance more circum-stantially at Emerson's literary apprenticeship at Harvard. The gen-eral conditions of that apprenticeship were not encouraging to a budding American literatus. Emerson himself notes, in an 1819 letter, that the College authorities had "just made a new law that no student shall go to the Theatre on penalty of 10 Dols. fine at first offence and other punishment afterwards." (In fact the ordinance forbade any undergraduate from being "an actor, or in any way a par-taker, in any stage plays, interludes, masquerades, or theatrical enter-tainments . . . or a spectator at the same"—this under the presumed liberal sway of a now Unitarian institution!)[4] When it came to writ-ing original verse, at least for public consumption, the approved form—apart from Greek and Latin hexameters—was the by now hackneyed Popean pentameter couplet that, Byron had already shown, could easily be turned to self-parody. So, Emerson's many efforts in the genre—from longish verse-essays delivered before lit-erary societies to his Valedictory Poem in 1821—were essentially exercises in ragging the literary establishment.

It is surely not without significance that Emerson described him-self to his brother Edward in 1820 as a "mock-Poetick Junior." It was only by mocking what was detrimental to his own development as a native writer that he could begin to find his way. Thus when Emerson wrote Edward in Alexandria, Virginia, three months later offering to send one of his ponderous Popean imitations for local reading to friends he made fun of the empty and essentially alien conditions imposed by literary tradition: "Always observe the rules of decorum due from poet to patron;—make a long preface on presentation, about the abject, prostrate, *down-to-the-ground* hu-mility of a luckless rhymer; tell of the unpropitious regards of the muses, the freezing glance of Apollo[,] of the scornful, horrificable *irrefrangefrackability* of the world;—& then, make a low bow & forthwith produce the Poem—This is the best & most approved way now practised in England."[5] Is it any wonder that seventeen years later Emerson would complain that "we have listened too long to the *courtly* muses of Europe," or that his disciple, Whitman, would insist: "take off your hat to nothing known or unknown"? Note also Emerson's humorously aggressive coinages—"horrificable *irrefrangefrackability*"—which amount to an assault on the presumably requisite Latinisms.

In an earlier letter to Edward—this time inviting him to try his own hand at original composition—Emerson said: "You may write in Latin, the language of Literature, or Greek the tongue of Herodotus &c or Gallic the language of Voltaire or vernacular the language of ourselves." That American vernacular, so frequently associated with native humor, might not be considered the "language of literature" in polite circles, but its use would be one of the cornerstones of Emerson's literary program—as in this famous passage from "The American Scholar":

> Life is our dictionary. Years are well spent in country labors; in town,—in the insight into trades and manufactures; in frank intercourse with many men and women; in science; in art; to the one end of mastering in all their facts a language by which to illustrate and embody our perceptions. . . . Life lies behind us as the quarry from whence we get tiles and copestones for the masonry of today. This is the way to learn grammar. Colleges and books only copy the language which the field and the work-yard made.[6]

Emerson was even more outspoken in his journal. "The language of the street," he would note in 1840, "is always strong":

> What can describe the folly & emptiness of scolding like the word *jawing?* I feel too the force of the double negative, though clean contrary to our grammar rules. And I confess to some pleasure from the stinging rhetoric of a rattling oath in the mouth of truckmen & teamsters. How laconic and brisk it is by the side of a page of the North American Review. Cut these words & they would bleed; they are vascular & alive;

they walk & run. Moreover they who speak them have this ele-
gancy, that they do not trip in their speech. It is a shower of
bullets, whilst Cambridge men & Yale men correct themselves
& begin again at every half sentence.

Guts, Emerson concludes, "is a stronger word than intestines." This
program for a strong vernacular speech would come to fruition most
immediately in the work of Thoreau and Whitman, who would say
things like "It is not necessary that a man should earn his living by
the sweat of his brow, unless he sweats easier than I do"; or "I do not
snivel . . . that life is a suck and a sell." But Emerson could get a good
native sentence off himself when he wanted to, as in the original version of "Self-Reliance": "But do your thing, and I shall know you."
It took the rest of us about a hundred and twenty years to catch up
with that![7]
    My point, then, is a simple one: namely, that the basic vacuity and
irrelevance of what passed for an American literary education at
Harvard, and indeed other colleges, during Emerson's time as a student acted as a positive incentive to him to fill the void with something else—that is, with a program for autochthonous writing that
could appeal equally to a Harvard graduate like Thoreau or a graduate of nowhere like Whitman. The familiar words are still stirring
and seminal: "Our logrolling, our stumps and their politics, our fish-
eries, our Negroes, and Indians, our boasts, and our repudiations, the
wrath of rogues, and the pusillanimity of honest men, the northern
trade, the southern planting, the western clearing, Oregon, and
Texas, are yet unsung. Yet America is a poem in our eyes; its ample
geography dazzles the imagination, and it will not wait long for
metres." The meters that Emerson's America found may not have
been made entirely at Harvard, but they were certainly prepared for
there, and in ways hard to predict. Writing once again to Edward
in 1818, Emerson announced that he was making a concerted effort
to win a Bowdoin prize with another "somniferous dissertation for
next year." And if that succeeded no better than its "elder brother"

the year before, he went on, why "I'll put them to sleep each suc-
ceeding year with one, till they, tired out by my Morphean draughts,
give me the long-expected prize." And he concluded: "Oh how sweet
is revenge!"[8]

Well, by learning to work the Harvard system while also working—
at first quietly and then more loudly—to undermine it, Emerson
got his Bowdoin prize as well as his revenge, for *we* got an American
literature that is decidedly not "somniferous" in the approved
Harvard style of 1820.

SEVEN

HOLMES'S EMERSON

The choice of Oliver Wendell Holmes to write the volume on Emerson in the American Men of Letters series must have seemed odd, if not positively perverse, to the sage's disciples.[1] Emerson had died very much in the odor of sanctity in 1882, and the prevailingly pious attitude toward the master was already finding reverent expression in hagiographic lectures, essays, and book-length memorials. The man who had almost single-handedly managed to unchurch the New England mind was well on the way to being enshrined as Boston's tutelary divinity. Transcendentalism, which forty years earlier had elicited public derision and execration, now found itself invested with the dignity of an ancestral creed. What business, then, had Dr. Holmes—with his skeptical scientific mind and biting wit—attempting to take the measure of so rarefied an emanation as the sainted Emerson?

Holmes himself would have been the first to admit that he had little patience with some of the more extravagant manifestations of New England's mid-century madness. Indeed he suggests in his biography that "Transcendentalist" might be considered simply a fancy word for "crank"; and he does not shrink from lampooning the most famous of Emerson's fellow travelers: Alcott, whose speculations "often led him into the fourth dimension of mental space; Hawthorne, who brooded himself into a dream-peopled solitude; Thoreau, the nullifier of civilization, who insisted on nibbling his asparagus at the wrong end." Holmes in fact admired Emerson for never losing his balance in such a heady atmosphere, for being able to judge his visionary friends with Franklinesque shrewdness and mother-wit. Emerson had a "sense of the ridiculous" almost as sharp as that of his biographer. And it may well be that Holmes undertook the difficult task of preparing his book precisely as a corrective to all the Transcendental stardust that was being flung in readers' eyes by the more uncritical Emersonians. Holmes's Emerson was less a mystic than a poet with a penchant for dabbling in the occult. But "he never let go the string of his balloon."

Although Holmes and the sage of Concord might have appeared to some as having inhabited very different worlds of discourse, the truth is that they had much in common; and Holmes undoubtedly realized that the writing of Emerson's biography gave him a unique opportunity to examine the cultural history of his own time and tribe. Both men stemmed from New England's Brahmin caste, or that subdivision which Holmes delineates as "the Academic Races"; both were educated at Harvard College; and though Emerson could boast (or occasionally lament) a weightier ecclesiastical heritage than Holmes, they were equally the sons of Congregational ministers.

Abiel Holmes has usually been described as more orthodox than William Emerson, but the difference between them was probably not significant: Holmes's father was not illiberal in his views, and Emerson's was scarcely a religious radical. Both, despite their love for polite literature, reared their sons in a fixed theological frame of reference that was manifestly burdensome to their modern-minded offspring, who valued intellectual and personal freedom above all else. When Holmes notes that "no man has done more for spiritual republicanism than Emerson, though he came from the daintiest sectarian circle of the time in the whole country," he is clearly not only describing his own background but also articulating a fundamental aspiration of his life as he, like Emerson, struggled to free himself from that background.

Holmes's career, of course, was shaped by his passion for science and exemplifies the now familiar contest in the nineteenth century between the new learning and hidebound tradition. Whether Holmes was agitating the medical establishment by insisting that puerperal fever was contagious or challenging received theological wisdom in his "medicated novels," he could align himself with Emerson as an "endless seeker" with no past at his back—or at least with a past that was being reshaped beyond recognition by the irresistible forces of evolution. Holmes's description of Emerson's "descent" from his Puritan ancestors has a decidedly Darwinian cast and, however humorously, signals an important motif in the biography. "A genealogical table," Holmes tells us, "is very apt to illustrate the 'survival of the fittest,'—in the estimate of the descendants." We are thus faced with a case not so much of "natural selection" as of conscious choice on Emerson's part: he could single out from his ample ministerial heritage the very best figures whom he might hope to emulate and refine in his own career. Emerson would therefore represent in nineteenth-century form the "descent" of his sturdier ancestors into more adaptable avatars. For Holmes this inevitable and highly desirable process describes not simply the progress of a family but the evolution of a whole culture—the survival of New England's spiritual genius in ever more liberal and flexible forms of belief: "From Edwards to Mayhew, from Mayhew to Channing, from Channing to Emerson, the passage is like that which leads from the highest lock of a canal to the ocean level. It is impossible for human nature to remain permanently shut up in the highest lock of Calvinism." The open sea of human experience and free speculation beckoned, and the Emersonian spirit found a way to lead New England out of bondage.

In reviewing the growth of Emerson's first book, *Nature*, Holmes is pleased to note that the 1836 epigraph from Plotinus was replaced in 1849 by some verses of Emerson's own making that evinced a more contemporary spirit:

> *A subtle chain of countless rings*
> *The next unto the farthest brings;*
> *The eye reads omens where it goes,*
> *And speaks all languages the rose;*
> *And striving to be man, the worm*
> *Mounts through all the spires of form.*

Holmes then points out that this was "ten years before the publication of Darwin's 'Origin of Species,' twenty years and more before the publication of 'The Descent of Man'":

> But the "Vestiges of Creation," published in 1844, had already popularized the resuscitated theories of Lamarck. It seems as if Emerson had a warning from the poetic instinct which, when it does not precede the movement of the scientific intellect, is the first to catch the hint of its discoveries. There is nothing more audacious in the poet's conception of the worm looking up towards humanity, than the naturalist's theory that the progenitor of the human race was an acephalous mollusk.

Emerson, in Holmes's view, dared affirm his kinship with the oyster and the worm because he believed, along with modern science, in "evolution of the best and elimination of the worst as the law of being." This was the message of *Nature,* and it agreed well with Holmes's own progressive beliefs, though timid academics would condemn Emerson's meteoric little book as "a stumbling-block to be got out of the well-trodden highway of New England scholastic intelligence."

Despite his manful attempt to rescue Emerson's writings from the category of Transcendental moonshine and align Emerson's notions with those of contemporary science, Holmes was perpetually nagged in his task by what he took to be the poet-idealist's tendency to "leave the laboratory and its crucibles for the sybil's cave and its tripod." Having worked so hard to get Emerson into his own camp, so to speak, Holmes struggled with the distance that nonetheless remained between them. Perhaps the real difficulty lay with Holmes himself, for as his active medical career drew to a close, he could still hear murmurings that he was little more than a dilettante in science, to be remembered, if at all, as a minor poet and a popular essayist and lecturer. Holmes sniffed at Emerson's reputation for mysticism and metaphysics as if he were at once castigating his own poetic vagaries and brandishing his credentials as a scientific critic: "He played with the incommunicable, the inconceivable, the absolute, the antinomies, as he would have played with a bundle of jack-straws," Holmes insists, dismissing "Brahma" as a mere Oriental amusement. "To the average Western mind it is the nearest approach to a Torricellian vacuum of intelligibility that language can pump out of itself." Presumably, readers of Emerson's poem in the *Atlantic Monthly* should have been warned that the sorcerer's apprentice was merely fooling around in the linguistic laboratory.

If Holmes feared that Emerson's visionary gleam was frequently little more than a will-o'-the-wisp, he nevertheless fervently shared Emerson's faith in America's mission. Holmes undoubtedly had to read much of Emerson's writing for the first time as he prepared his biography, but he hardly needed to be reminded of America's "intellectual Declaration of Independence," since he shared the platform with Emerson on that memorable August day in 1837 when "The

American Scholar" was first heard. This was the Emersonian music that was most acceptable to Holmes's ears, for he believed that Emerson was born to "preach the gospel of the New World, that here, here in our America, is the home of man; that here is the promise of a new and more excellent social state than history has recorded." With such a noble ground bass running through all his compositions, Emerson inevitably seemed the first of national writers to Holmes and perhaps, indeed, the most inspiriting voice on either side of the Atlantic.

The Emerson-Carlyle correspondence had been published just before Holmes began work on his book, and he naturally availed himself of the opportunity to compare these two nineteenth-century giants. Holmes was inevitably led, in contrasting Carlyle's endless lamentation to Emerson's song of joy, to an implicit comparison between the mind of the old world and the mind of the new: "The Duet they chanted was a Miserere with a Te Deum for its Antiphon; a *De Profundis* answered by a *Sursum Corda*. 'The ground of my existence is black as death,' says Carlyle, 'Come and live with me a year,' says Emerson"—and the clear implication of Holmes's juxtaposition of texts is that Emerson's Concord might have raised Carlyle out of his inferno. Though Emerson had the American habit of eating presumably sodden wedges of pie for breakfast, he never suffered from dyspepsia, physical or spiritual; whereas "there, on the other side, was Carlyle, feeding largely on wholesome oatmeal, groaning with indigestion all his days." If the American atmosphere could do so much for the stomach, Holmes believed along with Emerson, then its potential for the heart and mind was unlimited. "To the dark prophecies of Carlyle," Holmes notes in his final chapter, "which came wailing to him across the ocean, [Emerson] answered with ever hopeful and cheerful anticipations. 'Here,' he said, in words I have already borrowed, 'is the home of man. . . .'"

Emerson's America, provincial or even parochial as it might appear to the great world outside, was very much the home preferred by Dr. Holmes, and he was eminently qualified to take its measure.

He understood as well as anyone the evolution of New England's religion "from Edwards to Emerson"—understood, that is, how the "genial atmosphere" of Emersonianism had leavened and humanized all religious discourse. Reminding himself of Emerson's reputation in the 1830s as an "infidel" and an "atheist," Holmes made bold to tell his readers in 1884 that such terms were "fast becoming relinquished to the intellectual half-breeds who sometimes find their way into pulpits and the so-called religious periodicals." This refreshing smack at the lingering spirit of sectarianism was delivered in the name of Emerson by a compatriot who sympathized with his subject to a marked degree.

Holmes's book contains little of the gush or unction to be found in treatments of Emerson by more fervent disciples, but it is peppered with shrewd observations and sound judgments. He grasped the crucial fact that Emerson "writes his own biography, no matter about whom or what he is talking" and thus, in one ringing sentence, could counter the tendency to read the sage's works as a kind of disembodied wisdom-literature: "His books are all so full of his life to their last syllable that we might letter every volume *Emersoniana,* by Ralph Waldo Emerson." Holmes himself was so skilled at detecting the flavor of what he calls the "Emersonially Emersonian" that many of his critical pronouncements remain fresh and valid. In a strong chapter on Emerson's poetry, for example, he observes justly of that old chestnut "The Concord Hymn" that though it "is the most nearly complete and faultless" of all Emerson's poems, "it is not distinctively Emersonian"; it might have been written by someone else. But Holmes perceptively singles out "Threnody," Emerson's touching lament for his lost boy, as one of his most distinctive productions, noting that it has the dignity of Milton's "Lycidas" but not "its refrigerating classicism."

Holmes was not afraid of Emerson's rhetoric and, indeed, perceived shrewdly that the essence of his writing lay in the "splendid hyperbole," or *felix audacia,* which enlivens Emerson's best pages. "Over-statement, extravagance, paradox, eccentricity"—the qualities

Holmes admired most in his friend's mind and art he cherished and nurtured in his own discourse. "Without a certain sensibility to the humorous, no one should venture upon Emerson." If Emerson seems dull, Holmes may be suggesting, the reader might profitably examine the condition of his or her own susceptibilities.

"Consciously or unconsciously," Holmes observes, "men describe themselves in the characters they draw. One must have the mordant in his own personality or he will not take the color of his subject." Undoubtedly some of the most delicate Transcendental tints lost their sheen in being transferred to Dr. Holmes's pages, but at least a more vigorous and vital Emerson did react successfully with Holmes's intellectual chemistry. The Emerson who comes most vividly to life in Holmes's book is characterized by "a dash of science, a flash of imagination, and a hint of . . . delicate wit." It is not the only Emerson capable of being recreated through the biographer's art, but it is inimitably *Holmes's* Emerson, and deserves to endure longer than the one-hoss shay.

EIGHT

EMERSON'S FRENCH CONNECTION

Ce qu'on adore en lui, c'est lui-même. Son nom est son immortalité.
[What we adore in him is his very self. His name is his immortality.]
　　　　　—Lamartine on Fénelon

Fénelon—The name is enough.

　　　　　—Wallace Stevens

In tracing the contours of Emerson's "French connection," we can start from the premise that Fénelon's name was indeed one to conjure with throughout Emerson's career; but the name alone will *not* be enough. We will need to discover—or recover—the story of how Fénelon's doctrine, reputation, and spirit can be seen to draw together the seemingly disparate elements that comprise Emerson's relation to French writers and French culture generally. A useful place to start is with a basic question: how did this American

Protestant of all Protestants regard Catholicism—the root and ground of French culture as he understood it?

1. THE UNITARIAN MINISTER AND THE CATHOLIC CHURCH

In his still indispensable study, *America and French Culture* (1927), Howard Mumford Jones suggests that

> The great obstacle to a sympathetic reception of things French by the Americans has been, it appears, a *sense of religious differ-ence*. This sense of religious difference carries with it a suspicion of French morality, of French infidelity, and of French Catholicism. Weakest in the concluding quarter of the eigh-teenth century when both countries were dominated by a movement of tolerance and even of scepticism, this sense of difference is yet always present and is basic to an understand-ing of the American attitude. In the seventeenth century the Americans are suspicious of French Catholicism; in the last decade of the eighteenth century, they are suspicious of French infidelity, and they carry this attitude into the opening decades of the nineteenth century; and in the last twenty-five or thirty years of our study [1818–1848], they are impartially suspicious of both infidelity and Catholicism.[1]

Jones goes on to qualify his assertion by remarking that "this sense of religious difference is weakest among those who possess the cos-mopolitan spirit." Was Emerson one of them? Certainly we would need to observe that the Congregationalist/Unitarian Boston of Emerson's youth, provincial by any standards, was sufficiently intol-erant of religious difference—particularly as regards "Romanism."

And so in Emerson's earliest journals and letters (and sporadically later on) we do find evidence of some fairly conventional anti-Catholic sentiment. But the surprising thing, perhaps (perhaps, because we are dealing with Emerson), is how quickly these sentiments evapo-rate or undergo serious qualification. A more cosmopolitan view quickly takes over. By the late 1820's, in his sermons, Emerson is regularly invoking Fénelon, along with Socrates, Plato, Paul, Newton, and Milton, as an exemplar of moral power and one of the "best & greatest men." It might, in fact, be said that the fiercely sectarian spirit of Emerson's Boston ambiance was tempered early on in the very bosom of his family, for Robert D. Richardson, Jr., reports that Emerson's mother, a deeply pious woman whose books were not only "Unitarian, nor . . . Puritan, or even exclusively Protestant," was a devoted reader of Fénelon. Perhaps it was she who encouraged the thirteen-year-old Emerson to improve his French by undertaking to read Fénelon's *Télémaque*.[2]

Another crucial influence on the young Emerson was the liberalizing spirit of William Ellery Channing. In an 1829 essay on Fénelon published in the *Christian Examiner* (which Emerson read with great interest), Channing makes at the outset the important concession that Fénelon, "though a Catholic," was "essentially free." He then adds that he does not welcome the selection of Fénelon's writings under review "the less for coming from a Catholic." Perhaps, he continues, "we prize it the more; for we wish that Protestantism may grow wiser and more tolerant, and we know not a better teacher of these lessons than the character of Fénelon. . . . His virtue is broad enough to shield his whole church from that unmeasured, undistinguishing reprobation, with which Protestant zeal has too often assailed it." Noting the great number of Catholic believers, Channing insists that "it is time that greater justice were done to this ancient and wide-spread community" that "has produced some of the greatest and best men that ever lived." Channing then makes an interesting move:

To come down to our own times, has not the metropolis of New England witnessed a sublime example of Christian virtue in a Catholic bishop? Who, among our religious leaders, would solicit a comparison between himself and the devoted Cheverus? This good man, whose virtues and talents have now raised him to high dignities in church and state, who now wears in his own country the joint honors of an archbishop and a peer, lived in the midst of us, devoting his days and nights, and his whole heart, to the service of a poor uneducated congregation. . . . This good man, bent on his errands of mercy, was seen in our streets under the most burning sun of summer, and the fiercest storms of winter, as if armed against the elements by the power of charity. He has left us, but not to be forgotten. He enjoys among us what to such a man must be dearer than fame. His name is cherished where the great of this world are unknown. It is pronounced with blessings, with grateful tears, with sighs for his return, in many an abode of sorrow and want; and how can we shut our hearts against this proof of the power of the Catholic religion to form good and great men?[3]

Channing's stategy is worth attending to. Clearly inviting his reader to compare the character and career of Jean-Louis Lefebvre de Cheverus, first Bishop of Boston, with that of François de Salignac de la Mothe-Fénelon, Archbishop of Cambrai, Channing implicitly points up the ironies of preference in the Catholic church while praising it for producing two such saintly figures. During twenty-seven years in New England Cheverus moved steadily upward—from missionary work among the Indians in Maine to his preeminence in Boston—then returned to greater honors in France (the Archbishopric of Bordeaux, elevation to the peerage, nomination as a Cardinal); whereas Fénelon, initially raised to privilege by Louis the Fourteenth as tutor of the Duke of Burgundy but then, through the hypocrisy, envy, and intrigue of Bossuet, banished from the court and from Paris to Cambrai, where he experienced the horrors and dislocations caused by the wars in Flanders, died in official disgrace, though revered by his flock as an angel. Boston—Catholic and Protestant alike—remembers the "devoted Cheverus" who furthered the pious work of his illustrious predecessor and is now invited to reconsider the life and work of Fénelon. Emerson, while a student at Harvard College and already dipping into Fénelon's writing, finds his mother moving into a house in Boston opposite the Church of the Holy Cross, "the seat of Bishop Cheverus," as Ralph Rusk reminds us. Before long, in his journals, Emerson will begin making references to the "saintly" Fénelon while also praising Cheverus as a golden-tongued preacher. With the help of Channing, Emerson is learning to make connections that will clarify his attitude toward the Catholic church and some of its most distinguished French adherents.[4]

2. SAINT MICHEL DE MONTAIGNE

Early and late a favorite of Emerson's, Montaigne in *Representative Men* stands for the "skeptic." Unlike Thersites or Voltaire—mere scoffers who represent "the worst of materialism" because they have nothing but scorn for high-minded abstractions or what they take to be platitudinous posturing, weigh man "by the pound," and believe only "that mustard bites the tongue, that pepper is hot, friction-matches are incendiary, revolvers to be avoided, and suspenders hold up pantaloons"—the skeptic avoids the kind of worldly wisdom that runs "into indifferentism, and then into disgust." He refuses to be flatly dismissive of the claims of believers or non-believers alike because he occupies a middle ground: that of the considerer. He is here only to consider—to consider how things are. "Why fancy that you have all the truth in your keeping? There is much to say on all sides."[5]

Montaigne, then, is "Saint Michel," as Emerson dubs him, only whimsically. Emerson marks his "calendar-day" as a time for "counting or describing . . . doubts or negations." Thus the Saint of Skepticism is set up in the niche of non-belief only provisionally as representing a mood that may well come to us all. Indeed, Emerson argues, the most fervent believers themselves may sometimes suffer from "the cloy or satiety of the saints": "In the mount of vision, ere they have yet risen from their knees, they say, We discover that this our homage and beatitude is partial and deformed. We must fly for relief to the suspected and reviled Intellect, the Mephistopheles, to the gymnastics of talent." Was this the situation Fénelon found himself in when his "homage and beatitude" based, as he believed, on the pure and disinterested love of God was denounced by Bossuet and the casuists employed by Pope Innocent the Twelfth as mere Quietist nonsense imbibed from the writings and personal influence of Madame Guyon? Then, indeed, Fénelon was forced to employ his formidable scholarship and powers of logic and argumentation in order to save his neck.[6]

I circle back to Fénelon here not gratuitously, I hope, but rather because Emerson begins his chapter on "Montaigne, or the Skeptic" by invoking the name of Fénelon in support of his argument that we all belong to one of two classes: "One class has the perception of Difference, and is conversant with facts and surfaces; cities and persons; and the bringing certain things to pass;—the men of talent and action. Another class have the perception of Identity, and are men of faith and philosophy, men of genius." Emerson thinks that "each of these riders drives too fast. Plotinus believes only in philosophers; Fénelon, in saints; Pindar and Byron, in poets." Of course, Saint Michel de Montaigne is waiting in the wings, to be offered as a counterweight to the high-octane saintliness of a spiritual genius who will be overtaken by the police-powers of a state religion: the minions of Difference will inevitably collide with the fervent believers in Identity. A healthy skepticism must mediate between these two factions.[7]

But there is a bit more to be said about the Fénelon connection in *Representative Men.* In the chapter preceding the one on Montaigne, "Swedenborg, or the Mystic," Emerson anticipates the chapter which will follow "Montaigne" ("Shakspeare, or the Poet") by employing yet another taxonomy of "classes"—here producers, poets, philosophers, and adherents to the "moral sentiment." The latter, exemplified by Swedenborg, are of course high religious types. In what we can see is a gambit used throughout his book, Emerson concedes at the outset that "mystics"—those who live perpetually in "a region of grandeur"—may become tedious: "If we tire of the saints, Shakspeare is our city of refuge." And yet "all men are commanded by the saint." A "holy and godlike soul" capable of "being assimilated to the original Soul, by whom, and after whom, all things subsist," may easily become an object of awe to lesser beings. But Emerson, characteristically, issues a caveat:

> This path is difficult, secret, and beset with terror. The ancients called it *ecstasy* or absence, a getting out of their bodies to think. All religious history contains traces of the trance of saints; a beatitude, but without any sign of joy; earnest, solitary, even sad; "the flight," Plotinus called it, "of the alone to the alone." Μύεσις, the closing of the eyes, whence our word Mystic. The trances of Socrates, Plotinus, Porphyry, Behmen, Bunyan, Fox, Pascal, Guion, Swedenborg, will readily come to mind. But what as readily comes to mind is the accompaniment of disease. This beatitude comes in terror, and with shocks to the mind of the receiver.[8]

Lyceum-goers who heard Emerson deliver this lecture in the mid-1840's might or might not have had ready knowledge of all the figures he mentions, but the name "Guion"—or rather, Madame Guyon—though perhaps caviar to the general, was familiar in transcendentalist circles. Emerson's strategy, however, is certainly clear to us now. Fénelon's companion in the exercise of Quietistic meditation is named here to point proleptically to the introduction of Fénelon's name in the next lecture in Emerson's series (indeed the phrase from Plotinus's Sixth Ennead used in this passage is quoted in Greek in an 1841 journal passage in which Emerson criticizes the worldly St. Simon for misrepresenting Fénelon; Emerson's ambivalence toward "mysticism" is thus manifest). The saintly archbishop will be faulted for driving "too fast"; Madame Guyon, though included in a very distinguished group of mystics, is here tainted by the suspicion of "disease." The antidote to the spiritual excesses of both these figures appears to be the level-headedness of Michel de Montaigne. "His writing," Emerson observes, "has no enthusiasms."[9]

3. MADAME DE STAËL: MYSTICISM AND ENTHUSIASM

As we have seen, among Emerson's early forays into French literature was his attempt to read Fénelon's *Télémaque* at the age of thirteen, one year before he entered Harvard College. The year after he graduated, in 1822, Emerson began his lifelong engagement with Madame de Staël by at least beginning *Corinne* and *Germany*—the latter in an excellent translation published in London in 1813. Before long he was dipping into both her *Considerations sur la Révolution* and her *Mémoires*. As Robert D. Richardson, Jr., observes, Madame de Staël was one of Emerson's "early constant reference points, one of the people he read and reread, turning the books a little each time like a kaleidoscope, so that a new pattern could emerge from the familiar elements." By 1827, in an important journal entry entitled *"Peculiarities of the present Age,"* Emerson noted that "it is said to be the age of the first person singular. . . . The reform of the Reformation. . . . Transcendentalism. Metaphysics & ethics look inwards—and France produces Mad. de Stael . . ."[10]

For Emerson, Madame de Staël was the most eloquent exponent of what he would come to consider the quintessence of both his philosophy and his religion: the infinitude of the private self—the self being understood as the "higher" self as explained by Madame de Staël in her exposition of the philosophy of Fichte in *Germany*. The "permanent" self (as opposed to the "transient" self) is that "immoveable soul" to which Fichte, she explains, "attributes the gift of immortality, and the power of creating, or (to translate more exactly, of *drawing to a focus in itself the image of the universe*." Citing Madame de Staël in an 1831 journal entry, Emerson approves of her ability, even in the "most disagreeable circumstances," to hug herself "with the feeling of my immortality." Emerson goes on to insist that the "wise man," indifferent to circumstance, "can separate himself from impure contact & embosom himself in the sublime society of his recollections, of his hopes, & of his affections." In another journal entry from around the same time, Emerson (quoting from Marie Joseph de Gérando's *Histoire Comparée des Systèmes de Philosophie* [1804]), cites Anaximander's saying that "the Infinite is the principle (principe) of all things" and observes that "Anaximander revives in De Stael"—alluding, presumably, to Madame de Staël's belief that "the infinite" is that principle to which "the greater portion of German writers refer all their religious ideas": "The enthusiasm, which the beautiful in idea makes us feel (that emotion, so full of agitation and of purity at the same time), is excited by the sentiment of infinity." And "enthusiasm," Madame de Staël will insist in a late chapter in her book, signifies simply "*God in us.*"[11]

In her chapter on "The Religious Disposition Called Mysticism" Madame de Staël defines this tendency as "only a more inward manner of feeling and conceiving Christianity," the belief of those who wish to "confine [their religious fervor] to their own hearts." Among the fathers of the Church whom she claims for this belief are Thomas-A-Kempis, Fénelon, and St. François-de-Sales. These are men, she insists, "who have made religion a sort of feeling." For "there is nothing more simple and more pure than the connexions of the soul with the Deity, such as they are conceived by those whom it is the custom to call Mystics; that is to say, the Christians who introduce love into religion." A supreme instance of such a figure is the writer to whom Madame de Staël (raised a Calvinist) turned and returned frequently—so we are told by her cousin Albertine Necker de Saussure—in her times of inner distress:

> In reading the spiritual works of Fénelon, who is not softened? where can we find so much knowledge ["tant de lumières"], consolation, indulgence? There no fanaticism, no austerities but those of virtue, no intolerance, no exclusion appear. The differences of Christian communion cannot be felt at that

height which is above all the accidental forms created and destroyed by time.[12]

Emerson seems to have agreed. In a long journal entry set down in 1833, he identified the "error of religionists" with their inability to know "the extent or the harmony or the depth of their moral nature." So they cling to "little, positive, verbal, formal versions of the moral law" while ignoring "the infinite laws" within. True teachers, he continues, pass over falsehood and pitiful sectarianisms and descend to these bottom truths. Such "eminent men of each church" are "Socrates, A Kempis, Fenelon, Butler, Penn, Swedenborg, Channing." They all "think & say the same thing," Emerson argues: "A man contains all that is needful to his government within himself. He is made a law unto himself." And he concludes, clearly echoing Madame de Staël, "the highest revelation is that God is in every man."[13]

It is worth adding that a fervent admirer of Madame de Staël and her writing, Alphonse de Lamartine, who recreated an "enthusiastic" Romantic and republican Fénelon in his "dernier entretien du *Cours familier de littérature*," was moved precisely by Madame de Staël's concept of "the infinite." As Paul Viallaneix informs us:

Le jeune Lamartine apprend en lisant *Le Génie du christianisme* et surtout *De l'Allemagne* à nommer "infini" la donnée immédiate de l'existence qu'enregistre sa conscience, rebelle à la logique des mathématiques enseignées au collège. "Les Allemands, explique-t-il à Virieu, iront plus loin que nous n'avons été, parce qu'ils fondent tout sur un principe vrais et sublime: Dieu est infini." Le fidèle confident se plonge, à son tour, dans la lecture des derniers chapitres de l'ouvrage de Mme de Staël, qui traitent de la "religion" et de l' "enthousiasme." Et Lamartine le remercie de lui répéter la leçon qu'il en avait tirée lui-même, le premier: "Tu as trouvé le vrai mot: l'infini. Je l'avais dit souvent sans m'y fixer. Je l'avais dans l'esprit et tu l'as produit: c'est cela, il faut le mettre en réserve, tout est là. C'est l'âme de l'homme tout entière et, par conséquent, tout ce qui doit et peut agir sur son âme dans les arts mêmes, doit en tenir et y tendre par quelque point."

Lamartine's Fénelon, equally in love with "the infinite," considers himself a "prodigy" because, "being nothing, at least possessing only a dependent, limited, and transient existence, I hold by the infinite and immutable which I have conceived." Lamartine's biography of Fénelon, completed shortly before the poet's death, presents that saintly figure as reimagined through the filter of Madame de Staël's reflections on mysticism and enthusiasm.[14]

Richardson describes *Germany* as "one of the best books written on one country by a native of another." It is necessary to add, however, that Madame de Staël composed her book knowing full well that large numbers of French readers would be looking over her shoulder. Her book (at least the part we have been considering) is not simply a study of German philosophy and religion written by a foreign observer; it is rather a study that is comparative by design. Throughout, French culture is being set next to that of Germany and found wanting. In the large generalizations that frame her argument, Madame de Staël finds contemporary French philosophy to be external and materialistic, French religion dogmatic and shallow. She therefore concludes her book with a monitory apostrophe to her compatriots:

O France! land of glory and of love! If the day should ever come when enthusiasm shall be extinct upon your soil, when all shall be governed and disposed upon calculation and even the contempt of danger shall be founded only upon the conclusions of reason, in that day what will avail you the loveliness of your climate, the splendour of your intellect, the general fertility of your nature? Their intelligent activity, and an impetuosity directed by prudence and knowledge, may indeed give your children the empire of the world; but the only traces you will leave on the face of the world will be like those of the sandy whirlpool, terrible as the waves, and sterile as the desert![15]

4. FÉNELON AMONG THE TRANSCENDENTALISTS

As Howard Mumford Jones has observed, "Fénelon had ever been a favorite Catholic author in America." His "work was widely distributed throughout the seventeenth and eighteenth centuries." *Les Aventures de Télémaque,* Fénelon's overwriting of the *Odyssey* in the form of a manual for the education of young princes (Fénelon produced it for the instruction of his pupil, the Duke of Burgundy), was considered a proto-Republican treatise and became a popular school text; it went through at least two editions in America in the eighteenth century and more followed in the nineteenth century. Writing in 1824 to a young cousin whom he had taught in his brother William's school for girls, Emerson recommended "Telemachus & La Bruyère" as French chefs d'oeuvres, calling them "entertaining and instructive."[16]

Other works of Fénelon were also well known. His *Dissertation on Pure Love* (plus an account of Madame Guyon), published in Philadelphia in 1738, was often reprinted. And, as we have seen, William Ellery Channing, in the *Christian Examiner* for 1829, reviewed *"Selections from the Writings of Fenelon; with an Appendix, containing a Memoir of His Life. By a Lady"* (the author was Eliza Follen, the wife of Harvard professor Charles Follen; her book went through five editions by 1844). It is worth noting here that Channing studiously avoids any mention of Madame Guyon except perhaps obliquely when, after excusing Fénelon's "excesses," he rejects "common fanaticism" as being "essentially vulgar, the working of animal passions, sometimes of sexual love, and oftener of earthly ambition." But, he continues, "when a pure mind errs, by aspiring after a disinterestedness and purity not granted to our present infant state, we almost reverence its errors." Lamartine would confront the Fénelon/Guyon issue more directly, though with equal delicacy: "The resemblance in gentleness and elevation of these two spirits, equally pious, and guided by imaginations equally ardent, established at once between Fénelon and Madame Guyon a spiritual intercourse, in which there was no seduction but piety, and nothing to be seduced but enthusiasm."[17]

In the general recrudescence of interest in Fénelon during the Transcendentalist period (1830's to 1840's) Madame Guyon was not neglected—indeed, she became a kind of heroine. Thus in an article entitled "Lady Guion and some of her Religious Views," published in the *Christian Review* in 1838, the author remarks that she fell into "Catholic errors," but (as Howard Mumford Jones notes) "the chivalric writer 'would not speak lightly of that broken-hearted, holy woman.'" Jones goes on to offer a useful summary of the flurry of interest in Fénelon and Guyon:

> In 1843 the *Christian Examiner* believes that "everything of Fénelon is welcome"; his *Thoughts on Spiritual Subjects,* as translated at Boston, "breathes of heaven and devotion." This book was a kind of supplement to Mrs. Follen's *Selections.* . . . [the author] considers the demand for "so pure and elevated a writer as Fénelon" "an indication of sound public taste." In 1847 [Alfred H.] Upham's *Life and Religious Opinions and Experience of Madame de la Mothe Guyon with an Account of Fénelon* is "full of instruction and interest, an example of purified mind and exalted faith"; Fénelon is "the most tolerant and humble-minded of Roman Catholics," Madame Guyon "a pious transcendentalist"(!) To another reviewer the "Doctrine of Pure Love set forth in this volume is most misapprehended; to call Madame Guyon a fanatic, as many do, is to misjudge her diary, since she is as powerful in intellect as Bossuet." "Love constitutes my crime," she wrote, and Bossuet and the church are vigorously scourged for condemning her—albeit the Church of Rome is no more inconsistent than other churches.[18]

Much of this almost steamy commentary was not overlooked by Emerson and his circle. Perhaps the story of Fénelon and Madame

Guyon was associated in their minds—at least subliminally—with the celebrated romance of Héloise and Abélard (popularized for the English-speaking world by Alexander Pope's narrative poem, "Eloisa to Abelard," in 1717), wherein religious exaltation and sexual love fatally commingle. In any event, during his epistolary courtship of his wife-to-be, Lydia Jackson, in 1835, Emerson (addressing her in the third person) hyperbolically claims that she "apprehends, what it is grandeur to apprehend, that the height of human nature is in humility." Then, after quoting "noble lines" from Dante about the Virgin Mary's combined humility and sublimity that almost reconcile him "to popery," Emerson says of Lidian: "I am healed and exalted when I am near her & some virtue comes into me from her thought when I am away. So fare thee well my better than Guion." Eleanor Tilton, the editor of this volume of Emerson's letters, points out that "Emerson's role in this quietist romance would have to be that of Fénelon." Tilton goes on to note that Emerson and Lidian's daughter Ellen, who wrote a manuscript life of her mother, mentions a "vol by Mme Guyon called Les Torrents" as one of her mother's "favorite books." Tilton also informs us that Emerson's library has Madame Guyon's *Opuscules Spirituels* (Cologne, 1712).[19]

Does Emerson call Lidian "better than Guion" because, he believes, her spiritual intensity is untainted by any hint of carnal impulses? An odd thing for a would-be husband to suggest! This "quietist romance" would then be no romance at all. Or is Emerson saying that Lidian is "better than Guion" because her mystical tendencies do not issue from a "mind . . . impaired" (as the critic in the 1838 *Christian Review* said Madame Guyon's "unreasonable mysticism" did). The truth is, though, that in this period leading up to the publication of the transcendentalist journal *The Dial* (1840–44), Emerson was thinking a good deal about the curious mixture of interested and disinterested motives in transcendental friendships, especially in his relations with a group of perfervid female acolytes who would come to surround him (e.g., Margaret

Fuller, Caroline Sturgis, Anna Barker). In the peculiar love feast that would, to varying degrees, engulf them all, the question of the purity of motive would exercise them constantly. Thus in a strange and somewhat obscure letter to Caroline Sturgis in September of 1840, Emerson (who addresses Sturgis as "my dear sister") wonders if they can trust "that pure complacency . . . which gives us joy in the existence of others who live in the light of the same truth with ourselves." Emerson goes on:

> Can I not—I believe that I can—carry this office of dear love to its sacred height by simpl[y] following the law of the soul, so that there shall be no jar, friction, or impediment in it, for there shall be nothing of me in it, but it shall be all somewhat better than me, or, the joy of God in God.

If the modern reader is beginning to feel that this passage is redolent of Fénelon and Madame Guyon, the next sentence clinches the suspicion: "George Bradford is translating Fenelon & sent me yesterday two sheets concerning Friendship." And so Emerson continues:

> I am not so high that I can see & understand very well the ends of friendship which he stigmatizes—for profit, for honor, for consolation, & refined self love, but I can very easily see these departing out of all my higher friendships, and assure myself of the eternity of my bonds.

He concludes that in their friendship "love & religion, self trust and philanthropy are reconciled. But I think I waste too many words to try to say things so plain." Plain or not, these "things" continued to be a puzzle. When the beautiful Anna Barker decided—it seemed impetuously—to marry their mutual friend Sam Ward, Emerson's lower self was certainly piqued. Years later, long after the transcendental infatuations had died away, Emerson would fall back on Fénelon, but in a much more fundamental way, when offering Ward advice about his wife's conversion to Catholicism:

But for her church, she shares the exaltation shall I say? which belongs to all new converts in the dogmatic churches, & which gives so much pleasure that it would be cruel to check it if we could,—which we cannot. The high way to deal with her is to accept the total pretension of the Roman Church, & urge her through the whole rococo to the sentiment of Fenelon & A Kempis in its cloister,—which burns backward the whole church to foul smoke.[20]

5. EMERSON'S "FRANCE, OR URBANITY"

A list of French visitors who comment on life in America from the late eighteenth century to the late nineteenth century contains some very distinguished names: Brillat-Savarin, Brissot de Warville, the Marquis de Chastellux, Chateaubriand, Michel Chevalier, Crèvecoeur, Lafayette, La Rochefoucauld-Liancourt, Théodore Pavie, Moreau de Saint-Méry, Tocqueville. A corresponding list of well-known American visitors to France would be relatively short: James Fenimore Cooper, Franklin, Henry James, Jefferson, Tom Paine ... Up until now, Emerson's name would not have figured significantly among American commentators on French life and culture. Apart from journal entries made during his two brief visits to Paris—in 1833 and during the tumultuous spring of 1848—and remarks on French writers scattered throughout his journals and letters, Emerson appeared not to have spoken largely on French culture (as he did on England in *English Traits* [1856]). However, with the publication recently of *Emerson's Later Lectures*, edited by Ronald Bosco and Joel Myerson, we have learned that Emerson did in fact produce a substantial commentary on the country that, he understood, occupied a "central position" in "the system of Europe."[21]

"France, or Urbanity," a popular lecture Emerson delivered a number of times in the mid-1850's, is mainly intended to be entertaining—indeed, to mirror the character of a people who, Emerson claims, are devoted to amusement: "Everything comes to be valued for its entertainment." Accordingly, the lecture itself is *urbane*—suave and polished—and focuses mainly on Paris, *the* metropolis, the city that France has built "for the world." Noting repeatedly that France is famous for its fashion and cookery, Emerson at the outset introduces the figure of a *ragoût à modiste*— a stylish pot pourri. Referring to the French exhibition at the Crystal Palace in London (1851), he compares France to its neighbor across the Channel by arguing that "the national genius tends naturally to quality in variety; the English genius to quantity in uniformity"—so to speak, *ragoût à modiste* versus porridge.

The genre in which Emerson was working in his lecture on France was a familiar one in nineteenth-century letters: that of the exploration of "national" or "racial" character. Although this kind of collective "profiling" is, for the most part, no longer in good odor because it tends to trade in offensive stereotypes (e.g., "Scots are cheap"; "Jews are crafty"; "Italians are dirty") Emerson seemed willing to play the game both in *English Traits* and in this lecture. He does, however, signal his awareness that he is scarcely dealing in objective judgments. If "all people of Teutonic stock,—Germans, English, Americans,—do at heart regard it as a serious misfortune to be born a French native," that is largely owing to "Saxon" prejudices; but of course Emerson presents such a proposition as a kind of joke, which he immediately broadens by suggesting that the Saxons further believe that the "English head is round, the French head . . . angular,—and perhaps some essential defects are thus coarsely indicated." Coarse indications of this kind could be credited only by a physiognomist gone mad—and our speaker clearly does not belong to that class. In fact this shifty paragraph starts with Emerson's insisting that "in what I have yet to say of France, I shall not begin by canting." He is not going to make a fake claim of "impartiality"; he will not play the hypocrite. He is going, in short, to be *frank* with us, and in two senses: he freely admits that his "biases" may "impair the value of [his] testimony"; for that reason, distrusting his own "unsupported impressions," he intends when he has "unfavorable opinions to express" to draw his "witnesses" from the

French themselves. Emerson's *frankness* will then consist in his taking a French point of view when he undertakes to criticize the French. (The implicit pun here on being *frank* is made explicit later in the lecture when Emerson notes that "Napoleon was very frank in expressing his contempt of his compatriots"; but Emerson had already employed the pun in his "Montaigne," claiming that this favorite author "is the frankest and honestest of all writers. His French freedom runs into grossness . . .")[22]

Emerson's principal strategy in his lecture—the adopting of a French mask of rapier-like wit and sarcasm in order to educe (citing Napoleon) the "tomfoolery . . . vanity, levity, and caprice" of this "empire of *bagatelle*"—treads the brink of disgust even as he produces one of the cleverest and funniest paragraphs in his talk:

Of course, the conversation of this million of pleasure hunters can have nothing very serious. The only rule is that nothing serious shall be said. In all times, a malignant gaiety jokes alike at the good and bad fortune of the public. The best of kings is not less its butt than the worst tyrant. Epigrams, sarcastic sentences, caricatures, puns, are forever the favorite toy of this infant people. Persiflage or banter is the genius of the boulevard and the salon. It is the knife by which every rival is cut down. To be once ridiculous is to be stone dead. And where everybody talks incessantly, a bonmot flies with fatal effect. Is the new beauty slender? She is the Venus of the Père La Chaise. Is the Bishop of Autun fat? He was created and placed on this earth merely to show to what extent the human skin might be stretched. When the squinting man asked Talleyrand, "How things went in the cabinet?" he replied, "As you see." When it was rumored once and again M. Dupin's life was threatened, he was greeted, on entering the assembly, "*Comment vous assassinez vous,* M. Dupin?

French wit is *deadly:* it turns the slender beauty of today into the skinny corpse buried in Père La Chaise cemetery tomorrow.

Emerson's most telling phrase in this paragraph—"a malignant gaiety"—hints at whose spirit lies behind his critical thrusts: that of Madame de Staël. In *Germany,* in a chapter entitled "Of the Ridicule introduced by a certain Species of Philosophy," Madame De Staël castigates Voltaire for attacking all "philosophical opinions that exalt the dignity of man" and exerting the "effort of a diabolical gaiety" in *Candide.* It is the work of a "daemon or an ape" laughing at human misery, the expression of a "jester and a cynic" who has given himself over to a "scoffing philosophy." The real culprit, then, according to Madame de Staël, is the "materialistic" spirit of the philosophy of "sensation," introduced by Locke and developed by Condillac and Helvetius, which calls into question "the truth of everything that is not proved by the senses."[23]

Following in the footsteps of Madame de Staël's critique, Emerson faults the French for "pushing the joys of sense to the highest point of refinement. . . . They possess an erudition of sensation; they have a civility of condiments, of wine and cigars. Their philosophy ended in a dreary materialism." Though Emerson praises the Revolution because it "destroyed the feudal service, newly distributed property, and [gave] every man a right to vote"—"when an opportunity shall once more return to use it"!—it was also the expression of the French love of novelty and change for its own sake: "In the Revolution, they abolished the chronology of mankind, and begun with the year One; for the world is a slate to a Frenchman on which he wipes out all the old marks and lines to work out his whole problem anew." O brave new world! Emerson seems to be saying; but his trope betrays the presence of Locke's "tabula rasa."

Turning in his lecture to praise France, Emerson drops his witty mask and recuperates what is best in the French spirit as he conceives it:

Yet Nature, everlasting in beneficence, scatters here also beautiful and generous souls, and profound minds. Here was born Fénelon, the saint, a man whose nobilities were so apparent in his manners, that his contemporaries said, that you could not turn your eyes from his face without an effort. Here was Montesquieu, the wise, who "found the lost titles of the human race," and whose heart was as great as his head. Here was Pascal. Here were noble and beautiful women. Here was Guyon, the mystic and saint. . . . [and] Madame de Staël, whose pure genius has made bright every height and depth of thought and sentiment which she has approached . . .

The perennial France of Emerson's transcendentalist leanings brings him back to the soul of a nation whose intrinsic nobility of spirit cuts through all the familiar stereotypes of whim and bagatelle. Emerson closes his talk with an encomium to the "immense vitality" of an indomitable people: "They have a great industrious population. Men of honor have appeared in their late crises who did not bow the knee, and there exist in the nation multitudes of individuals nowise implicated in their bad politics, and nowise infected with the old giddiness of the Gauls."

6. NAPOLEON, WEBSTER, AND FÉNELON

Emerson was not alone in admiring Napoleon, in however qualified a fashion. From Byron's *Childe Harold* to Carlyle's *French Revolution* to Stendhal's *Chartreuse de Parme* to Tolstoy's *War and Peace,* and at many points in between, the little corporal who became an emperor exercised a tremendous fascination on nineteenth-century writers. Napoleon is a powerful unnamed presence throughout Madame de Staël's *Germany;* and even before he began reading Madame de Staël's book Emerson was meditating on Napoleon's career. When William Ellery Channing published a long two-part review of Sir Walter Scott's *The Life of Napoleon Bonaparte* in the *Christian Examiner* in 1827–28, just before turning to his Fénelon essay, Emerson fell upon it with considerable interest.[24] He would, of course, compose his own essay on Napoleon ("Napoleon, or the Man of the World") for the lecture series on "Representative Men" that he began to deliver in the mid-1840's. What has not been generally noticed, however, is that Emerson's strategy for his Napoleon piece—he paired it with his essay on Goethe ("Goethe, or the Writer")—was obviously influenced by Channing's reprinting of his Napoleon review in the last collection of his essays that he himself assembled shortly before his death (*The Works of William E. Channing, D.D.*, 1841). Emerson undoubtedly noted that in the first volume of this collection the Napoleon essay is paired, back to back, with Channing's reflections on Fénelon. The two figures are clearly juxtaposed so as to invite the reader to make a comparison. Though it is highly unlikely that Emerson was ever interested in attempting a similar pairing (*Representative Men* already has two Frenchmen among its six figures), Channing's strategy would have forestalled such a project on Emerson's part. In any case he obviously wanted to conclude *Representative Men* with sketches of two parallel contemporary lives. But Channing's implicit comparison of Napoleon and Fénelon surely gave Emerson something to think about.

As Howard Mumford Jones has observed, "American admiration for Napoleon began early, wavered only as he took on despotic character, and, after his death, his faults forgot, wove around him their own version of the Napoleonic legend."[25] This can stand as a succinct way of contrasting the diverse attitudes toward Napoleon of Channing and Emerson. Writing just six years after the death of Napoleon, Channing sees nothing in this tyrant's character or career that might mitigate the harshest criticism of a man he views as a "bandit and savage" who merits our everlasting opprobrium:

He who lifts a parricidal hand against his country's rights and freedom; who plants his foot on the necks of thirty millions of his fellow-creatures; who concentrates in his single hand the powers of a mighty empire; and who wields its powers, squanders its treasures, and pours forth its blood like water, to make other nations slaves and the world his prey,—this man, as he unites all crimes in his sanguinary career, so he should be set apart by the human race for their unmingled and unmeasured abhorrence, and should bear on his guilty head a mark as opprobrious as that which the first murderer wore.

Pronouncing Napoleon to be a second Cain, Channing is not moved by popular sympathy for the supposed wrongs visited upon Napoleon during his enforced exile on St. Helena: "Whoever gives clear, undoubted proof, that he is prepared and sternly resolved to make the earth a slaughterhouse, and to crush every will adverse to his own, ought to be caged like a wild beast." Channing considers the origin of Napoleon's crimes to lie in unchecked egotism—in that "self-relying, self-exaggerating principle, which was the most striking feature of his mind." Combined with the "*love of power,*" these two principles (mentioned repeatedly by Channing)—self-reliance and self-exaggeration—were the root causes of Napoleon's fatal lack of human sympathy. It is worth noticing that the year in which Channing chose to reissue these charges against Napoleon—1841—was the same year in which Emerson published his first series of *Essays,* containing the famous chapter on "Self-Reliance."

The Fénelon piece that immediately follows Channing's review of Scott's *Napoleon* presents the saintly French cleric and theologian as the direct opposite of the devilish Napoleon: Fénelon "looks on human error with an angel's tenderness, with tears which an angel might shed, and thus reconciles and binds us to our race, at the very moment of revealing its corruptions."[26] Fénelon, for Channing, "saw far into the human heart, and especially into the lurkings of self-love." The latter, the very principle that drove Napoleon to his destructive excesses, is what Fénelon was devoted to rooting out of human nature through "self-crucifixion or self-sacrifice, and love to God." Self, Fénelon teaches,

is the great barrier between the soul and its Maker, and self is to vanish more and more from our thought, desires, hopes, trust, and complacency, and God to become all in all. Our own interests, pleasures, plans, advancement, all are to be swallowed up in an entire and unreserved devotion to the love of God.

Such a doctrine, Channing believes, is "essentially just," though a liberal Protestant reader of the essay will have a strong feeling that this kind of excessive self-denial smacked, for Channing, of the self-immolating practices of the cloister and the monastery (and perhaps also of the fervent desire for self-annihilation that one finds, for example, in such a hyper-Calvinist document as Jonathan Edwards' "Personal Narrative").[27] Channing worries that Fénelon's doctrine, which will seem to some the work of an "enthusiast," may lead to "self-contempt, a vice as pernicious as pride." Instead Channing believes, consonant with his program for liberal Unitarianism, that we cannot do without a healthy self-respect and self-reverence. Self-love, he insists, "is an essential part of our nature and must not and cannot be renounced." Thus if in the Napoleon essay Channing seems to tilt away from Emersonian self-reliance, in the Fénelon piece he tilts back towards a constructive self-regard, or what he terms "self-remembrance." Emerson will call it "self-recovery."

For about a decade, from the mid-1840's when he was putting together *Representative Men* to the mid-1850's when he was working on The *Conduct of Life*, Emerson developed a fascination for the exercise of power and the uses of executive energy. An early hero of his, Daniel Webster, appeared to exemplify these qualities—and, indeed, to be linked somehow in Emerson's mind with Napoleon.[28] Thus, in an 1849 journal entry, Emerson compares the two:

It is true that Webster has never done any thing up to the promise of his faculties. He is unmistakeably able, & might have ruled America, but he was cowardly, & has spent his life on specialities. When shall we see as rich a vase again! Napoleon, on the other hemisphere, obeyed his instincts with a fine audacity, dared all, went up to his line, & over his line, found himself confronted by Destiny, & yielded at last.

Emerson would soon discover that Webster too would find himself "confronted by Destiny" with the Compromise of 1850 and the passage of the Fugitive Slave Law and would be forced to yield to his Waterloo. What he and Napoleon had in common was a forcefully unscrupulous nature ("Webster is no saint, but the wild olive wood, ungrafted yet by grace"; "Napoleon is thoroughly modern, and, at the highest point of his fortunes, has the very spirit of the newspapers. He is no saint") and the ability to seem to represent the rising business-class:

> Webster truly represents the American people just as they are, with their vast material interests, materialized intellect, & low morals. . . . [His] absence of moral faculty is degrading to the country.
>
> Bonaparte was the idol of common men, because he had in transcendent degree the qualities and powers of common men. There is a certain satisfaction in coming down to the lowest ground in politics, for we get rid of cant and hypocrisy. Bonaparte wrought, in common with that great class he represented, for power and wealth,—but Bonaparte specially without any scruple as to the means. All the sentiments which embarrass men's pursuit of these objects, he set aside. . . . He did all that in him lay, to live and thrive without moral principle.[29]

When Emerson's admiration for these two arch-egotists waned he would feel like echoing the general cry "of France and Europe, in 1814"—*assez de Bonaparte*—and of people of conscience in America in 1852—*enough of Webster*—and fall back on his deeply-rooted love of moral principle. "Man, we believe," notes Channing toward the end of his Fénelon essay, "never wholly loses the sentiment of his true good."

7. THE FÉNELON MOOD

Robert D. Richardson, Jr., has argued convincingly that

> [Emerson's] repeated calls for self-reliance were not empty egotism; they represent ground won back from dependency. This feeling of dependency went hand in hand with feelings of humility and self-deprecation, which can be considered Emerson's Fénelon mood.[30]

I think we need to add, though, that Emerson's Fénelon mood not only comprised "feelings of humility and self-deprecation" but also experiences of religious exaltation that could overtake him at any period of his life. Not linked to any established form of religious worship or sectarian belief, these elevations of spirit formed an important part of what we can call Emerson's perennial philosophy.

Returning from Europe in 1833, for example, Emerson thanked God that he had had the opportunity to see "the men I wished to see—Landor, Coleridge, Carlyle, Wordsworth." But he criticized them all for being deficient, "—in different degrees but all deficient—in insight into religious truth. They have no idea of that species of moral truth which I call the first philosophy." Amplifying this line of thought in his journal the following year, Emerson noted that "Goethe & Carlyle & perhaps Novalis have an undisguised contempt for common virtue standing on common principles. Meantime they are dear lovers, steadfast maintainers of the pure ideal Morality. But they worship it as the highest beauty; their love is artistic. Praise Socrates to them, or Fenelon, much more any inferior contemporary good man & they freeze at once into silence. It is to them sheer prose."[31]

As has often been observed, Emerson's "first philosophy," particularly with regard to religious experience, from early on owed something to "enthusiastic" or Quietist doctrine. Ralph Rusk, in his *Life of Ralph Waldo Emerson,* published more than a half-century ago, made note of Emerson's knowledge of Fénelon and suggested the likelihood that Emerson was "braced by the Frenchman's teaching that the soul, in the climactic experiences of the religious life, does not need the aid of form or method." To this conjecture Rusk added the name of the Quaker George Fox and his doctrine of the "inner light." Emerson himself, in 1830, two years before he decided to take a stand against religious "forms," and especially the ritual of the Lord's Supper, set down a pertinent entry in his journal:

A great deal may be learned from studying the history of Enthusiasts. They are they who have attained in different ways to this cultivation of their moral powers & so to the perception of God. The reason why they are *enthusiasts* is that they have cultivated these powers alone; if they had, with them, trained all their intellectual powers, they would have been wise devout men, Newtons, Fenelons, Channings. The Enthusiast enraptured with the grandeur of his discovery imagines that whosoever would make the same must think as he has thought. . . . The Swedenborgian thinks himself wholly different & infinitely more favored than the Quaker or the Methodist. Yet is nothing more like than the mode in which they severally describe this common experience. Their likeness is greater than their difference.—[32]

Expanding on this observation a few years later in a lecture entitled "Religion," Emerson mentioned the names of two "mystics," Jacob Behmen and Swedenborg, and then added:

What was in the case of these remarkable persons a ravishment, has in innumerable instances, in common life, been exhibited in less striking manner. Every where, the history of religion betrays a tendency to enthusiasm. The rapture of the Moravians and the Quietist; the "revivals" of the Calvinistic churches; the "experiences" of the Methodist are only varying forms of that shudder of awe and delight with which the individual soul always mingles with the Universal Soul.

It is worth noting that Madame de Staël includes a chapter on "Moravian Mode of Worship" in the last section of *Germany*—"Religion and Enthusiasm"—informing us that the "Moravians are the monks of Protestantism; and the religious enthusiasm of Northern Germany gave them birth, about a hundred years ago."[33]

Drawing on a journal entry of 1835, Emerson included in his "Religion" lecture what amounts to a paean in praise of "the sweetness of the ancient piety":

> The conscience of every age is drawn to the history and monuments of each religious epoch. For example in our own age we are learning to look as on chivalry at the sweetness of the ancient piety which makes the genius of A Kempis, Scougal, Taylor, Herbert. It is a beautiful mean, equidistant from the hard, sour Puritan on one side and the empty negation of Rationalism on the other. It is the spirit of David and Paul. Who shall restore to us the odoriferous Sabbaths that made the earth and the humble roof a sanctity. . . . That piety is a refutation of every skeptical doubt. These men are a bridge to us between the unparalleled piety of the Hebrew epoch and our own. These ancient men like great gardens with banks of flowers send out their perfumed breath across the great tracts of time. How needful is David, Paul, A Kempis, Leighton, Fénelon to our devotion! Of these writers, of this spirit which deified them, I will say with Confucius,—"If in the morning I hear about the right way, and in the evening die, I can be happy."

The least familiar name today on Emerson's list is that of Robert Leighton (1611–1684), a celebrated Presbyterian preacher who seems the perfect exemplar of Emerson's Fénelon mood. Tolerant of Quakers and Baptists, known for his charity to the poor, he put his professional career in jeopardy by trying to reconcile differences between Anglicans and Presbyterians. To Coleridge, Leighton's writings suggested "a belief of inspiration, of something more than human"; they were "the vibration of that once-struck hour remaining on the air."[34]

Emerson's interest in Fénelon, and his evocations of Fénelon's name, are not confined solely to his early, fervent years. As late as 1870, we see Emerson reflecting in his journal on the mutual interaction between Christian doctrine and the influence of great believers: "The Christian doctrine not only modifies the individual character, but the individual character modifies the Christian doctrine in Luther, in Augustine, in Fenelon, in Milton." As for Emerson's general interest in French writers, a very brief journal entry in the mid-1850's—possibly as he was working on his "France, or Urbanity" lecture—under the simple heading *"France,"* succinctly seems to summarize his indispensable French authors: "Rabelais, Montaigne, Pascal, LaFontaine, Fenelon, Moliere, Montesquieu, Sand, Beranger, DeStael." That final name itself, which might stand first and last for Emerson's Fénelon mood, may call to mind again the important journal entry for 1827, already cited, in which—under the title *Peculiarities of the present Age*—Emerson appeared to link the "reform of the Reformation" with Madame de Staël and the inwardness of contemporary transcendental philosophy, metaphysics, and ethics. It would be gratifying to think that Emerson could have had access to the following letter, written by Madame de Staël near the end of her life to Madame de Gérando:

> Je n'ai pas besoin de vous dire que liberté et religion se tiennent dans ma pensée; religion éclairée, liberté juste: c'est le but, c'est le chemin. Je crois le mysticisme, c'est-à-dire la religion de Fénelon, celle qui a son sanctuaire dans le cœur, qui joint

l'amour aux œuvres, je la crois une réformation de la *Réformation*, un développement du christianisme, qui réunit ce qu'il y a de bon dans le catholicisme et le protestantisme, et qui sépare entièrement la religion de l'influence politique des prêtres.[35]

NINE

HENRY THOREAU AND THE REVEREND POLUPHLOISBOIOS THALASSA

*En ce qui touche ma rêverie, ce n'est pas l'infini
que je trouve dans les eaux, c'est la profondeur.
[Concerning my reveries, it it not infinity
that I find in water, but rather profundity.]*

—Gaston Bachelard, *L'Eau et les Rêves*

... we looked off, and saw the water growing darker and darker
and deeper and deeper the farther we looked,
till it was awful to consider ...

—Henry Thoreau, *Cape Cod*

"**H**is riddles were worth the reading," Emerson notes, after quoting Thoreau's familiar parable of the hound, the bay horse, and the turtledove, whereby Emerson seems to grant his friend precisely that "pardon" for his "obscurities" which Thoreau had requested while introducing his mysterious little fable in *Walden*. "There are more secrets in my trade than in most men's," Thoreau apologized, "and yet not voluntarily kept, but inseparable from its very nature." Although it might be said that this particular riddle is scarcely worth all the ink that has been shed over it, both

Thoreau's plea and Emerson's concession seem much to the point. There *is* an enigma at the heart of Thoreau's quest, but we are emphatically cautioned not to attempt any solution of Thoreauvian mysteries that overlooks his "trade"—which is, of course, literature ("my work is writing"), or, better, poetry. We are advised, that is, to seek to fathom Thoreau's secrets in a spirit of imaginative extravagance that corresponds to his own. "Nothing memorable was ever accomplished in a prosaic mood," he insists in *Cape Cod*, for we must put ourselves "in a frame of mind fitted to behold the truth." There is "a mystery in all things," Thoreau noted in 1841, in the course of a long explication of Emerson's "The Sphinx"—"in infancy—the moon—fire—flowers—sea—mountain"; but "poetry is the only solution time can offer."[1]

What Thoreau meant, or achieved, by an extravagantly imaginative, inherently poetic, approach to his world is the heart of the matter, as I see it, and thus constitutes my fundamental concern. But since I shall root my discussion in Thoreau's *elementary* interest in and attraction to water, I must ask the reader to anticipate this subject (and particularly to focus both eye and ear on *Cape Cod* in the near distance). The concept, and critical practice, of associating the material fantasies of a given creative artist with a marked tendency toward one of the four elements—fire, water, air, or earth—is borrowed from the great phenomenological philosopher-critic, Gaston Bachelard (a devoted reader, be it noted, of Henry Thoreau), whose general theory of the creative imagination also has remarkable pertinence here. Like Thoreau, Bachelard makes a crucial distinction between nighttime dreams and daytime reveries. The first, as Thoreau says in *A Week*, "are the touchstones of our characters"; they belong to the realm of psychological analysis. But there is a mystery *in* things, or in our relation *to* things, which can best be explored through daydreams. "The dream worlds of wide-awake, diurnal reveries," Bachelard writes, "are dependent upon truly fundamental phenomenology." When these reveries become authentically poetic, they constitute "hypothetical lives which enlarge our lives by letting us in on the secrets of the universe. A world takes form in our reverie, and this world is ours. This dreamed world teaches us the possibilities for expanding our being within our universe." Thoreau's own formulation in *A Week* is more succinct: "Our truest life is when we are in dreams awake."[2]

As we know, Thoreau's reveries persistently concern that pastoral universe of things and nonhuman creatures in which he wishes to immerse himself—that "woodland vision" of Walden Pond which, he says, "for a long time made the drapery of my dreams." But his most impressive, most extravagantly poetic, indeed most puzzling imaginings have to do with what he called the "Wild"—nature as sheerly alien matter, awesomely personified in "Walking" as a "vast, savage, howling" beast. This lecture/essay, in fact, is a kind of touchstone of Thoreau's imaginative life, a fascinating and particularly revealing compendium of unbounded Thoreauvian fantasy. And the ever-present danger of approaching Thoreau's writing in the wrong frame of mind—in the spirit of ratiocination rather than of reverie—is especially sharp here. What are we to make, for example, of this remark about "Walking" offered by Leo Marx in 1962:

> Now he speaks as an extreme primitivist-anarchist. . . . It is one thing to repudiate the workaday world, as he had once done, for aesthetic purposes: to clear the ground for concentrated perception; but it is quite another to propose this regressive attitude as an overall prescription for living. In the end Thoreau's doctrine of "wildness" becomes indistinguishable from the shadowy bliss of infantile mindlessness.

Perhaps the four decades that passed after that observation was published are a sufficient comment on its decreasing relevance, for Thoreau's self-proclaimed "extreme statement" seems to have inspired a whole generation of budding ecologists (let us recall that the Sierra Club's lovely and influential *In Wildness is the Preservation of the World* also appeared in 1962). But we need to point to the perhaps unintended disparagement that laces the phrase "for aesthetic purposes." Thoreau's repudiation of State Street was as serious and sustained as his devotion to literature; and his aesthetic purpose was consciously "to make an extreme statement" if so he might "make an emphatic one." He traded not so much in prescriptions for living as in imaginative release and recreation.[3]

There is, however, a valid and it may be unanswerable criticism that can be leveled against "Walking": namely, that Thoreau's set of clichéd variations on the theme of "westward the course of empire takes its way" is virtually indistinguishable from the mindless political sloganeering in favor of expansion that Henry Nash Smith so ably documented in *Virgin Land*. Unquestionably, the true force of "Walking" does not lie in that direction, but rather in its radical revelation of that "syntax of metaphors," those "metaphorical coordinations," which in Bachelard's view are the hallmarks of a consistently poetic mind.[4]

Fundamental to the metaphoric syntax of "Walking" is a set of religious tropes that are clearly intended to underline the seriousness of Thoreau's quest. *Sauntering* Thoreau fancifully etymologizes at the outset as walking *à la Sainte Terre*—to the Holy Land. He is a walker in this sense, but his ultimate goal, his *Sainte Terre*, is an awesome, forbidding, even grim place, for he expects his life as a pilgrim to be "a divine tragedy" and warns whosoever would join him that we must be "prepared to send back our embalmed hearts only as relics to our desolate kingdoms." Although Thoreau does not believe in the Father, Son, and Holy Ghost, as he tells us in *A Week*, because in all his wandering he "never came across the least vestige of authority for these things," he offers his own Trinity in "Walking": "I believe in the forest, and in the meadow, and in the night in which the corn grows." He is sauntering toward the dark, holy Wild, and though he is presumably "in search of the springs of life" (a phrase that resonates widely in Thoreau's writings), his journey will necessarily carry him toward scenes of explicit "dreariness" and terror. He will look for "an impermeable and unfathomable bog" or "the darkest wood, the thickest and most interminable, and . . . most dismal swamp." This will be his "sacred place," his "*sanctum sanctorum.*" At the height of his seeming enthusiasm for this divine devastation, Thoreau ventures his most extreme—and perhaps most problematic—exclamation: "Give me the ocean, the desert or the wilderness!"[5]

We shall have occasion to reconsider this heady challenge shortly. Let me only note in passing that, despite his clearly hyperbolic (though distressingly masochistic) tone, Thoreau's extravagantly bleak vision here of the ultimate he seeks is entirely consistent with his familiar statement in *Walden* that he craves only reality, "be it life or death." But there is another, complementary set of metaphoric coordinates in "Walking" that invites special attention, whereby Thoreau expresses the more attractive, life-enhancing aspect of his reverie on sublime wildness. Everywhere in Thoreau's writings the site of his religious experience is given a location in space which he calls, variously, the "frontier," the "border," or the "neutral ground." As Edwin Fussell observes, "Pilgrim and Pathfinder, Thoreau was forever playing with the words frontier and front, trying to detach them from literality." In a very important sense, however, this "place" has physical reality for Thoreau: it is the dream-site where the supernal, or supremely poetic, experience impinges on mundane consciousness. As such, it invites what Bachelard calls a "topoanaly-sis," or "the systematic psychological study of the sites of our inti-mate lives." In context, Bachelard is thinking of houses—particularly of Thoreau's hut—but the concept lends itself in a suggestive way to "Walking." The "border" figure appears in what is presumably its purely metaphoric form in this sentence: "I feel that with regard to Nature I live a sort of border life, on the confines of a world into which I make occasional and transient forays only. . . ." The Wild, as an ideal, we surmise, is something Thoreau experiences only spo-radically. There is another passage in "Walking," however—one with the deepest reverberations in Thoreau's reveries—where that border experience is made flesh and dwells with the poet: "There are some intervals which border the strain of the wood-thrush, to which I would migrate,—wild lands where no settler has squatted; to which, methinks, I am already acclimated."[6]

The site, as it were, of Thoreau's most intimate experience of wildness *borders* where this particular bird sings; it lies *next to* the wood thrush. Any devoted reader of Thoreau's journal will recall that he was virtually obsessed by the wood thrush; its real importance in Thoreau's life can scarcely be overemphasized because it is the voice of that *wild* nature which Thoreau particularly seeks: "This sound most adequately expresses the immortal beauty & wildness of the woods. I go in search of him. He sounds no nearer. . . . [T]hough I am scarcely more than a rod off—he seems further off than ever." In other journal entries, this elusive bird of wildness gathers to itself an illuminating set of metaphoric attributes. Thoreau asociates it with water: its song is a stream that embodies "the liquid coolness of things that are just drawn from the bottom of springs"; it is "a medicative draught" to his soul, "an elixir" to his eyes, and "a fountain of youth" to all his senses. And the waters of the thrush are profound ones ("the bottom of springs"): "he deepens the significance of all things seen in the light of his strain"; for Thoreau, "he touches a depth in me which no other birds song does." These fathomless waters of song are "divine," the "truest and loftiest preachers" on earth; they are Thoreau's preferred religion, "the gospel according to the wood thrush." Finally, corresponding to the belief expressed everywhere in Thoreau's writings that the poetry of Homer represents literally the voice of the Wild ("it is as if nature spoke"), the wood thrush is proclaimed the Homer of birds: "Men talk of the *rich* song of other birds,—the thrasher, mockingbird, nightingale. But I doubt, I doubt. They know not what they say! There is as great an interval between the thrasher and the wood thrush as between Thomson's 'Seasons' and Homer." That *interval*, the space between ordinary nature and the Wild, is the borderland of Thoreau's ecstatic reverie, where, as he says in *Walden*, "both place and time were changed" and he "dwelt nearer to those parts of the universe and to those eras in history" that most attracted him. Or, to return to the journal:

> This minstrel sings in a true a heroic age. . . . I long for wildness—a nature which I cannot put my foot through. woods where the wood-thrush forever sings, where the hours are early morning ones, & there is dew on the grass, and the day is forever unproved—Where I might have a fertile unknown for a soil about me. . . . A New Hampshire everlasting & unfallen.[7]

Readers unsympathetic to Thoreau's rhapsodic praise of the Wild might be excused for disparaging him as "an extreme primitivist" mindlessly ranting in his "most unreasonably and unrealistically reckless" fashion, but the truth remains that we cannot really have Thoreau on any other terms. As Ellery Channing notes, "his love of wildness was real. . . . This was a religion to him; to us, mythical." Though his quest for the "fertile unknown" might appear to be psychologically dubious and socially and economically regressive, it represents the central commitment of his life and art: an experiment in imaginative *re-creation* through contact with the elementary sources of life. Beneath the undeniably miscellaneous character of everything Thoreau wrote palpitates this theme. *A Week*, for example, has not generally made its point. It represents Thoreau's search back in time, inland spatially, for the origins of all things: of history (particularly American), of religion, of literature, of nature, of being itself. When he reaches "Unappropriated Land" and attains the summit of Agiocochook, Thoreau implies that he has not only discovered the source of the Concord and Merrimack rivers, but of all seas and mountains, indeed of primal daylight. It is, as he quotes from George Herbert, "the bridal of the earth and sky," the marriage of Gaea and Uranos, at which he is present.[8]

A Week is very consciously, and even humorously, an *elemental* book. "There are earth, air, fire, and water," Thoreau asserts with Empedoclean certainty in the "Sunday" section, and the next day he continues: "The greatest appreciable physical revolutions are the work of the light-footed air, the stealthy-paced water, and the subterranean fire." Nor is Thoreau purely objective concerning what Bachelard calls "the natural dialectic of fire and water." He makes an impassioned plea for the element that most attracted him: "Cold and damp,—are they not as rich experience as warmth and dryness?" In the opening pages of "Wednesday" Thoreau seems to cast his lot for Thales (though Heraclitus was to get his due in *Walden* when the Hermit "sacrificed . . . to Vulcan" as he warmed his hut), for he becomes fascinated by a smaller bittern, "a bird of the oldest Thalesian school" who "no doubt believes in the priority of water to the other elements." Studying this "relic of a twilight antediluvian age" with its "melancholy and contemplative" air, Thoreau wonders whether it may not have "wrested the whole of her secret from Nature." He thinks that if he could penetrate to the core of the bittern's "dull, yellowish, greenish eye"—descend, that is, into the very heart of water–he might reach the bottom of his own soul.[9]

"In order for a reverie to be pursued with sufficient constancy to produce a written work," theorizes Gaston Bachelard in *L'Eau et les Rêves*, "in order that it not be simply the vacancy of a fugitive hour, it must find its *matter*, it is necessary that a material element nourish it with its own substance, its own pattern, its own specific poetics." Poetic thought, like pre-Socratic philosophy, must be marked by the elemental temperament of the poet, "linked to a primitive material reverie." It would, of course, be absurd to insist narrowly and rigidly on any particular scheme of things in this regard. Bachelard says elsewhere that he is talking about "orientation," that "it is not a question of being rooted in a particular substance, but of tendencies, of poetic exaltation." The true poet must have a concretely material imagination in order to be interested in the world and to interest us in *his* world, and this material imagination will always have a specific tendency.[10]

Can there be any doubt about Thoreau's primary orientation toward water? (In this respect of course he is not singular in his literary generation, for one thinks naturally of Poe, Melville, and Whitman.) We have only to glance at the titles of the two books Thoreau published in his lifetime to confirm this observation, and if we add *Cape Cod* we have a kind of aqueous Trinity: in *A Week,* the book of the River; in *Walden,* the book of the Pond; and in *Cape Cod,* the book of the Sea. For this last, despite its historical and humorous digressions, is thoroughly permeated and controlled by that "unwearied and illimitable ocean," that "grand fact," which Thoreau tells us he specifically went to see—which, indeed, he was "determined" to get "into" himself. In "Walking," as we have noticed, Thoreau begged for "the ocean, the desert or the wilderness." In his professedly unsentimental journey to the Cape, where "everything told of the sea," he found all three impressively combined ("the abyss of the ocean is nearly a desert"; "the ocean is a wilderness reaching round the globe"). Searching for the "springs of life," he found at Cape Cod the "spring of springs, the waterfall of waterfalls," a teeming jumble of actual and inchoate life perpetually being created and destroyed.

> The Greeks would not have called the ocean ἀτρύγετος, or unfruitful, though it does not produce wheat, if they had viewed it by the light of modern science; for naturalists now assert that "the sea, and not the land, is the principal seat of life. . . ." "[M]odern investigations," to quote the words of Desor, "merely go to confirm the great idea which was vaguely anticipated by the ancient poets and philosophers, that the Ocean is the origin of all things."

Here, on the "neutral ground" of the seashore, by the side of this mysterious element—at once "unfruitful" and "the origin of all things"—in which "the animal and vegetable kingdoms meet and are strangely mingled," Thoreau prepared himself for something like "the experience of Noah—to realize the deluge." It was primarily not a scientific but a poetic attitude and religious expectation that Thoreau brought to "the shore of the resounding sea."[11]

This last phrase in fact, drawn from a line in the *Iliad* (I. 34) that especially affected Thoreau, to judge by the frequency with which he returns to it, embodies the quintessence of oceanic poetry and religion. For Greek is Thoreau's *elemental* language, and Homer is its truest practitioner. His song, like that of the wood thrush, is the actual voice of that divine watery Wild which Thoreau sought:

> We were wholly absorbed by this spectacle and tumult [of the sea], and like Chryses, though in a different mood from him, we walked silent along the shore of the resounding sea,
>
> Βῆ δ' ἀκέων παρὰ θῖνα πολυφλοίσβοιο θαλάσσης.
>
> I put in a little Greek now and then, partly because it sounds so much like the ocean.

In *Cape Cod*, Thoreau puts in more than a little Greek, for as Sherman Paul notes, "allusions to Homer, especially for the sound and color of the sea," are particularly numerous. Here we have a crucial example of that "*philological* side" to Thoreau's writing which Ellery Channing said deserved thoughtful consideration, though it is not so much a question of etymological interest here as of the very sound and texture of words. "At times the sound of a vocable, or the force of a letter, reveals and defines the real thought attached to a word," observes Bachelard in a remarkably Emersonian mood. For someone extremely sensitive to words,

> language having achieved complete nobility, phonetic phenomena and the phenomena of the logos harmonize. But we should have to learn how to meditate very slowly, to experience the inner poetry of the word, the inner immensity of a word. All important words, all the words marked for grandeur by a poet, are keys to the universe, to the dual universe of the Cosmos and the depths of the human spirit.

So πολυφλοίσβοιο θαλάσσης suggests to Thoreau the posibility of an actual religious revelation being uttered from the depths of wild nature to the receptive soul:

> The attention of those who frequent the camp-meetings at Eastham, is said to be divided between the preaching of the Methodists and the preaching of the billows on the back side of the Cape, for they all stream over here in the course of their stay. I trust that in this case the loudest voice carries it. With what effect may we suppose the ocean to say, "My hearers!" to the multitude on the bank! On that side some John N. Maffit; on this, the Reverend Poluphloisboios Thalassa.

Even the revivalists are compelled by the power of water, for they too "stream over" to view the ocean. But for Thoreau Christianity can scarcely compete with the voice of the Wild. And he puts in a little Greek now and then to render physically present for us the force of what Wallace Stevens calls this "speech belched out of hoary darks," this "one vast, subjugating, final tone."[12]

Like Stevens's Comedian, however, Thoreau faces obvious problems in transcending Kantian prohibitions. "Here was the veritable ding an sich, at last" (indeed Thoreau calls the Cape and its ocean "the thing itself"), and here, as Crispin discovered, "was no help before reality." Both Crispin and Henry David are in danger of being "washed away by magnitude." Emerson noted with justice, in his memorial sketch of Thoreau, that he had "a natural skill for mensuration," but as Emerson moved from the scale of commodity to a more transcendental point of view, he unintentionally contradicted himself in an interesting way: "To him there was no such thing as size. The pond was a small ocean; the Atlantic, a large Walden Pond." Despite Emerson's confidence, not even Thoreau's customary tricks of rhetoric could carry him, a man used to measuring things by eye on a pastoral scale, over the shattering "immensity" of this "illimitable" ocean. As he stood looking on "the roaring sea, θάλασσα ἠχήεσσα," Thoreau became "gradually convinced," with Yankee understatement, "that fishing here and in a pond were not, in all respects, the same." He is roughly in the situation of Stevens's "Doctor of Geneva":

> *Lacustrine man had never been assailed*
> *By such long-rolling opulent cataracts. . . .*
> *[The sea] found means to set his simmering mind*
> *Spinning and hissing with oracular*
> *Notations of the wild, the ruinous waste . . .*[13]

Thoreau's ocean reveries darkened under the pressure of a particular perception the significance of which attentive readers of *Walden* will be quick to notice:

As we looked off, and saw the water growing darker and darker and deeper and deeper the farther we looked, till it was awful to consider, and it appeared to have no relation to the friendly land, either as shore or bottom,—of what use is a bottom if it is out of sight, if it is two or three miles from the surface, and you are to be drowned so long before you get to it, though it were made of the same stuff with your native soil?—over that ocean, where, as the Veda says, "there is nothing to give support, nothing to rest upon, nothing to cling to," I felt that I was a land animal.

This quasi-anacoluthic sentence, with its painfully suspended period, perfectly enacts the anxiety it expresses: the ocean appears to have no bottom. Thoreau is faced with a crucial dilemma, for the question of a *bottom* is fundamental to him. We recall his passionate concern in *Walden* to find "a hard bottom and rocks in place, which we can call *reality*, and say, This is, and no mistake," leading of course to his compulsion to measure Walden Pond; for although it is commonly believed to be bottomless, Thoreau is determined to fathom it. In large measure the optimistic assurances of *Walden* are based on Thoreau's belief that bottoms exist *commensurate* with man's ability to discover them. He concludes the book with an unequivocal assertion in this regard—"there is a solid bottom every where"—followed, however, by an illustrative anecdote which, in the light of *Cape Cod*, is finally not so funny:

> We read that the traveller asked the boy if the swamp before him had a hard bottom. The boy replied that it had. But presently the traveller's horse sank in up to the girths, and he observed to the boy, "I thought you said that this bog had a hard bottom." "So it has," answered the latter, "but you have not got half way to it yet."

Reinforcing the dubiousness of the humor here, that sentence from *Cape Cod* reverberates: "of what use is a bottom if it is out of sight, if it is two or three miles from the surface, and you are to be drowned so long before you get to it?"[14]

Thoreau claimed in *Walden* that he craved only reality, "be it life or death." Now, in the sea, he found a "fertile unknown" which he could not put his foot through because there *was* no bottom, and it made him ponder nervously. "Severance/Was clear," as Stevens writes:

> *The last distortion of romance*
> *Forsook the insatiable egotist. The sea*
> *Severs not only lands but also selves.*[15]

Thoreau found that the self of *Walden*, the "I" which could measure its own depth in the depth of Walden Pond, was now literally and philosophically at sea.

In this connection probably the most fascinating passage in *Cape Cod*, and the one that stands in the most striking contrast to *Walden*, concerns Thoreau's careful investigation of a "Charity-house," or "Humane-house," placed along the shore as refuge for shipwrecked sailors. In Thoreau's hands, this description of the locked and windowless hut, as seen through a knothole, becomes a

parodic deflation of the comforts of home and of the assurances held
out to us by exhortations to spiritual self-examination and religious
faith, vis-à-vis the dark depths of the Wild.

Looking with the eye of faith, knowing that, though to him
that knocketh it may not always be opened, yet to him that
looketh long enough through a knot-hole the inside shall be
visible,—for we had had some practice at looking inward,—by
steadily keeping our other ball covered from the light mean-
while, putting the outward world behind us, ocean and land,
and the beach,—till the pupil became enlarged and collected
the rays of light that were wandering in that dark (for the pupil
shall be enlarged by looking; there never was so dark a night but
a faithful and patient eye, however small, might at last prevail
over it,)—after all this, I say, things began to take shape to our
vision,—if we may use this expression where there was nothing
but emptiness,—and we obtained the long-wished-for insight.

Then, with an ironical flourish borrowed from the opening of book
3 of *Paradise Lost* ("Hail! Holy Light"), this diminished "I" ("eye,"
"pupil") offers us his desolate "insight":

A little longer, and a chimney rushed red on our sight. In
short, when our vision had grown familiar with the darkness,
we discovered that there were some stones and some loose
wads of wool on the floor, and an empty fire-place at the further end; but it *was not* supplied with matches, or straw, or hay,
that we could see, nor "accommodated with a bench" [as adver-
tised in a "Description" of the Cape that Thoreau read].
Indeed, it was the wreck of all cosmical beauty there within.
Turning our backs on the outward world, we thus looked
through the knot-hole into the humane house, into the very
bowels of mercy; and for bread we found a stone. It was literally a great cry (of sea-mews outside), and a little wool.
However, we were glad to sit outside, under the lee of the

humane house, to escape the piercing wind; and there we thought how cold is charity! how inhumane humanity! This, then, is what charity hides! . . . So we shivered round about, not being able to get into it, ever and anon looking through the knot-hole into that night without a star, until we concluded that it was not a humane house at all, but a sea-side box, now shut up, belonging to some of the family of night or chaos.[16]

We might well speculate on the possibility of Melville's having read this passage while composing *The Confidence-Man,* but let us not lose sight of Thoreau. He discovers that this uninviting hut by the sea is merely a poor imitation of a *human* house, for instead of light, warmth, and nourishment it contains only a cold chimney and a bit of disorder. In fact, through a kind of terrible attraction, it has been appropriated by the sea and has ceased to be a human habitation at all. Its secrets are not human ones, but rather the elemental

> *secrets of the hoary deep, a dark*
> *Illimitable Ocean without bound,*
> *Without dimension, where length, breadth, and highth,*
> *And time and place are lost; where eldest Night*
> *And* Chaos, *Ancestors of Nature,* hold
> *Eternal* Anarchy.[17]

From a structural point of view, the situation presented in this section of *Cape Cod*—the situation, that is, of a hut next to a body of water—corresponds to the central motif in *Walden;* but the differences in meaning are crucial and worth close examination. In his "topoanalysis" of "inhabited space . . . the non-I that protects the I," Gaston Bachelard—thinking especially of Thoreau—describes the hut as a "centralized solitude" that "gives us access to absolute refuge." I believe we can and should extend the notion to Walden Pond itself. The pond, like the hut, is "inhabited" by Thoreau. It is "like a hermit in the woods," and Thoreau identifies with it thoroughly. Both hut and pond are scaled to human size and can be comprehended and measured by Thoreau. Though the hut is associated with fire and the pond with water, both express and enclose Thoreau's vital self: fire is the self that rises; water the self that descends. One might say finally that the hut and the pond represent two forms of intimacy.[18]

In the hut by the sea, on the other hand, the chimney is bare and there is no fire: the self is annihilated. Insofar as this hut represents Christianity, it is an *inhuman* "Humane-house," an uninhabited ark of divinity, expressing the emptiness and despair Thoreau finds in the "profundity" of religious promises. But to the extent that this cheerless habitation has simply been assimilated by the sea, it stands for the awesome *bottomlessness* of the Wild. Thus this hut and the body of water it lies beside may be seen as two forms of immensity, or boundless depth, inspiring in man a sense of alienation, terror, and helplessness. The only possible reactions, as in *Moby-Dick,* are defiance (Ahab), reverence (Starbuck), or a species of cosmic humor (Ishmael). Thoreau's response contains none of the first, some of the second, and a good deal of the third. Perhaps it is this last that accounts for the frequent descriptions of *Cape Cod* as Thoreau's "sunniest, happiest book,"[19] despite the undeniable seriousness of its oceanic reveries.

What lesson, then, did Thoreau learn from the sea, what was the doctrine preached by the Reverend Poluphloisboios Thalassa? Mainly this, it seems: that a man who has gotten the Wild into his soul may stand anywhere and put, not only all America, but every place and thing behind him. Some lines from Santayana's "The Genteel Tradition in American Philosophy" may be useful here. We recall that Santayana delivered this talk in 1911 during his first visit to California. In his summation he, too, appealed to the lesson of the Wild, to the voice of the forests and sierras of the great West:

In their non-human beauty and peace they stir the sub-human depths and superhuman possibilities of your own spirit. It is no transcendental logic that they teach; and they give no sign of any deliberate morality seated in the world. It is rather the vanity and superficiality of all logic, the needlessness of argument, the relativity of morals, the strength of time, the fertility of matter, the variety, the unspeakable variety, of possible life. . . . Everywhere is beauty and nowhere permanence, everywhere an incipient harmony, nowhere an intention, nor a responsibility, nor a plan. . . . They allow you, in one happy moment, at once to play and to worship, to take yourselves simply, humbly, for what you are, and to salute the wild, indifferent, non-censorious infinity of nature . . . through wonder and pleasure, you are taught speculation. You learn what you are really fitted to do, and where lie your natural dignity and joy, namely in representing many things, without being them, and in letting your imagination, through sympathy, celebrate and echo their life. Because the peculiarity of man is that his machinery for reaction on external things has involved an imaginative transcript of these things, which is preserved and suspended in his fancy; and the interest and beauty of this inward landscape, rather than any fortunes that may await his body in the outer world, constitute his proper happiness.[20]

The sea, with its annihilating force, teaches us that our world can be possessed only in imagination—that it is the imaginative spirit alone, as Emerson once said, which builds itself a permanent house, world, and heaven. Thoreau's faith in the constitutive power of poetry was the same and his conclusion, already quoted, deserves to be heard again: "Our truest life is when we are in dreams awake."[21]

TEN

SOCIETY AND SOLITUDE

Though it is tricky to attempt to summarize a complex career in a few phrases, Thoreau lends himself well to a certain kind of summary because of the calculated intensity with which he did one thing. For, despite the varied and voluminous nature of his writings, it is in and through a single book that Thoreau immortalized a personal experiment and burned an image of himself on the consciousness of the world that more than one hundred years of criticism have scarcely been able to modify. The experiment, as everyone knows, was an attempt to live a solitary life, and the image thus created was that of Henry Thoreau as the celebrated hermit of Walden Pond.

Many people, of course, have lived totally alone before and since Thoreau's time, so that what he did was not in itself unique, nor did it represent an especially protracted sentence of solitary living—as such a thing often occurs to others—for Thoreau himself tells us that he lived at Walden for only two years and two months. But here, in fact, lies the very point of Thoreau's sojourn: it was an experiment consciously and willfully undertaken for the purpose of learning something about the nature of man and his relation to the world, and when Thoreau thought that he had found what he went to Walden to find, he left the woods, as he tells us, for as good a reason as he went there. "Perhaps it seemed to me that I had several more lives to live, and could not spare any more time for that one."[1] There were other learning experiences awaiting him, and his major business in life was education. Many people live alone, but few perhaps do so for the express purpose of discovering something about themselves, and with the intent of publishing their discoveries in a form that has permanent value and meaning for us all.

Why is it that Americans (at least literate ones) remain perennially fascinated by Thoreau's example? "To judge from the number of editions now in paperbacks and the volume of their sales, the vogue of Thoreau is a phenomenon that no modern" observer should ignore, Perry Miller noted in 1961. Miller argued that Thoreau's growing popularity in America was mainly owing to his triumphant—indeed, defiant—opposition of the human spirit to the ever-increasing dominance of the machine, a dominance that all of us feel threatened by. "It does seem clear," Miller continued, "that the appeal of Thoreau is not mainly to beatniks who have signed off from the reign of the machine, but to hundreds most abjectly enslaved by it. Thoreau appeals to those prisoners of megalopolis who from him gain at least a passing sight of blue sky. He keeps alive the flicker of an almost extinguished fire of the mind amidst piles of nonflammable steel and concrete—and chromium." And Miller concluded: "I rejoice when told that in the lower echelons of Wall Street there are young executives who, once they have contrived through the rush hour to reach their ranch-type homes in Scarsdale, mix a bit of Thoreau with their martinis."[2]

Though I think that this quasi-Luddite analysis of Thoreau's popularity has much truth in it, I want to suggest a slight shift of emphasis. The major opposition I find exemplified in Thoreau's writings is that of the spirit of an individual against the domination of society—the spirit of the herd. *Walden* is mainly an attempt to debate these opposed claims, and I believe it still and increasingly fascinates us because of our profoundly ambivalent attitudes on this subject. Almost by definition, Americans (post-Emerson) believe in the dignity and importance of the individual. Whether we speak of the major role that individual initiative has played in the development of our country, or emphasize the individual's right to freedom of conscience and belief; whether we insist on the great fact of political democracy, in which every person has one vote and each vote is equally significant, or point pridefully to a long tradition of respect for individual eccentricity and dissent—in all these instances we like to remind ourselves that although our nation is a union, it is a union of many individuals, each of whom reserves the right to be different from his or her neighbors and to be heard as a distinct voice. As Alexis de Tocqueville wrote when Henry Thoreau was a young man, "Individualism is a novel expression, to which a novel idea has given birth." That novel idea was, of course, democracy. And Tocqueville insisted that a new kind of literature would come to birth as a result of this new social idea. "The destinies of mankind, man himself taken aloof from his country and his age and standing in the presence of Nature and of God, with his passions, his doubts, his rare prosperities and inconceivable wretchedness, will become the chief, if not the sole, theme of poetry among these nations."[3]

But at the same time that Tocqueville was predicting an American literature devoted to describing man alone, he was also warning about the tyranny of the majority in America, describing the forces that tended to make for a uniformity of character and opinion in this democratic nation. Tocqueville thus seemed to expose a fundamental paradox at the heart of American life: our crying up of individual initiative is undercut by a widespread desire for group activity; our emphasis on freedom of belief is offset by an undeniable pressure for community consensus; electoral manipulation and control often make a mockery of democratic theory, rendering every person's vote equally *in*significant; and our presumed respect for eccentricity is frequently offset and nullified by an exaggerated fear of being different. Such an irrepressibly optimistic writer as Walt Whitman might try to relax the tensions of this paradox—the contradictory claims of individualism and conformism—by frankly and exuberantly incorporating both positions in his large nature: "One's-self I sing, a simple separate person, / Yet utter the word Democratic, the word En-Masse." Or he could try to solve the problem by asserting instead of proving, attempting through brag—a kind of good-natured bullying—to force all of America to let him be its spokesman: "I celebrate myself, and sing myself, / And what I assume you shall assume." But this sort of bare and hopeful assertion of identity between the individual and the mass was precisely the kind of solution that Henry Thoreau was not prepared to accept. "I did not get far in conversation with him," Thoreau reported of his meeting with Whitman, ". . . and among the few things which I chanced to say, I remember that one was, in answer to him as representing America, that I did not think much of America." Here, with a vengeance, is the voice of Thoreauvian individuality set against the plea for community. But the fine thing about Thoreau is that he was open to contradiction, willing to explore alternative possibilities and debate opposed claims—much less dogmatic than he often seemed. Another sentence from his letter on Whitman, less frequently quoted, also deserves to be remembered: "He may turn out the least of a braggart of all," he conceded of Whitman, "having a better right to be confident."[4]

Let us, however, make no mistake about it: Thoreau's example increases our uneasy suspicion that a radical paradox, a set of conflicting impulses, underlies the whole American experience. New generations of Americans read *Walden,* I suggest, with unabated fascination because, although the book partially argues for social reform and seems to be the first step toward a new and perfected American community, it really (as I have said elsewhere) represents "a description of Thoreau's dream, to a large extent realized, of perfected self-indulgence and self-possession."[5] We are fascinated, I argue, because some part of ourselves profoundly shares this desire to be free, to cut oneself loose from the complications, responsibilities, and conformities of American life. Is it extravagant to see in Thoreau's example part of a larger pattern in American history?

The words that naturally occur to one are separation, flight, withdrawal. William Bradford and his Mayflower pilgrims were, of course, literally separatists—physically from England and spiritually from the Church of England. And the same might be said of the Massachusetts Bay people: for, despite their royal charter and their stout insistence that they had never separated from the English Church, they were in spirit, as in church polity, almost as separatist as the earlier settlers. The impulse toward purification and radical reform engendered in these idealists a desire to remove themselves from the established order for the greater glory of God and the salvation of their individual souls. Spiritual and physical restlessness became characteristic of Americans. One thinks of Roger Williams, Samuel Gorton, and Anne Hutchinson—banished, to be sure—but nonetheless drawing off to Providence, the latter two continuing in the spirit of secession when they felt so moved; one thinks of Thomas Hooker removing to Connecticut, of Edward Taylor choosing to live in the then wilderness of Westfield, of Jonathan Edwards retiring to Stockbridge. The pattern of separation and flight becomes a familiar one in American history, myth, and literature, culminating perhaps in the related, even merged, figures of Daniel Boone and Natty Bumppo—the withdrawing American hero who finds it inconvenient to have a neighbor within even one hundred miles of himself. Why did the Pilgrim Fathers come here? asks D. H. Lawrence: "They came largely to get away—that most simple of motives. To get away." And extending Lawrence's suggestion, Lewis Mumford builds this notion of withdrawal into a tentative theory of American writing in general: "The hope of making a fresh start in this new land," he writes, "explains the constant note of rebellion that underlies our greatest literary expressions: rebellion against the political state, against the caste system, against property, against religious ceremony and ritualism, even, in Huckleberry Finn, against tidy routine and mechanical punctuality, as against every kind of cowed conformity."[6]

To be sure, the rationale for flight is always that the isolate American hero, disgusted with the imperfections of the actual society in which he finds himself, has run away to establish the foundation of a more perfect union; by this argument, his rebellion is not merely in the service of a cantakerous individualism, but actually the first step toward a reconstituted social order. However, we must not lose sight of our paradox: because no actual society is ever good enough for our American hero, we are led to suspect that his act is a selfish, not a social, one. Emerson pointed to the issue in a journal entry made, probably, in 1860: "Thoreau's page," Emerson observed, "reminds me of Farley, who went early into the wilderness in Illinois, lived alone, & hewed down trees, & tilled the land, but retired again into newer country when the population came up with him. Yet, on being asked, what he was doing? said, he pleased himself that he was preparing the land for civilization." Without going into the question of Mr. Farley, the point of Emerson's comparison is clear enough. Like the other man, Thoreau is forever preparing the land for a society that he cannot abide, making one feel that his basic purpose is asocial and personal. I please myself, Thoreau says in "Resistance to Civil Government" ("Civil Disobedience")

> with imagining a State at last which . . . would not think it inconsistent with its own repose, if a few were to live aloof from it, not meddling with it, nor embraced by it, who fulfilled all the duties of neighbors and fellowmen. A State which bore this kind of fruit, and suffered it to drop off as fast as it ripened, would prepare the way for a still more perfect and glorious State, which also I have imagined, but not yet anywhere seen.

Thoreau's idea of Paradise is a solitude where, like the poet, he can loaf and invite his soul isolated from the cares and confusions of the modern world. "I live," he states in the last chapter of *Walden*, "in the angle of a leaden wall, into whose composition was poured a little alloy of bell metal. Often, in the repose of my mid-day, there reaches my ears a confused *tintinnabulum* from without. It is the noise of my contemporaries. . . . They tell me of California and Texas, of England and the Indies, of the Hon. Mr.——— of Georgia or of Massachusetts, all transient and fleeting phenomena . . . I delight . . . not to live in this restless, nervous, bustling, trivial Nineteenth Century, but stand or sit thoughtfully while it goes by."[7]

Now I have purposely, perhaps unfairly, stressed this reclusive and anti-social side of Thoreau's personality and writings because I think we do him and ourselves a disservice when we try to gloss over the radically subjective nature of his experiment at Walden Pond. Subjectivity is not a word that we like very much, for we as a nation are supposed to be outgoing and sociable, and the kind of intense self-concern suggested by the notion of subjectivity seems almost un-American. *Walden*, we like to insist, is really a book about economics, teaching us how we can live on less money or with fewer possessions; or we say that it is a guide to life in the woods, including a treatise on what books we should take along, and telling us how to cultivate our garden and how to fish in winter or summer. Of course it is all these things; in fact, it is somewhat of a miscellany. But at the heart of the book lies an experiment in self-discovery that is never lost sight of for long. And this, paradoxically, is what makes *Walden* so American a book, for Americans, besides being sociable, are also a withdrawing and self-scrutinizing people. At least such a tradition is part of our heritage—that heritage of intense spiritual self-examination, perhaps Puritan in origin, which makes the confession, the diary, the journal, the autobiography, such important forms in American writing. Thus, we can look upon Thoreau's solitary life at Walden Pond as the spiritual exercise of a man who has lost his interest in formal religion but not in the habits that it once engendered.

But we must remember that Thoreau was an American Romantic and represents, we might say, the culmination, in this country, of a literary tradition that begins at least as far back as Rousseau and continues on through Wordsworth, Byron, and beyond. All of these Romantics made a cult of solitude, at least on paper, because they believed it is only in solitude that one can truly come to oneself and get to know the twistings and turnings of one's innermost soul. This mood of aloneness, subjectivity, and introspection is, as Emerson pointed out in various places ("The Transcendentalist," "Historic Notes of Life and Letters in New England"), one of the essential things to be associated with the general rubric Transcendentalism. In his journal for 1827 (the year of Beethoven's death, it should be recalled) Emerson made the following entry under the heading "Peculiarities of the present Age": "It is said to be the age of the first person singular. . . . Transcendentalism. Metaphysics & Ethics look inwards." Emerson could have added that literature—art in general—was also looking inwards, for we should notice how directly Emerson's statement about his age looks forward to the opening page of *Walden*: "In most books," Thoreau writes, "the I, or first person, is omitted; in this it will be retained; that, in respect to egotism, is the main difference. We commonly do not remember that it is, after all, always the first person that is speaking. I should not talk so much about myself if there were any body else whom I knew as well"[8]

The humor is characteristic, for instead of whining pathetically that he has no friends (he usually saved the whining for his journal) Thoreau simply asserts that he is his own best acquaintance. But the humor is complicated by irony, for here on the first page of his book Thoreau calculatedly begs the very question that his whole experiment is designed to explore: just how well does he, or any man, know himself? One way of achieving that end is, as it were, to speak in the first person, and thereby to discover and finally to develop the self. Here we need to emphasize the enormous importance for Thoreau and his contemporaries of a notion, often associated with William Ellery Channing, which was to have continuing significance in American life: namely, the idea of self-culture. In the second issue of *The Dial,* dated October 1840, the twenty-three-year-old Henry Thoreau certainly read an article, entitled "The Art of Life,—The Scholar's Calling," in which, with notable eloquence, Frederick Henry Hedge expatiated upon that idea which was to become Thoreau's ruling passion:

> The work of life, so far as the individual is concerned, and that to which the scholar is particularly called, is self-culture,—the perfect unfolding of our individual nature. To this end above all others the art, of which I speak, directs our attention and points our endeavor . . . the business of self-culture admits of no compromise. Either it must be made a distinct aim, or wholly abandoned. . . . Of self-culture, as of all other things worth seeking, the price is a single devotion to that object,— a devotion which shall exclude all aims and ends, that do not directly or indirectly tend to promote it.[9]

Hedge went on to attack what he called the "cultus" and "worship of the age," "an endless multiplication of physical conveniences—an infinite economy": "The end is lost in the means," he wailed. "Life is smothered in appliances [!]. We cannot get to ourselves, there are so many external comforts to wade through. Consciousness stops half way. Reflection is dissipated in the circumstances of our environment." Then, reaching the climax of his address, the author announced that the only environment suitable for the pursuit of self-culture is solitude:

> The business of self-culture requires a renunciation of present notoriety, and a seclusion more or less rigorous from the public eye. The world is too much with us. We live out of doors. An all-present publicity attends our steps. Our life is in print. At every turn we are gazetted and shown up to ourselves. Society has become a chamber of mirrors, where our slightest movement is brought home to us with thousandfold reflection.

This kind of reflection, he suggested, is false and diseased:

> The consequence is a morbid consciousness, a habit of living for effect, utterly incompatible with wholesome effort and an earnest mind. No heroic character, no depth of feeling, or clearness of insight can ever come of such a life. All that is best in human attainments springs from retirement. Whoso has conceived within himself any sublime and fruitful thought, or proposed to himself any great work or life, has been guided thereto by solitary musing.

Hedge then instanced Gibbon, Klopstock, Newton, and Luther as examples of the advantage of solitude for the creative mind. "In retirement," he continued, "we first become acquainted with ourselves, our means, and ends. There no strange form interposes between us and the truth. No paltry vanity cheats us with false shows and aims. The film drops from our eyes. While we gaze the vision brightens; while we muse the fire burns. . . . whoso would perfect himself," he concluded, "and bless the world with any great work or example, must hide his young days in 'some reclusive and religious life out of all eyes, tongues, minds, and injuries.'"

One cannot overstress the formative influence that such an argument as this, this aspect of the Romantic Zeitgeist, must have had on Thoreau's decision to live alone in the woods. Solitude and self-culture were absolutely inseparable notions for him. "How shall I help myself?" he asks in his journal for 1840: "By withdrawing into the garret . . . determining to meet myself face to face sooner or later."[10] In this entry self-help is equated with self-discovery, and Thoreau could think of no better environment for such an activity than the solitude of Walden Pond. The results of this confrontation, of course, would form the bulk of his second and most famous book. Which brings us quite naturally to the major issue: what did solitude teach Henry Thoreau?

Not surprisingly, one of the first things he seems to have learned was that he had to wean himself from his dependence on society, that the social habit had weakened his ability to be throughly comfortable with himself. "I have never felt lonesome, or in the least oppressed by a sense of solitude, but once," Thoreau confesses, "and that was a few weeks after I came to the woods, when, for an hour, I doubted [i.e., questioned] if the near neighborhood of man was not essential to a serene and healthy life. To be alone was something unpleasant. But I was at the same time conscious of a slight insanity in my mood, and seemed to foresee my recovery." I think that Thoreau is offering us a particularly valuable insight here which has something to do with a primitive existential fear of our own being that we all share. Ordinarily, this fear is dissipated by society; quite literally, we lose ourselves in the company of others. But in total isolation, deprived even of the promise or expectation of social distraction, we may feel indefinably threatened from within. It is not the darkness outside that Thoreau is complaining of—at least not for himself—for he comically assures us in this same chapter on "Solitude" how comforted he was to know that "the witches are all hung, and Christianity and candles have been introduced." No, the "insanity" that menaced him was an inner one: the danger either of an internal void or of some alien presence within that threatened to subvert or overwhelm the confident normal self. What Thoreau is describing, of course, is a painful sense of division—of the reflective spirit from the animal body or of the total human organism from the environment. The "insanity" he feels amounts to a feeling of alienation, of separation, and the cure clearly lies in the ability to reintegrate oneself—both internally and with the totality of the creation.

Readers of Kierkegaard (Thoreau's contemporary, by the way) may notice that Thoreau's "slight insanity" bears some resemblance to Kierkegaard's "Despair," that "sickness unto death" which amounts to a spiritual and existential disrelationship. Like Thoreau, Kierkegaard insisted that one of the chief ways in which we try to hide our state of spiritual disease from ourselves is by losing individual consciousness in the crowd. Society thus serves to mask the central problem of the self from view, thereby prolonging the disease. And if solitude is initially painful, it is so mainly because it exposes and sharpens our awareness of divison and alienation. But such knowledge is the necessary beginning of our cure, for the problem must be worked through, not shunted off or forgotten about. "Our only health," as Eliot writes, "is the disease . . . to be restored, our sickness must grow worse." Made aware by solitude of his "insanity," Thoreau also seems to foresee his own recovery, and that recovery, as I have noted, lies in the ability to reintegrate oneself— both internally and with the totality of the creation. Both kinds of integration come together and reinforce one another. Here is how Kierkegaard puts it: "This then is the formula which describes the condition of the self when despair is completely eradicated: by relating itself to its own self and by willing to be itself the self is grounded transparently in the Power which posited it."[11]

Thoreau's description of his cure can be characterized as a dramatization of Kierkegaard's abstract formulation. Having, through his choice of solitude as it were, willed to confront and be only himself and to come into relation with himself, Thoreau is rewarded by an awareness of continuity between his own being and Nature's that dispels his "insanity," his feeling of fearful separateness and division:

> In the midst of a gentle rain while these thoughts prevailed [Thoreau is speaking of his "insanity"], I was suddenly sensible of such sweet and beneficent society in Nature, in the very pattering of the drops, and in every sound and sight around my house, an infinite and unaccountable friendliness all at once like an atmosphere sustaining me, as made the fancied advantages of human neighborhood insignificant, and I have never thought of them since. . . . I was so distinctly made aware of the presence of something kindred to me, even in scenes which we are accustomed to call wild and dreary, and also that the nearest of blood to me and humanest was not a person nor a villager, that I thought no place could ever be strange to me again.

Thoreau is now sane again—spiritually integrated with himself and nature—and thus can say: "This is a delicious evening, when the whole body is one sense, and imbibes delight through every pore. I go and come with a strange liberty in Nature, a part of herself."[12]

Having experienced that sense of spiritual freedom and rebirth which he came to Walden Pond to find, Thoreau can now even suggest that solitude is not really a place—a solitary cell or the like—but rather a state of mind, in which the self feels truly and individually alive and at peace, supported, accompanied, and transparently grounded, as Kierkegaard says, "in the Power which posited it." "Any prospect of awakening or coming to life to a dead man," Thoreau writes, "makes indifferent all times and places":

> The place where that may occur is always the same, and indescribably pleasant to all our senses. For the most part we allow

only outlying and transient circumstances to make our occasions. They are, in fact, the cause of our distraction. Nearest to all things is that power which fashions their being. *Next* to us the grandest laws are continually being executed. *Next* to us is not the workman whom we have hired, with whom we love so well to talk, but the workman whose work we are.

Thoreau has arrived at that point of understanding, it seems to me, which Spinoza called our truest good: namely, at a "knowledge of the union existing between the mind and the whole of Nature." This is Spinoza's intellectual love of God, the ability to see all things, oneself included, under the form of eternity. It amounts to a kind of faith in the whole created universe, and in fact Kierkegaard says that his formula for describing the condition of the self without despair, willingly and confidently grounded in the Power which posited it, is also a definition of faith. Such a faith, apparently, was one of the great lessons taught Thoreau by his solitary life in the woods.[13]

My heading for this chapter—"Society and Solitude"—is drawn of course from Emerson. Perhaps it is less well known that Santayana also wrote a short essay with the same title. Both of these pieces of writing, but especially Santayana's, have some bearing on Thoreau's experiment. I have already mentioned Thoreau's notion that solitude is really, or at least can be, a state of mind, not a condition of the body. Let us expand a bit on this. "We are for the most part more lonely when we go abroad among men," Thoreau writes, "than when we stay in our chambers." Now this is a familiar notion—the idea that a person can feel terribly solitary in the midst of a crowd. Paradoxically, society can foment a feeling of intense solitude. "Let us not be the victim of words," says Emerson. "Society and solitude are deceptive names. It is not the circumstance of seeing more or fewer people, but the readiness of sympathy, that imports." Where there is no sympathy, Emerson suggests, there is no true companionship, and a person might as well be alone. Sadly, Emerson considers this to be too often the actual condition of social intercourse. "How insular and pathetically solitary are all the people we know!" he writes. Afraid to tell the truth to one another, we deal in "superficial and treacherous courtesies"; and the knowledge that we are neither speaking nor being spoken to honestly drives "each adult soul as with whips into the desert"—that is, makes us all feel miserably dishonest and cut off. Emerson's solution—and it is typical—amounts to a suggestion of synthesis: that we mix the honesty of our solitary meditations with the pleasures of society. "The remedy is to reinforce each of these moods from the other," he writes. "Conversation will not corrupt us it we come to the assembly in our own garb and speech and with the energy of health to select what is ours and reject what is not. Society we must have; but let it be society, and not exchanging news or eating from the same dish."[14]

Now, Thoreau would not necessarily have rejected Emerson's synthesis or his conclusions on the problem of society versus solitude, but by nature Thoreau was not one to lean toward compromise. What especially delighted him, as we know, was to dwell in paradox. Having discovered that a person can feel extremely lonely in the midst of society, it then occurred to him to explore the opposite paradox, namely that in solitude we can create our own society. Here is where Santayana's essay proves a useful guide to the mood of Thoreau's musings on solitude. Santayana begins this way: "O solitudo, sola beatitudo, Saint Bernard said; but might he not have said just as well, O societas, sola felicitas? Just as truly, I think." Santayana argues that whether one is prompted to insist that the only happiness in the world lies in solitude or society depends on one's temperament, for in the abstract neither situation is necessarily better than the other. But he defends Saint Bernard's preference, insisting moreover that his "beatific solitude . . . was filled with a kind of society," for we are by nature a social creatures: "That the wilderness to which hermits flee must be peopled by their fancy," Santayana says, "could have been foreseen by any observer of human nature." Therefore, "all Saint Bernard could mean . . . is that happiness lies in this substitution of an ideal for a natural society, in converse with thoughts rather than with things. . . . To substitute the society of ideas for that of things is simply to live in the mind."[15]

Admittedly, Santayana's tacit equation of people with "things" here is rather odd—perhaps a good example of that chilliness of temperament which caused many who knew him to revere him as a philosopher but dislike him as a person. At all events, the point of Santayana's essay is still well taken: namely, that humans have the gift of imagination, which enables us to compensate in our minds for the defects of the real world. Accordingly, a life lived totally in the mind can achieve a perfection denied to actual existence. This notion was certainly one of the tenets of Transcendentalism in its purest and most unyielding form. As Hedge writes in his *Dial* essay on "The Art of Life": "The highest life,—the highest enjoyment, the point at which, after all our wanderings, we mean to land, is the life of the mind—the enjoyment of thought." It is quite clear that the Romantic cult of solitude owes a great deal to this formulation: an idealist, thwarted in his attempt to make the world conform to his own model, is pleased to retire into the mind, where at least he reigns supreme. Seen in this light, Romantic self-culture becomes a kind of compensatory self-absorption.

Thoreau, of course, was no Saint Bernard, nor did he always live alone or spend all of his time traveling in his own brain. But he saw clearly and seized upon this advantage of solitude: the opportunity it affords us to create an ideal society. Thus, Thoreau writes:

I have heard of a man lost in the woods and dying of famine and exhaustion at the foot of a tree, whose loneliness was relieved by the grotesque visions with which, owing to bodily weakness, his diseased imagination surrounded him, and which he believed to be real. So also, owing to bodily and mental health and strength, we may be continually cheered by a like but more normal and natural society, and come to know that we are never alone.[16]

Pursued rigorously and unremittingly, of course, this advantage of solitude can prove a vice—dehumanizing us and rendering us unfit for normal society. But that is not, I think, what happened to Thoreau; nor is his point that we should permanently and exclusively substitute the creatures of the mind for real society. Rather, his experience of solitude reminded him that the gift of imagination can be used to people the void when we are left, willingly or not, to our own devices. This, for Thoreau, was another valuable lesson of his life in the woods, and he offers it to us, not as the whole of wisdom, but simply as one more portion of usable human truth.

ELEVEN

"GOD HIMSELF CULMINATES IN THE PRESENT MOMENT": THOUGHTS ON THOREAU'S FAITH

We do not know if Thoreau was present on that great occasion when Emerson delivered his Divinity School Address. Thoreau was working hard in the small school he had opened in Concord just a month earlier and probably had no desire to spend Sunday, too, indoors—even if the sermon *was* unorthodox and the preacher Ralph Waldo Emerson. Just five weeks later, on August 19, 1838, Thoreau would in fact complain in his journal that the pealing of the sabbath bell disturbed him as he sat on the cliffs. It was, he said, "the sound of many catechisms and religious books twanging a canting peal round the world"; and he pronounced himself "sick at heart of this pagoda worship." No, it is unlikely that Thoreau was himself in the chapel of Divinity Hall on that momentous Sunday evening; but he had in fact anticipated Emerson's own mood and message in the Address the previous May when he jotted down this poem in his journal:

> *So mild the air a pleasure 'twas to breathe,*
> *For what seems heaven above was earth beneath.*
> *The school boy loitered on his way to school,*
> *Scorning to live so rare a day by rule.*[1]

In view of the striking consonance of perceptions and attitudes that was already uniting Emerson and Thoreau, it would be impossible to say whether Thoreau's language in journal entries made during August and September actually echoed Emerson's words about its having "been a luxury to draw the breath of life" in that "refulgent summer" of 1838. "The crackling flight of grasshoppers is a luxury," Thoreau exclaimed one day; "it is a luxury to muse by a wall-side in the sunshine of a September afternoon," he insisted on another. Whether through coincidence or actual influence, Thoreau had come to share Emerson's belief that one's "faith should blend with the light of rising and of setting suns, with the flying cloud, the singing bird, and the breath of flowers." Though the orthodox would loudly condemn such talk as nature-worship or pantheism, Thoreau was no more afraid of these labels than Emerson was.[2]

Feeling himself fundamentally nourished and sustained by the physical world, the young Thoreau already knew that any definition of "faith" which would have meaning for him must blend with his experience in nature. He knew, too, that taking such a position would put him radically at odds with most of his neighbors. On September 3 he wrote: "The only faith that men recognize is a creed—But the true creed which we unconsciously live by, and which rather adopts us than we it, is quite different from the written or preached one." Like Emerson, Thoreau had been adopted by the refulgent summer and the luxury of living; and he would therefore always have trouble convincing his more conventional neighbors that he was any better than a mere village atheist. Perhaps this is why Emerson felt obliged, in his funeral oration on Thoreau, to insist that "whilst he used in his writings a certain petulance of remark in reference to churches or churchmen, he was a person of a rare, tender, and absolute religion, a person incapable of any profanation, by act or by thought."[3]

Thoreau's petulance in regard to what he considered the merely nominal Christianity of many of his neighbors was abundantly in evidence in his first book, *A Week on the Concord and Merrimack Rivers,* and undoubtedly contributed greatly to the commercial failure of that venture. In the "Sunday" section of the book Thoreau pronounced himself a follower of "the great god Pan" and mused sadly over the paradox that the all-loving and self-abnegating Jesus should somehow have given birth, in modern times, to the factionalism and exclusiveness of the various Christian sects. "What are time and space to Christianity," he writes, "eighteen hundred years, and a new world?—that the humble life of a Jewish peasant should have force to make a New York bishop so bigoted." Thoreau, we should note, is in fact not attacking Christ but rather the uses to which his teachings have been put. "It is necessary not to be Christian," he insists, "to appreciate the beauty and significance of the life of Christ." Since such is his logic, Thoreau must necessarily speak from the outside—as a self-declared non-Christian—in order to weigh the merits of Christ as a religious leader. "I know," he goes on, "that some will have hard thoughts of me, when they hear their Christ named beside my Buddha, yet I am sure that I am willing they should love their Christ more than my Buddha, for the love is the main thing, and I like him too." This is not petulance; it is insolence: "*Their* Christ . . . *my* Buddha . . . I *like* him too."[4]

All of this is calculated, of course—calculated to get a rise out of his audience; for Thoreau loves a good fight and he is fighting mad over the realization that religious intolerance and bigotry have turned the religion of love from its true path. The divine is multiform, in Thoreau's view; and he is in actuality less concerned with debating the opposed claims of Pan or Buddha or Christ than he is with defining the fundamental religious impulse: "for the love is the main thing." "God," he continues, quoting Rammohun Roy, "is the letter Ku, as well as Khu." Do we, Thoreau is asking, in fact know how to spell or pronounce the name of God? Should it matter whether it is spelled B-u-d-d-h-a or C-h-r-i-s-t? How, he goes on to ask, can we "presume to fable of the ineffable"—which is to say, speak of the unspeakable? This is the posture, as Emerson says, of "a person of a rare, tender and absolute religion, a person incapable of any profanation"; for with an almost Hebraic awe, Thoreau forbears to utter the holy name or even to claim that he knows what it is.[5]

Indeed, the attributes of the divine are an equally mysterious business; and Thoreau understands that we shall never clarify our religious principles until we purify our understanding of how it is possible to make meaningful predications: "Pythagoras says, truly enough, 'A true assertion respecting God, is an assertion of God'; but we may well doubt if there is any example of this in literature." Thoreau did not need a Wittgenstein to tell him that theological problems are, at base, linguistic ones. Divinity, it seems, is the thing whereof, as yet, we may not truly speak; for "Divinity" is nothing less than the truth itself, and even our best words are but raids upon that inarticulate center.[6]

The *experience* of that ultimate we may have, as others have had it before us, Thoreau insists: "The oldest Egyptian or Hindoo philosopher raised a corner of the veil from the statue of the divinity; and still the trembling robe remains raised, and I gaze upon as fresh a glory as he did." What is problematic is our *articulation* of that experience, since it is not a matter of logic, but rather of the "fringe" or atmosphere, the overtones, the poetic or extravagant aura that surrounds or accompanies our most serious or exalted speech. "The volatile truth of our words," Thoreau writes, "should continually betray the inadequacy of the residual statement. Their truth is instantly *translated;* its literal monument alone remains. The words which express our faith and piety are not definite; yet they are significant and fragrant like frankincense to superior natures." Let me emphasize what seems to be Thoreau's main point here: since the truth of the words that express our faith and piety is instantly *translated*—that is, gets away from us, flying off into some meta-language of the spirit—we must work hard to infer that higher, or deeper, sense of language from the residual monument we find on the page. Each word must be a kind of spiritual depth-charge, capable of exploding when it touches the bottom of our consciousness. And Thoreau's own practice is to load his language, even to the point of seeming obscurity, with that potential energy, that tendency toward literal instability, which makes them volatile and alive. "I fear chiefly lest my expression may not be *extra-vagant* enough," he writes, "may not wander far enough beyond the narrow limits of my daily experience, so as to be adequate to the truth of which I have been convinced."[7]

What is this truth of which Thoreau was convinced and which he worked so hard to express? Here we might invoke a distinguished imaginary academic, Wallace Stevens's Professor Eucalyptus of New Haven, who said: "The search / For reality is as momentous as / The search for god." That is a sentence Thoreau could have written—did in fact write in another form. Thoreau was not afraid of the notoriously indefinite word *reality;* on the contrary, it was one of his favorites. It expressed his faith and piety and was significant and fragrant to him. If it seems to us a dubious linguistic item as it sits there abstractly on the page, ravaged by time and usage, that may be only because we lack the imagination, or courage, to confront it boldly and try to understand what it signifies in our lives. Thoreau did not avoid the challenge. To judge only by the second chapter of *Walden,* reality was the chief thing he craved and lived for—the object of his researches and the goal of his quest. "Shams and delusions are esteemed for soundest truths," he writes, "while reality is fabulous. If men would steadily observe realities only, and not allow themselves to be deluded, life, to compare it with such things as we know, would be like a fairy tale and the Arabian Nights' Entertainments."[8]

At this point, as readers, we ought to stop and briefly interrogate our experience of this difficult concept, especially as we find it used in Transcendentalist writings. Though he did not need to, Thoreau could have gotten a standard philosophical definition of *realism* from Emerson, who tells us in various places that it implies Idealism or Platonism. The Realists, Emerson says, in their "famous dispute with the Nominalists . . . had a good deal of reason." For they believed, as did Emerson himself, that "general ideas are essences. They are our gods: they round and ennoble the most partial and sordid way of living. Our proclivity to details cannot quite degrade our life, and divest it of poetry." Leaning on the traditional, technical meaning of the word, Emerson argues that the *real* is the idea, or essence, which lies behind or above the details of ordinary life and fills them with meaning. Pure ideas are the gods which hover over the illusions, or appearances, among which we live and provide them with their only true poetry. We must therefore look beyond ordinary experience to the reality—the *truth*—of which it is only a representation.[9]

Is this what Thoreau means by *reality*—the ultimate truth which is concealed by the appearances among which we live and breathe? Such would seem to be the drift of the paragraph quoted above:

> I perceive that we inhabitants of New England live this mean life that we do because our vision does not penetrate the surface of things. We think that that *is* which *appears* to be. If a man should walk through this town and see only the reality, where, think you, would the "Mill-dam" go to? If he should give us an account of the realities he beheld there, we should not recognize the place in his description. Look at a meeting-house, or a court-house, or a jail, or a shop, or a

dwelling-house, and say what that thing really is before a true gaze, and they would all go to pieces in your account of them.

Thoreau does seem here to be ratifying Emerson's Transcendental notion that our perceptions are merely skin deep and do not penetrate to the hidden meaning. The poet, or visionary, could thus be defined as a kind of Platonic *enfant terrible* who, as Arthur Rimbaud says, "through a long, immense and reasoned *derangement of all the senses*" habituates himself to seeing realities not available to ordinary views of the world—"a mosque instead of a factory, a school of drummers composed of angels, calashes on the roads of the sky, a drawing-room at the bottom of a lake: monsters, mysteries. . . ." Why not conclude, with Rimbaud, by "finding sacred the disorder of [one's] intelligence" if thereby ordinary life might be transformed into something strange and wonderful—"like a fairy tale and the Arabian Nights' Entertainments"?[10]

Though Rimbaud actually seems to have been talking about the metaphor-making power of the poet's eye, I have purposely reduced the Idealist/Platonic notion of *realism* to an absurdity with the help of his extravagances in order to highlight the dangers of seeing abstractly. I believe that Thoreau was in fact complaining that his neighbors were living according to a debased version of the Platonic scheme—in their case, however, seeing the world through eyes dimmed by received opinions and stock ideas. We conduct our lives in terms of the conventional fables in which we have come to believe and fail to notice that reality--the world in which we actually live our lives—is truly fabulous and inexhaustible. "May we not *see* God?" Thoreau asks.[11]

To return to our paragraph, we note that Thoreau *perceives* the truths that he reports to us. When Thoreau walks down the main street of Concord, he does not think of something called the "Mill-dam" but rather experiences that place in all its concrete particularity—in the fullness of its being. His neighbors see a meeting-house, a court-house, a jail, a shop, a dwelling-house—that is, they see, superficially, a function, an institution, an abstract notion reified. But Thoreau wants to know "what that thing really is" as we come upon it in the street. He does not want to be awed and subdued by the idea that it represents. Such abstractions are "shams and delusions," what he calls the "mud and slush of opinion, and prejudice, and tradition." To the penetrating eye of a true *seer* the jail, as jail, with all it stands for, would simply "go to pieces" and show forth for the poor item it really is. "When we are unhurried and wise," Thoreau says, "we perceive . . . that petty fears and petty pleasures are but the shadow of the reality." We struggle with those shadows, Thoreau argues, and thus allow our preoccupations, prejudices, and habits to take the pith and substance out of life as it actually presents itself to us from moment to moment:

> Men esteem truth remote, in the outskirts of the system, behind the farthest star, before Adam and after the last man. In eternity there is indeed something true and sublime. But all these times and places and occasions are now and here. God himself culminates in the present moment, and will never be more divine in the lapse of all the ages. And we are enabled to apprehend at all what is sublime and noble only by the perpetual instilling and drenching of the reality which surrounds us.[12]

Do those sound like the words of an ordinary kind of Platonist? Thoreau's "God"—the truth—is not somewhere off in space and time, separated from his being in the world, but rather embedded in "the reality which surrounds us." Nor is Thoreau some sort of literal-minded materialist for whom words are reducible to things and things to their physical substance. The word "reality," let us remember, is significant and fragrant for Thoreau, and not only points to our *perceptions* of the universe but also to our *conceptions*. Neither modality of the "real" must be allowed to overpower the other; if this happens, we are in danger of succumbing to "shams and delusions." Ideas are the realities that give meaning and value to physical experience; substance is the reality that links us to the world and gives weight and veracity to our conceptions. The intellect, as Thoreau says, "is a cleaver; it discerns and rifts its way into the secret of things."[13] Without the solidity of reality there would be nothing for the intellect to work in; and if there were no "secret of things," that work would be meaningless.

In his appropriation of the world as a writer, Thoreau begins with things as they are and then proceeds to celebrate them in language that adds meaning to their substance and translates what is fleeting to the level of permanent truth. But that permanent truth must continue to culminate in the present moment; we must be able to test and reanimate it in our own experience. It is not an abstract truth that Thoreau is after, but one that can still be discovered in reality as we know it. Henry Thoreau of Concord seeks God *in* Concord, as Stevens says of Professor Eucalyptus,

> . . . *with an eye that does not look*
>
> *Beyond the object. He sits in his room, beside*
> *The window, close to the ramshackle spout in which*
> *The rain falls with a ramshackle sound. He seeks*
>
> *God in the object itself, without much choice.*
> *It is a choice of the commodious adjective*
> *For what he sees, it comes in the end to that:*
>
> *The description that makes it divinity, still speech*
> *As it touches the point of reverberation—not grim*
> *Reality but reality grimly seen*
>
> *And spoken in paradisal parlance new . . .*[14]

As Stevens says, it does not matter much which object or experience we choose; the present moment is always good enough, and Professor Eucalyptus's evening is an ordinary one in New Haven. What matters is how our spirit greets that occasion with the commodious adjectives, the descriptions that make it divinity (such as Emerson's "refulgent summer" or Thoreau's phrase "sky water" for

Walden Pond). No, reality is not grim, but it must be *seen* "grimly"—
fiercely, severely, honestly—if it is to divide us through the heart and
marrow and leave us with the assurance that we have lived truly and
deliberately. Thoreau's great sentence—"God himself culminates in
the present moment, and will never be more divine in the lapse of all
the ages"—is a kind of "paradisal parlance new" that arises out of the
"now and here" and attempts to redeem and revitalize the world for
those who share its faith. That faith is simply a faith in the world
that adopted Thoreau, as it adopts us all for a time. We have need,
he writes, "not only to be spiritualized, but *naturalized*, on the soil of
earth." For the man who thus places his faith in the creation,
Thoreau continues, "who shall conceive what kind of roof the heav-
ens might extend over him, what seasons minister to him, and what
employment dignify his life!"[15]

Such a man would claim, at the end of his life, that he did not
need to make his peace with God because they had never quarreled.
"God could not be unkind to me if he should try," Emerson reports
Thoreau as saying. Thoreau believed, to appropriate Emerson's
phrase, in the "perfection of this world, in which our senses converse"; and he could therefore insist, "here or nowhere is our heaven."
It is hardly surprising, then, that he never felt obliged to turn his
thoughts to another world. With the return of spring, Thoreau said,
he recovered his innocence and the world re-created itself for him.
In that perpetual morning light, he entered into the joy of his Lord,
and thus was enabled, in Wallace Stevens's words, to find

> *the brilliant mercy of a sure repose,*
> *on this present ground.*[16]

TWELVE

"In Wildness Is the Preservation of the World": The Natural History of Henry David Thoreau

1. THOREAU AS "NATURAL HISTORIAN"

I begin by glossing the second part of my title first: "The Natural History of Henry Thoreau." This phrase implies, as we know, that Thoreau was employed throughout his life in producing writing that can be located in the genre of "natural history"; it also implies that the history of his life was a "natural" one that situated him radically in nature and linked him closely with the environment. He lived, we might say, a more natural life than most of us do because he chose deliberately to study nature. And he did so in the spirit of his mentor, Emerson, when the older man insisted that the ancient injunction, "know thyself," was to be joined to a newer one, "study nature." Thoreau would not only study nature but also study *himself* in nature.[1]

Thus his most famous book, *Walden,* has a double focus: both on the place in Concord, Massachusetts, where he lived in a small cabin next to a pond for two years, two months, and two days, and on the reportorial and reflective "I" through whose keen vision we share the experience. In his hands, "natural history" becomes autobiography as well as scientific-seeming investigation of the environment. The observer is present not simply to record data but to reflect on their possible meaning and value in relation to himself. He will accordingly reserve the right to include poetry, parable, mythology, and moral aphorism along with scientific data in order to round out the account he is producing.

When Thoreau died in 1862, the town clerk listed his occupation as "natural historian"; but Thoreau himself had provided a more comprehensive definition some years before: "The fact is," he said, "I am a mystic—a transcendentalist—& a natural philosopher to boot." Students of Thoreau have often considered these categories to be mutually exclusive, but he thought otherwise. In his first significant publication, "Natural History of Massachusetts," Thoreau insisted that "nature is mythical and mystical always, and works with the license and extravagance of genius." The true man of science, he argues,

> will know nature better by his finer organization; he will smell, taste, see, hear, feel better than other men. His will be a deeper and finer experience. We do not learn by inference and deduction, and the application of mathematics to philosophy, but by direct intercourse and sympathy.[2]

As it happens, the genre of natural history writing into which Thoreau was self-consciously inserting himself at a time when the distinction between "amateur naturalist" and "professional scientist" had not yet firmed up was essentially personal and literary—what E. D. H. Johnson calls "genially informal records of regional flora and fauna." Gilbert White, with whose enormously popular book *The Natural History of Selbourne* Thoreau's work has often been compared, was engaged in what he himself calls *autopsia*—a Greek word which we now exclusively apply to the grim job of examining corpses for forensic purposes but which White uses in the root sense to mean "seeing for one's self." It denotes, as Johnson tells us, "the observer's open-minded reliance on the evidence of his own eyes. Shorn of abstract speculation and hearsay, [such] descriptions have the authenticity of direct experience." Naturalists like White, Johnson continues, were concerned "with animate nature, unlike the closet scientist who anatomizes his specimens in the laboratory. This means that in their writings they were constantly endeavoring to capture and portray the living drama of the natural world in all its vibrant inter-relatedness." This was also Thoreau's goal, which was why he fell on White's book with evident pleasure. Another book, first published, like White's, in 1789, probably elicited a similarly enthusiastic response from Thoreau. Thomas Jefferson's *Notes on the State of Virginia,* though not devoid of "abstract speculation and hearsay," insists nevertheless on precise observation, mensuration, and the weighing of evidence while allowing itself spasms of poetic description and moralizing commentary. Closer to Thoreau's own lifetime was the early work of another gifted amateur, Charles Darwin, whose *Voyage of the Beagle*—a great favorite of Thoreau's—is an amiable mixture of personal observation, raw data, taxonomical catalog, and wide-ranging theory. This kind of natural history writing, in the words of John Hildebidle, "can thus be described as informal, inclusive, intensely local, experiential, eccentric . . . and utilitarian, yet in the end concerned not only with fact but with fundamental spiritual and aesthetic truths." It is "this broad notion of natural history, a paying of attention to the past *and* the present, firmly based in the local and the immediate but not refusing any possible source until it has been assessed and weighed, which can stand as a home, in literary terms, for *Walden* and for much else of Thoreau's work."[3]

One needs to add, however, that this generic "home" and the natural observation it domesticated was put under increasing pressure, even in Thoreau's own lifetime, by the relentless tendency toward professionalization and the consequent denigration of "amateur" work. The tension between the two is nicely exemplified in Clarence King's *Mountaineering in the Sierra Nevada*, which records the youthful experience of a budding geologist, just out of Yale College, in 1863—the year after Thoreau's death. Traveling alone in a stagecoach on his way to Bear Valley, King found himself "preyed upon by self-reproach, and in an aggravated manner," because on his arrival in the Sierras the senior palaeontologist—apparently observing King mooning at an impressive landscape—said "with unwonted severity, 'I believe that fellow had rather sit on a peak all day, and stare at those snow-mountains, than find a fossil in the metamorphic Sierra.'" Stung by the remark, King brooded over the implications of the incident: "Can it be? I asked myself; has a student of geology so far forgotten his devotion to science? Am I really fallen to the level of a mere nature-lover?"[4]

It may be that a similar mood of self-reproach, but in reverse, overtook Thoreau in the spring of 1847, when he was living at Walden Pond, and allowed himself, briefly, as Laura Walls puts it, a "flirtation with institutionalized science." Contacted, apparently, by James Elliot Cabot (later to be Emerson's literary executor and biographer), who was working for Louis Agassiz, Havard's new Professor of Geology and Zoology, Thoreau over a period of some weeks trapped, packed, and sent off to Harvard assorted fish, tortoises, snakes, mice, and even a live fox, asking in return only that Cabot and Agassiz might answer some of his own questions about scientific nomenclature. During this period—from spring 1846 to spring 1847—as Walls tells us, Thoreau seems to have been "taking his first steps toward a methodized approach to nature: measuring the [fish], surveying the ponds and taking their temperature, collecting specimens as part of a scientific network." At the same time, Walls continues, Thoreau "also regarded what he was doing with uncertainty and suspicion, warning himself that method alone was insufficient, that measurements diminished the sublime, that 'fact' and accuracy were gained at the expense of 'genius.'" Perhaps Thoreau was remembering what he had written only a few years earlier in the conclusion to "Natural History of Massachusetts": "It is with science as with ethics,—we cannot know truth by contrivance and method; the Baconian is as false as any other, and with all the helps of machinery and the arts, the most scientific will still be the healthiest and friendliest man, and possess a more perfect Indian wisdom."[5]

Despite his lifelong infatuation with scientific nomenclature, Thoreau's interests did not really coincide with those of a Louis Agassiz, as we might surmise from a strange and wonderful passage in the "Spring" chapter of *Walden* in which Thoreau responds ecstatically to the song of a robin: "O the evening robin, at the end of a New England summer day! If I could ever find the twig he sits upon! I mean *he;* I mean *the twig.* This at least is not the *Turdus migratorius.*" Thoreau is not interested in generic birds. Rather he longs to experience the quiddity of this individual bird in the very place in which he sings. Thoreau means to engage, not in scientific investigation, but in a confrontation. This robin is not the *Turdus migratorius* in two senses: first, in its particularity it is not the abstract bird named in the Latin nomenclature for the genus of thrushes; and second, it equally eludes the category *migratory* thrush because it is a permanent resident of Thoreau's holistic vision of Walden Woods— as firmly fixed in his imagination as Keats's nightingale was in his. The song of the robin calls to Thoreau not from the pages of an ornithological manual but from the depths of wild nature, as does the singing of another member of the *Turdidae* family, the wood thrush (discussed above, in Chapter Nine), whose note, as we have seen, satisfies Thoreau's longing "for wildness—a nature which I cannot put my foot through. woods where the wood-thrush forever sings. . . .

where I might have a fertile unknown for a soil about me. . . . A New Hampshire everlasting & unfallen."[6]

2. "IN WILDNESS IS THE PRESERVATION OF THE WORLD"

Now let me draw our attention back to 1962 when, as I have already observed, the Sierra Club of California published a volume of exquisite nature photographs by Eliot Porter that he executed as an accompaniment to selections from the writings of Henry Thoreau. The title of the book, *In Wildness is the Preservation of the World,* was drawn from Thoreau's lecture "Walking; or, the Wild," first published in 1863, one year after Thoreau's death. The appearance of that Sierra Club volume (along with the publication of Rachel Carson's *Silent Spring* in the same year) proved to be a watershed event—effectively the beginning of the modern ecology movement, with its heightened concern for the protection and preservation of the natural environment. The book enjoyed wide circulation and helped to set the tone for the emerging decade of the 60's—a time, as we know, not just of Green awareness but also of Thoreauvian protest and civil disobedience.

It is important to note that in his famous sentence Thoreau wrote "wildness" and not "wilderness." Although the concept of "wilderness" may exemplify what Thoreau meant by "wildness," they are not the same thing. The best concise gloss on Thoreau's distinction is offered by the late Sherman Paul—a leading Thoreauvian: "Thoreau didn't say wilderness, he said wildness because . . . more than the actual wilderness itself he valued its psychic correlative: wildness, the instinctual; wildness as willed-ness, the expression of will, in the interest of keeping open one's vital, instinctual life."[7]

If that sounds more like William Blake or D. H. Lawrence than Thoreau it is because he was early appropriated by bland nature-lovers who preferred their hermit of Walden Woods purged of his wildness. Thus Waldo Frank, an important American cultural critic of the 1920's and '30's, could write: "When we were boys, we all had tedious uncles who professed to be very fond of Thoreau. They said that Thoreau was a great naturalist; that he wrote delightfully of butterflies and mushrooms. These uncles were typical good citizens of old America: altogether dull—mindless and sober paragons. We decided that their favorite author could be no favorite of ours. We took it for granted that Thoreau also was a stuffy bore."[8]

Though Thoreau may be a bore to some, he is certainly not stuffy. As E. B. White observes, "Thoreau was a master of prose . . . at once strictly disciplined and wildly abandoned." Thoreau's butterflies may be generally delightful, but he is quick to notice that they begin their careers as "voracious caterpillars"; he is the poet not only of immortal robins and sportive loons but also of vultures feeding on carrion and dead horses spicing the air as he strolls near his cabin. He loves nature when it is pretty and charming, but he also needs "the tonic of wildness." He is "earnest to explore and learn all things," and that includes an "infinitely wild" nature that is "mysterious and unexplorable"—"unsurveyed and unfathomed by us because unfathomable." His mushrooms, as we shall see, are less the fairy-tale book toadstools on which are perched enchanted bullfrog princes than they are the dark funguses that embody some of nature's unspeakable secrets.[9]

Thoreau's journal entries on funguses are invariably noteworthy—evidence that they represent and embody for him the rankest and most primitive aspects of that wild nature he claimed to be unable to get enough of. Undoubtedly one of the strangest passages Thoreau ever wrote exemplifies the bizarre attraction he felt toward these earthy artifacts that strained to an extreme degree the tensions he felt as "a mystic—a Transcendentalist—& a natural philosopher to boot." The passage in question (partially reproduced here from Thoreau's manuscript journal) offers us Henry David Thoreau at the limits of his quest for the wild, anticipating, mutatis mutandis, Conrad's Kurtz in *The Heart of Darkness* confronting the "horror" that appears to do him in. This "remarkable fungus"—actually less "rare" than Thoreau thought it was—he learns from Loudon's *Encyclopedia* has the Latin nomenclature *phallus impudicus*, which

Thoreau, as an expert Latinist, understands to mean "immodest" or "unchaste" phallus. In fact, given Thoreau's obsession with etymology, it is worth noting that such English derivatives from the Latin *pudere,* to be ashamed, as *pudency, pudic,* or *pudical* ("pertaining to the parts which modesty requires to be concealed") and *pudicity* ("modesty") were all current terms, as is evidenced by Webster's 1853 edition of *An American Dictionary of the English Language.* Today we have only *pudency, impudent* (which has traveled away from its root meaning), the rare *impudicity,* and the more familiar *pudendum* or *pudenda*— meaning, of course, "external genital organs" (*American Heritage Dictionary*) or "the parts of generation," to use Webster's 1853 definition. This would have been the etymological background— without doubt fully present to Thoreau's consciousness—as he investigated this fungus that he calls "a perfect phallus." The question I see forming in Thoreau's mind is, simply, this: are the organs of generation—the focus of the most powerful natural instincts we possess—truly "shameful," as the Latin derivation of *pudenda* implies? Notice that Thoreau's stinkhorn—to use its common name—is, to him, "in all respects a most disgusting object," yet, nevertheless, "very suggestive."[10]

The copious quasi-scientific details that follow in Thoreau's entry (measurement, minute observation and description) function, I think, as a kind of distancing strategy, allowing Thoreau to employ his status as an objective scientific investigator in order to hold at bay, temporarily, other issues of a more speculative or philosophical kind that are obviously pressing in on him. The fascination of the abomination is clearly driving him—forcing him to take this "offensive" object into the Thoreau house (one wonders what the family's reaction was!) so that he might get to know it as well as he learned to "know beans" in *Walden.* (Let us remember one of the most celebrated moments in the book, when Thoreau tells us of his determination "to drive life into a corner, and reduce it to its lowest terms, and, if it proved to be mean, why then to get the whole and genuine meanness of it and publish its meanness to the world.")[11] Now he

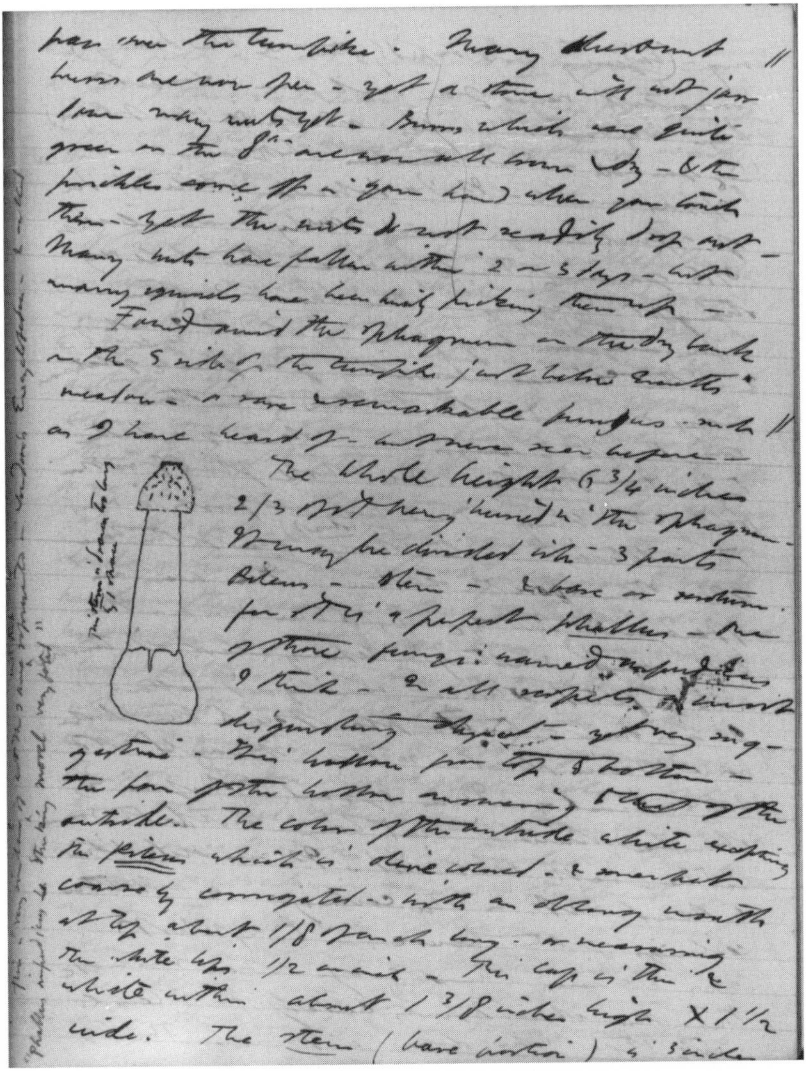

Thoreau's journal page, October 16, 1856.

Photography: Joseph Zehavi.

has cornered the phallus impudicus—he likens it to a "dead rat"—and the question that occurs to him as he faces down this disgusting representative of nature's wild generative energy is undoubtedly among the most interesting he ever asked: "Pray, what was Nature thinking of when she made this? She almost puts herself on a level with those who draw in privies."

Thoreau's question is consciously arch because he knows perfectly well that Nature does not "think" in our sense of the word, or rather "thinks" only through its creations (to cite *Walden* again: "Nature puts no questions and answers none which we mortals ask"). So he will have to do Nature's thinking for her and provide his own answer—and why not? since he describes himself as "leaves and vegetable mold." Nature, it seems, was "thinking" of propagation—at least of propagation of the species *phallus impudicus*. But Thoreau's question presses him and us further into our speculative corner, for Nature was doubtlessly thinking of Thoreau himself and other males, with their organs of generation. Are they "shameful"? Is Nature itself shameful or rather simply shameless—blindly furthering its ends through whatever means it evolves (one thinks inevitably of Molly Bloom's "its only nature")? If Nature, in producing the stinkhorn, "almost puts herself on a level with those who draw in privies," what are we to think of our own provincial Virgil—our guide through the Inferno of Nature's generative underworld who himself, as we can see, draws a picture of the *phallus impudicus* in the privacy of his journal? So, as we are led to conclude, Thoreau too is implicated in Nature's grand design—or in its almost unspeakable "meanness." I say "almost unspeakable" because Thoreau is in fact determined to speak and to represent the truth of the natural world. "I hesitate to say these things," Thoreau tells us in *Walden*, "but it is not because of the subject,—I care not how obscene my *words* are,—but because I cannot speak of them without betraying my impurity.... We are so degraded that we cannot speak simply of the necessary functions of human nature." When we do learn to speak simply of them, Thoreau implies—to use without shame every resource of language and art at our disposal to represent the world and ourselves in it—we shall no longer be fallen creatures, but rather "wild" and "good" at the same time. We shall be at once perfect naturalists and perfect Transcendentalists.[12]

If I seem to place undue emphasis on one strange passage in Thoreau's massive journal I do so because other entries on funguses throughout his journal point to the same nexus of concern. Thus, for example, on a warm and muggy August day in 1853 he comes upon a fungus more than a foot in diameter that has already begun to deliquesce and tells us that the ground around it "is covered with foul spots" where it has dissolved. For most of his walk, he continues, "the air is tainted with a musty, carrion-like odor, in some places very offensive, so that I at first suspected a dead horse or cow. They impress me like humors or pimples on the face of the earth, toddy-blossoms, by which it gets rid of its corrupt blood. A sort of excrement they are." Employing the rhetorical trope of prosopopeia, or personification, Thoreau views this offensive natural object as the face of a corrupt nature disfigured by what he likens to blotches on the face of a drunkard. Nature, through a process which presumably is also natural, is bleeding itself, casting out its filth; and this would appear to be part of its vigor—its ability to change and prosper.[13]

Thoreau's giving a human face to nature in this passage corroborates, I think, what we have already seen—that he is very close to identifying with the process he observes; and, indeed, further confirmation is not far to seek. In another journal entry he observes that "the simplest and most lumpish fungus has a peculiar interest to us, compared with a mere mass of earth, because it is so obviously organic and related to ourselves, however mute. . . . the humblest fungus betrays a life akin to my own. It is a successful poem in its kind." Perhaps Thoreau was thinking of Keats's line—"The poetry of earth is never dead"—but he is certainly ringing changes on it, roughing it up, so to speak. This is a living poetry of earth but it is not pretty or delicate; and it implicates us in the evidence it gives of primitive, seemingly impure, energy. "It is in vain," Thoreau writes in 1856—the year of the *phallus impudicus* entry—"to dream of a wildness distant from ourselves. There is none such. It is the bog in our brains and bowels, the primitive vigor of Nature in us, that inspires that dream. I shall never find in the wilds of Labrador any greater wildness than in some recess in Concord, i.e., than I import into it." The word "bog," I need to point out, has a double meaning, for it refers not only to a swamp or mud-hole but also (in British slang then and now that Thoreau was well aware of) to a privy or toilet.[14]

Thoreau's point is startling and seems to anticipate a notion we might loosely call Freudian: our dream of a sublime and fecundating wildness to be found in the environment is the upward and outward displacement of our natural functions—or as Thoreau puts it in what seems to be a prudish passage in the "Higher Laws" chapter of *Walden:* "the spirit can for the time pervade and control every member and function of the body, and transmute what in form is the grossest sensuality into purity and devotion. The generative energy, which, when we are loose, dissipates and makes us unclean, when we are continent invigorates and inspires us." That may sound like Thoreau's own peculiar Transcendental "Joy of non-Sex" or the colonel in *Dr. Strangelove* worried about preserving his precious bodily fluids, but let us remember Freud's dictum that the repression of sexual energy may issue either in a neurotic symptom or in a work of art.

Thoreau's point is that the so-called "lower" functions and the so-called "higher" ones are not distinct but correlative forms of the same energy. That is why he insists on saying, again in the same chapter of *Walden,* "I found in myself, and still find, an instinct toward a higher, or, as it is named, spiritual life, as do most men, and another toward a primitive rank and savage one, and I reverence them both. I love the wild not less than the good."[15]

It was certainly in the spirit of Thoreau that D. H. Lawrence expressed his desire to "escape . . . into the vital cosmos, to a sun who has a great wild life." For all of us, Lawrence argues, "the vast marvel is to be alive"; for humans "as for flower and beast and bird, the supreme triumph is to be most vividly, most perfectly alive." We "ought to dance with rapture," he continues, "that we should be alive and in the flesh, and part of the living, incarnate cosmos." In similar fashion, Thoreau seems to harken back to William Blake, for whom "every thing that lives is holy" and whose devilish wisdom proclaims that Energy—the Blakean equivalent of Thoreau's Wildness—"is the only life and is from the Body, and Reason is the bound or outward circumference of Energy," which is "Eternal Delight." When imagination reunites with and redeems humanity's fallen sexual energy, as at the end of Blake's prophetic poem *Milton,* the moment of "psychic transformation" (Morton Paley's phrase) is associated by Blake with "the wild thyme, the lark, and the dawn." It is an eminently Thoreavian moment, whereby regeneration is achieved in a natural setting through a new union of body and spirit.[16]

Let us return once more to my title—to Thoreau's famous sentence, "In Wildness is the preservation of the World." Why "preservation"? Why does Wildness *preserve* the world? The simplest answer is one that is frequently given by concerned ecologists— namely, that the zealous guarding of wild land, wild creatures, and wild flora is the only way to protect the earth from despoliation. That is certainly one of the implications of Thoreau's sentence—the reason why he is considered to be the patron saint of the modern Green movement. But, as Captain Ahab would say, there is a "little lower layer"—something further lurking in Thoreau's sentence. Of course we have already noticed that Thoreau loves the instinctual— the generative energy with which we are all endowed, the potential energy lying dormant in seeds, the indefatigable push of the seasons and turning of the world on its axis—because it preserves the world by perpetually offering a fresh start. There is a lovely passage in the "Spring" chapter of Walden that captures Thoreau's excitement at the wild energies that pulse through Walden Woods as the time of renewal gets under way:

In April the pigeons were seen again flying express in small flocks, and in due time I heard the martins twittering over my clearing. . . . In almost all climes the tortoise and the frog are among the precursors and heralds of this season, and birds fly with song and glancing plumage, and plants spring and bloom, and winds blow, to correct this slight oscillation of the poles and preserve the equilibrium of nature.

A curious ending to Thoreau's sentence: he figures the coming of spring as a "slight oscillation of the poles" which is held in check by the wild activity he observes—activity that "preserve[s] the equilibrium of nature." It is as if Thoreau were saying that the world is "preserved" from being overwhelmed by cosmic forces through the seasonal tug-of-war that any of us can take note of locally.[17]

Another hint about how Wildness preserves the world is provided by Sherman Paul, whom I have already cited on the importance of "keeping open one's vital, instinctual life." Paul goes on: "The will to change: In that, paradoxically, is the preservation of the world." Perhaps the paradox is only apparent, since the loss of the impulse to change—to achieve new growth—would lead not only to physical decay but also to spiritual stagnation. This is "preservation" in the dictionary sense of "preparing things for future use" or preventing them from "decaying and spoiling." Thoreau himself provides a gloss—again in the "Spring" chapter—on this all-important function of the will, or instinct, to change:

In a pleasant spring morning all men's sins are forgiven. Such a day is a truce to vice. While such a sun holds out to burn, the vilest sinner may return. Through our own recovered innocence we discern the innocence of our neighbors. You may have known your neighbor yesterday for a thief, a drunkard, or a sensualist, and merely pitied or despised him, and despaired of the world; but the sun shines bright and warm this first spring morning, re-creating the world, and you meet him at some serene work, and see how his exhausted and debauched veins expand with still joy and bless the new day, feel the spring innocence with the innocence of infancy, and all his faults are forgotten. There is not only an atmosphere of good will about him, but even a savor of holiness groping for expression, blindly and ineffectually perhaps, like a new-born instinct, and for a short hour the south hill-side echoes to no vulgar jest. You see some innocent fair shoots preparing to burst from his gnarled rind and try another year's life, tender and fresh as the youngest plant.[18]

Though Thoreau is surely in dead earnest here, he is nevertheless having some fun as he tries to sound like an evangelical preacher (the tip-off is the sentence, "While such a sun holds out to burn, the vilest sinner may return"—Thoreau's rewriting of a line from the popular hymn by Isaac Watts ["And while the lamp holds out to burn, the vilest sinner may return"]; it is tempting to read the part beginning "You may have known your neighbor yesterday for a thief . . ." in the tones, say, of a Billy Graham). Still the point seems to be the one he has already made: the "instinctual" self, even in the most hardened reprobate, should be capable of provoking the will to change—the "good will"—in the season of new growth. That "willed-ness," as Sherman Paul argues, is the psychic correlative of Thoreau's belief in Wildness as the great preserver of worlds. (Sometimes destroyer and preserver together: we think of Shelley's "West Wind.")

There is finally, and I think most importantly, another sense for Thoreau in which "Wildness is the preservation of the World," and it has to do with his work as a writer. As we know, Thoreau believed passionately in the power of writing to change people's lives if it is willing to take the chance of being exaggerated—to be writing that is "without bounds"; that takes off for the wilder margins of expression and puts the reader's mind on the stretch. "It is a ridiculous demand," he says at the end of *Walden*, "which England and America make, that you shall speak so that they can understand you. Neither men nor toadstools grow so." How do they grow? Secretly, mysteriously, incomprehensibly. Thoreau wants his writing to be "*extra- vagant,*" so that it might be released to wander freely and be "adequate to the truth of which [he has] been convinced." Writing that fails to provoke the reader in these ways will not preserve the world—that is, get experience convincingly and vitally down on the page. Wildness is the preservation of the word as well as the world—or, rather, world and word are tightly bound together, since, as Wallace Stevens says, "words of the world are the life of the world."[19]

A peculiar corollary of this theory, for a writer such as Thoreau, is that words of the natural world are the life of the page. He wants and needs to produce a "literature which gives the expression to Nature," as he argues in "Walking; or The Wild":

> He would be a poet who could impress the winds and streams into his service, to speak for him; who nailed words to their primitive senses, as farmers drive down stakes in the spring, which the frost has heaved; who derived his words as often as he used them,—transplanted them to his page with earth adhering to their roots; whose words were so true and fresh and natural that they would appear to expand like the buds at the approach of spring, though they lay half-smothered between two musty leaves in a library,—ay, to bloom and bear fruit there, after their kind, annually, for the faithful reader, in sympathy with surrounding Nature.

Accordingly, words that are true to their natural origins have the power, in Thoreau's view, to keep the world alive even in what appears to be pages that are "musty leaves in a library."[20]

The pun in that last phrase, as natural for Thoreau as it was for Whitman, is amplified by Thoreau in a radiant late essay, "Autumnal Tints":

> I formerly thought that it would be worth the while to get a specimen leaf from each changing tree, shrub, and herbaceous

plant, when it had acquired its brightest characteristic color, in its transition from the green to the brown state, outline it, and copy its color exactly, with paint in a book which should be entitled, "October, or Autumnal Tints";—beginning with the earliest reddening,—Woodbine and the lake of radical leaves, and coming down through the Maples, Hickories, and Sumachs, and many beautifully freckled leaves less generally known, to the latest Oaks and Aspens. What a memento such a book would be! You would need only to turn over its leaves to take a ramble through the autumn woods whenever you pleased. Or if I could preserve the leaves themselves, unfaded, it would be better still.

Not only is Wildness the life of the book Thoreau imagines; it might also become the very book itself—a collection of brilliant autumnal leaves that, though fallen, remain forever "unfaded," preserving for us what Thoreau in another place calls "the actual glory of the universe."[21]

THIRTEEN

WRITING AND READING NEW ENGLANDLY

I n Richard Poirier's *Poetry and Pragmatism* we find him picking up and expanding on issues already broached in *The Renewal of Literature*:[1] the healthy skepticism of Emerson's attitude toward language and the project of writing; the necessity of constant "troping"; the links, in these connections, between Emerson and William James; the baneful influence of Modernism, with its cult of "difficulty," its "boned-up erudition" and "religious and cultural nostalgias." Poirier is concerned in *Poetry and Pragmatism* with identifying a school of American writing committed to no orthodoxies, nervous about the truth-value of literature, willing to believe in little more than the power of writing to create its occasions in an alliance with ordinary language and ordinary work, unashamed of its extravagances and lack of final clarity. At the center of this tradition, for Poirier, lie Emerson and William James, and especially the latter's "pragmatism."

One might describe this book in another way. The key players in Poirier's portrait of "the tribe of Waldo" are almost all New England writers: Emerson himself, Thoreau, Dickinson, Dewey, James, Frost, Stein, and Stevens. If Dewey and Stein seem not entirely to fit that description, one can be more specific. With the exception of Dewey, who graduated from the University of Vermont, Poirier's cast of characters has a rather parochial provenance—and, indeed, centers in two particular academic parishes, Harvard and Amherst. It is probably no accident that these two places are also the ones that nurtured Richard Poirier, himself a New Englander by birth. In pointing to the understated but clearly personal side of Poirier's project, I mean to suggest not only that this is criticism underwritten by a specific human commitment but also that there is an interior coherence to Poirier's interest in these New England places and their writers/critics. The "pragmatist" line that Poirier identifies from Emerson through James and beyond places special weight on temperament and goes in fear of abstractions; it relies on voice, the sound of sense, the dramatic nature of literary encounter; it is tentative, open-ended, experimental. On the pedagogical side, the Amherst school of literary criticism that Reuben Brower brought to Harvard, where it reinforced the Richardsonian "practical criticism" already in place, was committed to "reading in slow motion." It was skeptical about literary absolutes, wary of metalanguages, chary of drawing conclusions. Poirier's own allegiances lie in these directions. He is essentially "writing off the self."

Though Poirier does not do so, we might view the argument of his book in terms of two key Emersonian concepts—"Prudence" and "Heroism" (the titles of two consecutive and dialectically paired essays in the First Series). The former, which Poirier essentially seems to want to associate with pragmatism, is content to work on the surface of things, in line with Wittgenstein's notion that "all the facts that concern us lie open before us." It feeds on common life and clear perceptions—on hands that handle, on eyes that "measure and discriminate." (To be sure, as Poirier observes and Cavell had noted before him, the world for Emerson may turn "unhandsome," lubricious; but that is only a sickness of prudence, not its normal condition.) Emerson's sense of the "American character"—really, the Yankee character—is that it is "marked by a more than average delight in accurate perception," and loves to be able to say "no mistake." On the literary side, Emerson wants poetry and prudence to be "coincident." Literary banknotes may be good, bad, or indifferent, may not really stand for bullion in the vaults, but the shrewd Yankee writer moves them along quickly, knowing that their cash-value is a matter of trade, not of individual accumulation. Literary skating *always* takes place over thin ice and is therefore concerned to keep going: the complacent writer is forever in danger of a good ducking. But the Emersonian pragmatist writer, in Poirier's terms, will resort to "continuous troping, turning, transforming, transfiguring," and be ever ready to "move on to the next transition."[2]

There is, however, another side to Emerson, one that Poirier seems less willing to recognize. Under the rubric of "Heroism" life rises above itself. The hero believes "he is born into the state of war." Committed to the "*strong* life," in William James's phrase, he insists on "the absolute truth of his speech" and his ability to master experience. Bestriding the narrow world like a colossus, convinced of his own superiority, the hero spurns the "common" in favor of "great and transcendent properties" and consorts with "angels and the Supreme Being." Poirier wants his Emersonian pragmatist tradition to be "unique for the privileges it accords to casual, extemporized, ordinary idiom, to uses of language that translate into little more than ordinary idiom," to bring its force to bear against "literature's claims to transcendence or the incorporation of values." But Emerson, in his heroic mood, would seem to spurn such diminished goals, affirming that he is no mere mortal but rather "a native of the deeps of absolute and inextinguishable being." Possessed by "the God, and the sacrifice and the fire he will provide," the Emersonian hero rejects "the laws of arithmetic" because "the soul of a better quality thrusts back the unseasonable economy into the vaults of life." Here, cash-value is of no concern for the poet of "transcendent properties," who will skate to his own stately measure and take his ducking whenever it may be necessary. He is centered in himself, and let the devil take the hindmost.[3]

Poirier, I am arguing, is inferably uncomfortable with the transcendental Emerson who does not fit a purely pragmatist program. Demonstrably distressed by the Arnoldian Great Tradition and its contemporary avatars (William Bennett, Allan Bloom), with their deference to the past and belief in "touchstones" and the "best that has been thought and said," Poirier has felt compelled to shape an Emerson, and an Emersonian "tribe," who are skeptical of "the fraudulent notion that literature is a monument to redemptive [here I read "heroic"] values and that it can help save us from the ravages of history." The irony is that Poirier has enlisted Emerson precisely as the American literary authority who can redeem us, through his own tradition, from the oppressive tradition that relies so smugly on tradition.

But if literary language is so precarious and unstable a medium as Poirier claims, how can Emerson do anything for us that can be described as *cultural* work? Poirier skewers Judge Robert Bork and the party-line writers in *The New Criterion* or *The American Scholar* for "longingly evok[ing] a past that never existed, never can have existed, in large part because language, in which the past comes to us, is too agitated a medium ever to allow any such fixity of meaning or value as they are able . . . to conjure up. Nor does language as found in literary or philosophical or political writings ever sustain the astonishing fantasy that these are the places where redemption is available for the damages and wastes of contemporary history."

Ever? Surely Lincoln's "Gettysburg Address" is a piece of political literature. Is its language so "agitated a medium" that it can *never* underwrite some "fixity of meaning or value" or provide a modicum of redemptive consolation?

Where, in any case, does Emerson stand on these questions? As we might expect, he stands in a variety of places. "Experience" would appear to give us no solid stance, no place to under-stand: "Gladly we would anchor, but the anchorage is quicksand." However, further along in the Second Series, in the important essay "Nominalist and Realist," Emerson seems to give full credence to a different view of the stability of language and its monumental (read *memorial*) function. "We infer the spirit of the nation," he writes, "in great measure from the language, which is a sort of monument, to which each forcible individual in a course of many hundred years has contributed a stone. And, universally, a good example of this social force, is the veracity of language, which cannot be debauched." That, too, is Emerson, and an Emerson who sounds by some definition "conservative." The same Emerson can be heard in other, even if arguably lesser, places, such as "Art and Criticism," where "the art of writing" is said to bring

> man into alliance with what is great and eternal. . . . [T]here is much in literature that draws us with a sublime charm—the superincumbent necessity by which each writer, an infirm, capricious, fragmentary soul, is made to utter his part in the chorus of humanity, is enriched by thoughts which flow from all past minds, shares the hopes of all existing minds; so that, whilst the world is made of youthful, helpless children of a day, literature resounds with the music of united vast ideas of affirmation and of moral truth.[4]

Here "literature" surely is an institution that seems to function apart from the vagaries of "capricious" and "fragmentary" souls, like Emerson, whose faith in the "slender human word" may sometimes appear infirm. As Poirier himself argues, no member of the tribe of Emerson is more capricious in his use of language than Thoreau, whose *Walden* is a perpetual trap for the linguistically unwary. As vagrant a writer as ever set pen to paper in America, with the possible exception of Whitman, Thoreau seems continually to betray and undermine his meanings. Instability is his middle name (indeed, his middle-name was once his first name). But Thoreau, like his mentor, can slip into moods of high-minded essentializing of "literature" that issue in language fit to adorn all the *Criterions* past, present, and to come. Despite his pragmatist work in "The Bean-Field" in search of fresh and extravagant tropes, Thoreau has more conservative turns. Poirier, once again, emphatically denies that Emerson and his followers ever support "the fraudulent notion that literature is a monument to redemptive values and that it can help save us from the ravages of history." Here, however, is Thoreau in the "Reading" chapter of *Walden:*

> Two thousand summers have imparted to the monuments of Grecian literature, as to her marbles, only a maturer golden and autumnal tint, for they have carried their own serene and celestial atmosphere into all lands to protect them against the corrosion of time.[5]

I do not intend, by any means, to align Thoreau or Emerson securely with Matthew Arnold, or Justice Bork, or the tribe of Bennetts and Blooms who have been trying to beat a presumably wayward academy into submission to traditional literary "values." That project is thoroughly repugnant to me, since I fervently believe in the healthfully subversive nature of good writing in general and that of Emerson and Thoreau in particular. But neither am I content simply to enlist Emerson and his followers on the side of the current angels (or salutary devil's children) as I see them. Emerson, Thoreau, and the rest of the "tribe" remain for me neither pragmatists nor rationalists, neither liberals nor conservatives. They are ineluctably themselves—complex, self-contradictory, endlessly fascinating and fecundating—and not ourselves. I do not want an Emerson who is deconstructive *avant la lettre,* for then he is no longer Emerson but rather largely a figure in the current polemical imagination.

That, to my mind, is what Poirier has done—fashioned an Emerson who stands mainly for "a form of linguistic skepticism," an anxiety about "the actual *inadequacy* of language to the task of representing reality," which Poirier identifies with "poststructuralism," itself defined as "some late conversions to a kind of linguistic skepticism, allied to pronounced theological and cultural skepticisms, already familiar to a number of readers and critics in England and the United States." Such a framing of "Emersonian pragmatism" comes perilously close to aligning Emerson with the uncompromising linguistic and cultural skepticism of a Paul de Man. Arguing, in "The Return to Philology," against Walter Jackson Bate's defensive call for a return to humanistic literary study, de Man (as Poirier notes) invokes Reuben Brower's Humanities 6 at Harvard, which he twice describes as "pragmatic" (not noted by Poirier). Though de Man claims that Brower's brand of pragmatic reading derived from I. A. Richards's "practical criticism," he implies—contra Bate—that it really descends from the still active linguistic skepticism of Hume. This perennial philological skepticism, in de Man's view, is also the source of "a principle of disbelief" in "standards of cultural excellence that, in the last analysis, are always based on some form of religious faith."[6]

It becomes fairly clear that Poirier's linking of poststructuralist "linguistic skepticism" with "pronounced theological and cultural skepticisms" is very close to de Man's own position—especially since *Poetry and Pragmatism* concludes with a chapter on Brower and Hum 6 ("Reading Pragmatically") that makes a point of mentioning de Man's presence in the course. Indeed, Poirier explicitly claims that Hum 6 was "a more subtle and ideologically neutral version of New Criticism" because the latter remained "subservient to quite specific social and even religious forms of authority." As a result he faults de Man for associating deconstructive practice with New Criticism, as if de Man had thereby compromised or blurred the very position that made Hum 6 formative for both of them in the first place.[7] For Poirier, as I have already observed, literature rightly read can never serve as "a monument to redemptive values." Its function is essentially and necessarily an autotelic one, busy as it must be with questioning its own linguistic structures, building its rhetoric, and doing its tropic dances. This is the "skeptical" pragmatic program that Emerson and William James are made to underwrite in Poirier's book.

I must confess that I do not see where Poirier finds the real, textual basis for claiming that Emerson and William James are serious linguistic skeptics and, further, that Jamesian pragmatism is to be identified with such a position. Poirier himself admits that "only a very few calculated discussions about language [are] to be found in their works." It is true that James, in *Pragmatism,* does inveigh against the mystification, in metaphysics, of such terms as "God," "Matter," "Reason," "the Absolute," "Energy" because he regards them as so many fake "solving names" or petrified sphinxes that serve to block the healthfully instrumental nature of language. He says, famously, that "you must bring out of each word its practical cash-value, set it at work within the stream of your experience." But that, I take it, represents a proto-Wittgensteinian call for an investigation of our language use, not a program for thoroughgoing linguistic skepticism. In fact my copy of *Pragmatism* (first edition, second printing, 1907) has no entries in its index for either "language" or "skepticism." Of course James insists that any concept of "*The* Truth" is an empty one—and we all hear Stevens's "Man on the Dump" waiting in the wings ("Where was it one first heard of the truth? The the"). But this sort of critique calls for a freshening of language, not for a theoretical rejection of it.[8]

Poirier invokes Santayana's phrase about "the kindly infidelities of language" to underwrite his belief that Emersonian pragmatists are worried about "the actual *inadequacy* of language to the task of representing reality." Well, it was in fact Santayana who, a long time ago, linked Emerson with pragmatism and argued that the "economical faith" that enables "one to dissolve the hard materialistic world into a work of mind, which mind might outflank, was traditional in the radical Emersonian circles in which pragmatism sprang up." Mind, of course, in Emerson's idealistic scheme, "outflanks" the world by turning it into a discourse—a linguistic opportunity. Far from being inadequate to represent its world, language for Emerson is an instrument of power—a sign of our command over nature and fate. "Good writing and brilliant discourse are perpetual allegories," he says, because they blend "experience with the present action of the mind." Our writing and discourse allegorize reality, coaxing it into conformity with the stories we tell about it.[9]

Thus Santayana, writing about James, insists that "experience, as memory and literature rehearse it," will always be nearer to us than the hypostatizing discourses of science, because "it is something dreamful, passionate, dramatic, and significative." And it was this "personal human experience, expressible in literature and in talk, and no cosmic system however profound," Santayana argues, that "James knew best and trusted most." For the

> pragmatic nature of truth . . . would never suggest itself in the presence of pure data; but a romantic mind soaked in agnosticism, conscious of its own habits and assuming an environment the exact structure of which can never be observed, may well convince itself that, for experience, truth is nothing but a happy use of signs—which is indeed the truth of literature.[10]

Santayana's crucial phrase here—"a happy use of signs"—should be underlined, for it is a fundamental faith in discourse, and its potential truth-value, not linguistic skepticism, that conjoins Emerson and James. Words, Santayana was to write, "should . . . not be blamed for being only words, symbolic and wholly unlike their objects. Rather they should be used freely, with sympathy towards the genius of words; so that through the plastic network of their sound and syntax something of the structure of things may be revealed." Can there be any doubt that this faith in the "genius of words," shared by Emerson, James, Santayana, and Stevens, prompted Stevens to express his profoundest homage to his teachers by finally insisting that amidst the irremediable poverty of experience, "the gaiety of language is our seigneur"? The "realist" of Stevens's poem is clearly a Jamesian pragmatist whose passion for saying "yes" can never be broken. As Stevens says elsewhere, the future world depends on that yes—the consent which is the essence of our speech, "a speech / Of the self that must sustain itself on speech."[11]

Poirier's concern for what he conceives to be Emerson's linguistic skepticism could have been clarified, I think, if he had entered into a more thorough engagement with the contemporary philosopher most identified with these problems, namely Stanley Cavell. There are some references to Cavell's writings in *Poetry and Pragmatism*, but they are not adequate to the case. In his *In Quest of the Ordinary* Cavell does appear to ratify Poirier's claims about Emerson's linguistic skepticism when he acknowledges that, for Emerson, "our relation to our language—to the fact that we are subject to expression and comprehension, victims of meaning—is . . . a key to our sense of our distance from our lives, of our sense of the alien, of ourselves as alien to ourselves, thus alienated." But, Cavell goes on to argue, Emerson's reaction to the "irresistible dictation" of fate issues in writing that is "a struggle against itself, hence of language with itself, for its freedom." This also seems to accord with Poirier's sense that "the invention of language . . . measures both the restraint upon and the expression of human freedom."[12]

But there is another essay by Cavell, not cited in Poirier's book, that takes the argument a good deal further.[13] In "The Politics of Interpretation," engaging de Man directly, Cavell argues that "skepticism would not be possible unless ordinary language is such that it can, sometimes must, repudiate itself, put its own naturalness into question." Emerson certainly engages in this process. However, Cavell goes on to say (echoing *The Claim of Reason*) that "it is skepticism that produces as a reaction to itself the idea of language as essentially conventional. But skepticism, as I have conceived it, is a repudiation of the naturalness of language (by means of the power of this naturalness itself), not a theoretical observation about it." This means, I take it, that skepticism (Emerson's, let us say) is not a "theoretical observation" about language itself but only a repudiation of its naturalness as we use it by the very force of our use. We have the power to call our own faith in language into question, thus to correct and redirect the way we employ that faith. It is not *language* that is inadequate but rather our ability, at times, fruitfully to reposition ourselves in respect to it. Skepticism, then, is not doubt or despair about language itself but rather about our sense of the possibility, through it, of uniting world and word. That possibility must exist as much for living as for literature. As Cavell goes on to say, wonderfully, in response to de Man's doubts about referentiality,

> the access of skepticism and poetry to one another means to me that a theory of referentiality or textuality designed to explain, say, our relation to Wallace Stevens's jar in Tennessee or to Heidegger's jug in the Black Forest is of no use to me if it fails to explain my relation to the chipped mug from which I drank my coffee this morning, I mean to explain its vulnerability to doubt, or say to imagination. It does not help to picture language as being turned from the world (say troped) unless you know how to picture it as owed to the world and given to it. I do not expect de Man disagrees with this.

Unfortunately, de Man did, most emphatically, disagree.[14] I hope Poirier does not. It must be clear, in any case, that Emerson is on Cavell's side and Cavell on Emerson's. If this is linguistic skepticism it does not seem very different from something like belief in language. Let Emerson have a potent final word from the opening paragraph of "Worship":

> I have no fears of being forced in my own despite to play, as we say, the devil's attorney. I have no infirmity of faith; no belief that it is of much importance what I or any man may say: I am sure that a certain truth will be said through me, though I should be dumb, or though I should try to say the reverse. Nor do I fear skepticism for any good soul. A just thinker will allow full swing to his skepticism. I dip my pen in the blackest ink, because I am not afraid of falling into my inkpot. . . . We are of different opinions at different hours, but we always may be said to be at heart on the side of truth.[15]

ABBREVIATIONS

CC Henry D. Thoreau. *Cape Cod.* Ed. Joseph J. Moldenhauer. Princeton: Princeton University Press, 1988.

CS *Complete Sermons of Ralph Waldo Emerson.* Ed. Albert J. von Frank, et al. 4 vols. Columbia: University of Missouri Press, 1989–92.

CW *The Collected Works of Ralph Waldo Emerson.* Ed. Alfred R. Ferguson, et al. 5 vols to date. Cambridge: Harvard University Press, 1971–.

EEL *Emerson: Essays and Lectures.* Ed. Joel Porte. New York: Library of America, 1983.

EEM   Henry D. Thoreau. *Early Essays and Miscellanies*. Ed.
Joseph J. Moldenhauer and Edwin Moser, with
Alexander Kern. Princeton: Princeton University Press,
1975.

EJ   *Emerson in His Journals*. Ed. Joel Porte. Cambridge:
Harvard University Press, 1982.

EL   *The Early Lectures of Ralph Waldo Emerson*. Ed. Stephen
E. Whicher et al. 3 vols. Cambridge: Harvard
University Press, 1959–72.

EPP   *Emerson's Prose and Poetry: A Norton Critical Edition*.
Ed. Joel Porte and Saundra Morris. New York: W. W.
Norton & Co., 2001.

EXCURSIONS   Henry D. Thoreau. *Excursions*. Boston: Ticknor and
Fields, 1863.

J   *The Journals of Henry David Thoreau*. Ed. Bradford
Torrey and Francis H. Allen. 14 vols. Boston:
Houghton Mifflin, 1906.

JMN   *The Journals and Miscellaneous Notebooks of Ralph Waldo
Emerson*. Ed. William H. Gilman et al. 16 vols.
Harvard University Press, 1960–82.

LETTERS   *The Letters of Ralph Waldo Emerson*. Ed. Ralph L. Rusk
and Eleanor Tilton. 10 vols. New York: Columbia
University Press, 1939–95.

MW   Henry D. Thoreau. *The Maine Woods*. Ed. Joseph J.
Moldenhauer. Princeton: Princeton University
Press, 1974.

PJ   Henry D. Thoreau. *Journal*. Ed. John C. Broderick
et al. 7 vols. to date. Princeton: Princeton University
Press, 1981–.

RP   Henry D. Thoreau. *Reform Papers*. Wendell Glick.
Princeton: Princeton University Press, 1973.

WALDEN   Henry D. Thoreau. *Walden*. Ed. J. Lyndon Shanley.
Princeton: Princeton University Press, 1971.

WEEK   Henry D. Thoreau. *A Week on the Concord and Merrimack Rivers.* Ed. Carl F. Hovde, William L. Howarth, and Elizabeth Hall Witherell. Princeton: Princeton University Press, 1980.

NOTES

PREFACE

1. Perry Miller, *Consciousness in Concord* (Boston: Houghton Mifflin, 1958), 33–35.

2. PJ 5, 469; WALDEN, 3; EPP, 174.

3. EPP, 102; *Works of William Ellery Channing, D.D.* (Boston: American Unitarian Association, 1841), 354–55, 363–64; WALDEN, 49.

4. EJ, 264, 269.

5. See Ralph L. Rusk, *The Life of Ralph Waldo Emerson* (New York: Columbia University Press, 1957), 360–87; *Later Lectures of Ralph Waldo Emerson* (Athens: University of Georgia Press, 2001), 343; EPP, 672.

6. See Susan J. Turner, *A History of the Freeman* (New York: Columbia University Press, 1963). Emilie McMillan is mentioned on page 29.

ONE EMERSON, THOREAU, AND THE DOUBLE CONSCIOUSNESS

1. *The Dial* 2 (July 1841): 41; CW 4, 157.

2. Everett cited in Frederick B. Wahr, *Emerson and Goethe* (Ann Arbor: G. Wahr, 1915), 41; Emerson, "The Man of Letters," in *Lectures and Biographical Sketches* (Boston: Houghton, Mifflin, 1890), 234; "Do you understand German? Do you know 'Faust'?" said Olive. "'*Entsagen sollst du, sollst entsagen!*'" (Henry James, *The Bostonians,* vol. 1 [London: Macmillan & Co., 1921], 102); Emerson cited in *Emerson and Goethe,* 117.

3. EPP, 415, 417.

4. Ibid., 416; Emerson's remark to Norton and Lewes cited in *Emerson and Goethe,* 117; *Faust,* trans. Bayard Taylor, rev. and ed. Stuart Atkins (New York: Collier Books, 1963), 108–9.

5. EPP, 102.

6. Cf. Perry Miller, *Consciousness in Concord* (Boston: Houghton Mifflin, 1958), 34; EPP, 28, 97, 209 (Edward Waldo Emerson glosses "the discovery" here as meaning "the discovery of our lower self, warping the divine universal self"); EPP, 44.

7. *The Christian Examiner* 16 (July 1834): 365, in *The Transcendentalists,* ed. Perry Miller (Cambridge: Harvard University Press, 1950), 78.

8. CW 4, 166; *Faust,* 114–15; *Pierre,* ed. Henry A. Murray (New York: Hendricks House, 1949), 321.

9. Sherman Paul, *The Shores of America* (Urbana: University of Illinois Press,1958), 53.

10. WEEK, 184.

11. WALDEN, 131, 134.

12. Ibid., 135.

13. Ibid., 138.

14. The Therien episode is at WALDEN, 144–50. Thoreau's changing attitudes toward Therien throughout his life are conveniently summarized by Robert W. Bradford in "Thoreau and Therien," *American Literature* 34 (Jan. 1963): 499–506. Although Bradford fails to explore Therien's significance in the structure of *Walden,* he does suggest that the problem of attaining a "'degree of consciousness' while not ceasing to be 'simple and natural' seems to underlie the whole portrait of Therien" and that Thoreau created an image "not of Therien, but of the conundrum of his poised faith."

15. Cf. Emerson in his "The Character of Socrates" (*Two Unpublished Essays,* ed. Edward Everett Hale [Boston: Lamson, Wolffe & Co., 1896], 25):

"[Socrates] directs his disciples . . . to shun vice,—τό θηρίον,—the dreadful monster which was roaring through earth for his prey."

16. WALDEN, 96. At points of intense personal reference in *Walden,* Thoreau tends to rely on parables or anecdotes apparently tailor-made by himself to suit the occasion, such as the anecdote of the Indian basket weaver in "Economy" and the parables of the king's son and the artist of Kouroo in "Where I Lived" and "Conclusion." For illuminating comment on Thoreau's method of constructing the artist of Kouroo parable see *The Shores of America,* 353.

17. Regarding the parable of the king's son, a comparison of the first version of *Walden* with the final version is instructive. The parable is not to be found in the original version except by implication in a passage just following the Therien episode, where Thoreau discusses other visitors, all "natural men": "One is a pacha or Sultan—Selim—or Mustapha or Mahmoud in disguise." Nor does Thoreau, in the first version, include the sentence about Therien's being a "prince in disguise." It seems clear that the development and placement of the parable, as well as the suggestive linking of Therien with it, were all worked out together, when the parabolic potential of the Therien episode became clear to Thoreau (his remark that Therien had so "suitable and poetic a name" is also missing from the first version). See J. Lyndon Shanley, *The Making of Walden* (Chicago: University of Chicago Press, 1957), 173–74.

18. WALDEN, 210–22.

19. Ibid., 97.

20. EPP, 527. Emerson continues: "Yet it gave him every advantage in conversation: For who that found him always skilled in facts, real experience in objects which made their objects & experiences appear artificial[,] could tax him with transcendentalism or over-refining." This passage would suggest that Emerson was irked at coming out second-best in conversation or comparison with Thoreau; but Emerson's conclusion handsomely acknowledges Thoreau's paradoxical ability to unite the low and the infinite: "and yet his position was in Nature, & so commanded all its miracles & infinitudes."

TWO   TRANSCENDENTAL ANTICS

1. EEM, 235; Bacon, *Essays,* XXXII, "Of Discourse"; Joyce, *Finnegans Wake* (New York: Viking Press, 1947), 197.

2. "Thoreau," in *The Shock of Recognition,* ed. Edmund Wilson (New York: Modern Library, 1955), 229–30.

3. See "Man the Reformer," EEL, 146.

4. *The Life of the Mind in America: From the Revolution to the Civil War* (New York: Harcourt, Brace and World, 1965), 7; *Religion and the American Mind: From the Great Awakening to the Revolution* (Cambridge: Harvard University Press, 1966), 544.

5. *American Humor* (Garden City: Doubleday Anchor, 1953), 111–12.

6. See EPP, 93, 97, 101.

7. *The Dial* 1 (July 1840): 1–4.

8. *American Humor*, 112–13.

9. *The Dial* 4 (Oct. 1843): 250.

10. See "Spiritual Laws," in EPP, 151.

11. "Chardon Street and Bible Conventions," in *The Dial* 3 (July 1842): 101.

12. From "New England Reformers," in EPP, 221–33.

13. WALDEN, 98.

14. *Pierre: Or, the Ambiguities*, ed. Henry A. Murray (New York: Hendricks House, 1949), 314.

15. See *Hawthorne: Tales and Sketches*, ed. Roy Harvey Pearce (New York: Library of America, 1982), 1146, 1141.

16. See *Nature*, in EPP, 27–55.

17. Ibid., 436–37.

18. *The Shock of Recognition*, 238.

19. WEEK, 100–101.

20. See EPP, 625.

THREE   THE PROBLEM OF EMERSON

1. Stephen E. Whicher, "Emerson's Tragic Sense," in *Emerson: A Collection of Critical Essays*, ed. Milton Konvitz and Stephen Whicher (Englewood Cliffs: Prentice-Hall, 1962), 39.

2. All quotations from Henry James may be found in EPP, 615–28; Santayana's remarks are taken from "Emerson," in EPP, 633–39.

3. George Edward Woodberry, *Ralph Waldo Emerson* (reprinted, New York: Haskell House, 1968), 1. In his *American Prose Masters* (1909; reprinted, Cambridge: Harvard University Press, 1963), 94, W. C. Brownell said that Emerson's presence was "suggestive of some new kind of saint—perhaps Unitarian." Twelve years earlier John Jay Chapman commented on the irony that this radical, who believed that "piety is a crime," should have been "calmly canonized and embalmed in amber by the very forces he braved. He is become a tradition and a sacred relic. You must speak of him under your breath, and you

may not laugh near his shrine." See *The Shock of Recognition*, ed. Edmund Wilson (New York: Modern Library, 1955), 645. Mary Moody Emerson's remark is cited in Perry Miller, *The Transcendentalists: An Anthology* (Cambridge: Harvard University Press, 1950), 11; Emerson's quip is in CW 4, 16.

4. For a detailed history of this debate, see Richard Ruland, *The Rediscovery of American Literature* (Cambridge: Harvard University Press, 1967). Also useful in this connection is René Wellek's "Irving Babbitt, Paul More, and Transcendentalism," in *Transcendentalism and Its Legacy*, ed. Myron Simon and Thornton H. Parsons (Ann Arbor: University of Michigan Press, 1966), 185–203.

5. Eliot's remark is cited by F. O. Matthiessen in *The Achievement of T. S. Eliot* (New York: Oxford University Press, 1959), 24; Eliot, *Complete Poems and Plays, 1909–1950* (New York: Harcourt, Brace, 1952), 18.

6. Malcolm Cowley, *Exile's Return* (New York: Viking Press, 1956), 227; *A Dial Miscellany*, ed. William Wasserstrom (Syracuse: Syracuse University Press, 1963), 151.

7. Harold Bloom, "Emerson: The Glory and the Sorrows of American Romanticism," *Virginia Quarterly Review* 47 (1971): 550.

8. Jonathan Bishop, *Emerson on the Soul* (Cambridge: Harvard University Press, 1964), 6.

9. *Emerson on the Soul*, 130, 15, 106, 184, 131, 151; Matthew Arnold, *Discourses in America* (London, 1889), 179.

10. William James, "Address at the Emerson Centenary in Concord," is reprinted in EPP, 639–43. W. C. Brownell manages to echo both James's at once. Though "no writer ever possessed a more distinguished verbal instinct, or indulged it with more delight" than Emerson, his style is that "of a writer who is artistic, but not an artist." Emerson had "no sense of composition; his compositions are not composed. They do not constitute objective creations. They have no construction, no organic quality—no evolution . . . art in the constructive sense found no echo in Emerson's nature." See *American Prose Masters*, 125–27.

11. Charles Feidelson, Jr., *Symbolism and American Literature* (Chicago: University of Chicago Press, 1953), 150. An example of how much Emerson needed protection from his "friendly" critics is afforded by this quotation from Norman Foerster's "Emerson on the Organic Principle in Art": "To Emerson . . . it was a fundamental conception capable of answering all our questions about the nature and practice of art. It is true that in his own writing, his own practice of art, Emerson was notoriously deficient in the organic law in its formal aspect; his

essays and poems are badly organized, the parts having no definite relation to each other and the wholes wanting that unity which we find in the organisms of nature. Rarely does he give us even a beginning, middle, and end, which is the very least that we expect of an organism, which, indeed, we expect of a mechanism. Yet if he could not observe the law of organic form, he could interpret it; in this matter his practice and theory are not equivalent—happily, he could see more than he could do" (*Emerson: A Collection of Critical Essays,* 109–10). The Emerson who was too impotent artistically to produce even a respectable machine was thus "praised" for envisioning what a truly living art might be! Though one might be tempted to say something harsh about such jejune remarks as these, Foerster's blandly thoughtless "happily" simply baffles judgment.

12. There are some valuable observations on "Emerson as literature" in James M. Cox, "Emerson and Hawthorne: Truth and Doubt," *Virginia Quarterly Review* 45 (1969): 88–107. Professor Cox writes of "metaphor as action" in Emerson's work.

13. *English Traits,* ed. Howard Mumford Jones (Cambridge: Harvard University Press, 1966), xv. Though Philip Nicoloff, in his exhaustive study of *English Traits,* also sees little justification for the opening and concluding chapters (indeed, he claims that the whole book is "not so shapely a production as has often been suggested, either in its entirety or in its parts"), he does find an intellectual pattern in *English Traits* based on Emerson's belief in the necessity of racial and historical evolution—growth and decline. Emerson's theories thus led him to see England as an exhausted species passing on its genetic heritage to the country of the future, i.e., America. My argument here is that the metaphoric structure of *English Traits* precisely reinforces this doctrine. See Philip Nicoloff, *Emerson on Race and History* (New York: Columbia University Press, 1961). Cf. also Ralph Rusk, *The Life of Ralph Waldo Emerson* (New York: Columbia University Press, 1957), 393 ff.

14. Still, the impulse to comment on this strange paragraph is hard to resist, though it may threaten to carry one far afield. Emerson's desire to express what he seems to feel is the primitive source of America's natural power leads him into a quasi-Frazerian fantasy in which he creates a myth-figure, "the great mother," who has the sort of terrifying appeal of that Yeatsian "rough beast" which "slouches toward Bethlehem to be born." Emerson's rank goddess seems to live in a solitude which is at once sad from the human point of view *(tristesse)* and yet necessary, for what man—even a mammoth American hero—could marry such a creature, a thing of night and water which "sleeps and murmurs and hides" like some holy out-

cast? The operative word here is *sloven*, not simply because it contrasts America's sprawling disorder with England's enclosed neatness, but more crucially because it suggests a kind of fecund dirtiness and lewdness ("lewd" is in fact an old meaning of the word) which constitutes the secret force of the American earth. Thus, Emerson seems to see the two countries in sexual terms, England being an "aged" and "exhausted" woman worn out "with the infirmities of a thousand years," whereas the American mother maintains a frightening but fertile attractiveness. With her will mate Emerson's superhuman national Poet, whose thought, "ejaculated as Logos, or Word," arises like the mother's body from the dark and dank substratum of human life ("Doubt not, O poet, but persist. Say 'It is in me, and shall out.' Stand there, baulked and dumb, stuttering and stammering, hissed and hooted, stand and strive, until, at last, rage draw out of thee that *dream*-power which every night shows thee is thine own; a power transcending all limit and privacy, and by virtue of which a man is the conductor of the whole river of electricity" [EPP, 197]). One moves directly from all of this to section 21 of "Song of Myself":

> *I am he that walks with the tender and growing night;*
> *I call to the earth and sea half-held by the night.*
> *Press close barebosomed night!*
> *Press close magnetic nourishing night . . .*
> *Smile O voluptuous coolbreathed earth!*
> *Earth of the slumbering and liquid trees! . . .*
> *Smile, for your lover comes!*

I am also reminded of another American genius who combined spiritual fastidiousness with a taste for the "arrant stinks" of the new world. Wallace Stevens' aesthetician of *mal*, like the Emerson of the paragraph we have been examining,

> *sought the most grossly maternal, the creature*
> *Who most fecundly assuaged him, the softest*
> *Woman with a vague moustache and not the mauve*
> *Maman. His anima liked its animal*
> *And liked it unsubjugated, so that home*
> *Was a return to birth, a being born*
> *Again in the savagest severity . . .*

[*The Collected Poems of Wallace Stevens* (New York: Knopf, 1957), 321.]

15. Sherman Paul, *Emerson's Angle of Vision* (Cambridge: Harvard University Press, 1952), 72–73; Vivian C. Hopkins, *Spires of Form: A Study of Emerson's Aesthetic Theory* (Cambridge: Harvard University Press, 1951), 3; Stephen Whicher, "Emerson's Tragic Sense," in *Emerson: A Collection of Critical Essays*, 42.

16. Some treatments of vision in *Nature* are: Kenneth Burke, "I, Eye, Ay— Emerson's Early Essay 'Nature': Thoughts on the Machinery of Transcendence," in *Transcendentalism and Its Legacy*, 3–24; Tony Tanner, *The Reign of Wonder* (New York: Harper and Row, 1967), ch. 2, "Emerson: The Unconquered Eye and the Enchanted Circle"; Richard Poirier, *A World Elsewhere* (New York: Oxford University Press, 1966), ch. 2, "Is There an I for an Eye?: The Visionary Possession of America." See also Warner Berthoff, *Fictions and Events* (New York: Dutton, 1971), "'Building Discourse': The Genesis of Emerson's *Nature*," esp. 209–13.

17. See EPP, 189–91.

18. Emerson uses the same sentence from Luke in "Experience." Cf. M. H. Abrams, *Natural Supernaturalism: Tradition and Revolution in Romantic Literature* (New York: Norton, 1971), 47; see also 411 ff. For an understanding of the Romantic context of *Nature*, one could hardly do better than to study Professor Abrams's brilliant exposition of the central Romantic motifs (the transvaluation of religious "vision"; the reinterpretation of the fall of man; the significance of the Romantic spiral). Professor Abrams's key text, by the way— Wordsworth's "Prospectus" to *The Recluse*—might have served Emerson as doctrine for *Nature*.

19. EPP, 266, 267, 271. For Bishop's remark see *Emerson on the Soul*, 210.

20. See EEL, 271, 300–302, 311, 334, 345, 350, 353, 389, 404, 405, 451, 463, 458, 460, 463.

21. EPP, 200, 198, 207; *The Collected Poems of Wallace Stevens*, 62; cf. "The Man Whose Pharynx Was Bad," 96; Yeats's line is from "The Circus Animals' Desertion."

22. Newton Arvin, "The House of Pain," in *Emerson: A Collection of Critical Essays*, 59; Jean-Paul Sartre, *Nausea*, trans. Lloyd Alexander (New York: New Directions, 1964), 177.

23. EJ, 184. A useful treatment of the evolution of Emerson's notion of the preacher-poet, especially in relation to the Unitarian background, is Lawrence I. Buell, "Unitarian Aesthetics and Emerson's Poet-Priest," *American Quarterly* 20 (1968): 3–20. See also Frederick May Eliot, "Emerson and the Preacher," *Journal of Liberal Religion* 1 (1939): 5–18.

24. For the text of the "Address" See EPP, 69–81.

25. Ibid., 76. The hapless preacher referred to here was actually Barzillai Frost, and Emerson's experience is recorded in JMN 5, 463. Conrad Wright's "Emerson, Barzillai Frost, and the Divinity School Address," *Harvard Theological Review* 49 (1956): 19–43, contains an absorbing discussion of the event. Noticing that Frost was only one year younger than Emerson, Professor Wright conjectures that Emerson viewed Frost as the lifeless preacher he himself might have become had he not left the Unitarian ministry in 1832. The vehemence of Emerson's reaction to Frost in his journal certainly does suggest a complex personal dimension to what, in the address, is presented simply as a generic problem in contemporary preaching.

26. Compare Robert Spiller's introduction to the address in CW I, 71.

27. It is worth noting that the journal passage that Emerson worked up here for the address, though it parallels the finished paragraph rather closely, does not mention "the beautiful meteor of the snow." That represents the touch of the poet, shaping remarks into literature. By a stroke of metaphysical wit, Emerson suggests that Frost's "cold preaching" (as it was sometimes called in the period) makes the snow seem positively hot. O. W. Firkins, in his *Ralph Waldo Emerson* (Boston: Houghton, Mifflin, 1915), 163, mordantly observes: "Emerson's discourse drew its matter and coloring largely from private experience, and the bitter hours which he had passed under the ministrations of Mr. Frost of Concord—a preacher who seems to have justified his name in the congealing effect he produced upon the most distinguished of auditors—and other clergymen of the glacial type spoke out in these biting and restive paragraphs."

28. EPP, 69; *Freedom and Fate: An Inner Life of Ralph Waldo Emerson* (Philadelphia: University of Pennsylvania Press, 1953), 74 [in "The Rhetoric of Apostasy," *Texas Studies in Literature and Language* 8 (1967): 547–60, Mary Worden Edrich argues persuasively that Emerson's language throughout the address was carefully calculated to shock]; *Emerson on the Soul*, 88. It is instructive to survey definitions of *luxury* in American dictionaries which Emerson might have consulted. Webster's first edition (1806) gives simply "excess in eating, dress, or pleasure." By 1830 this entry had been expanded, and the first meaning is "a free or extravagant indulgence in the pleasures of the table; voluptuousness in the gratification of appetite; the free indulgence in costly dress and equipage." The Latin sense of *luxuria*, "lust; lewd desire," is offered as definition number 4 and marked obsolete. However, the 1832 American edition of Johnson's dictionary gives as its first meaning "voluptuousness; addictedness

to pleasure," and cites Milton ("lust; lewdness"). As late as 1846 Worcester's dictionary gives "voluptuousness" as the first meaning. Emerson's own use of the word in the 1820s and 1830s tends to lean, not surprisingly, in Milton's direction. Thus, in 1821–22, "wealth induces luxury, and luxury disease" (JMN 1, 300); in 1831, "I am extremely scrupulous as to indulging my appetite. No <splendour> luxury, no company, no solicitation can tempt me to <luxury> excess . . . because . . . I count my body a temple of God, & will not displease him by gratifying my carnal lust" (JMN 3, 225). In a letter to Carlyle in 1834 Emerson says, "to write luxuriously is not the same thing as to live so, but a new & worse offence. It implies an intellectual defect also, the not perceiving that the present corrupt condition of human nature (which condition this harlot muse helps to perpetuate) is a temporary or superficial state. The good word lasts forever: the impure word can only buoy itself in the gross gas that now envelopes us, & will sink altogether to the ground as that works itself clear in the everlasting effort of God." See *The Correspondence of Emerson and Carlyle,* ed. Joseph Slater (New York: Columbia University Press, 1964), 108.

29. See, for example, Jonathan Edwards's *Images or Shadows of Divine Things,* ed. Perry Miller (New Haven: Yale University Press, 1948), entry nos. 40, 50, 54, 80, 85, 110, and 111.

30. EPP, 617.

FOUR REPRESENTING AMERICA

1. Arnold, *Discourses in America* (New York: Macmillan, 1906), 196; Nietzsche's phrase is cited in Hermann Hummel, "Emerson and Nietzsche," *NEQ* 19, 1 (March 1946): 66; Conway, *Emerson at Home and Abroad* (Boston, 1882), 7; *The Letters of William James,* ed. Henry James (Boston: Atlantic Monthly Press, 1920), II, 190.

2. See *The Awakening,* chap. 24; James, *The Bostonians* (New York: Modern Library, 1956), 183, 35, 184; Adams, *The Education* (New York: Modern Library, 1931), 35; for Eliot's remark, see above, ch. 3, note 5.

3. Perry, *Emerson Today* (Princeton: Princeton University Press, 1931), 19.

4. Ibid., 32.

5. Anderson, *The Imperial Self* (New York: Knopf, 1971), 25, 31; Douglas. *The Feminization of American Culture* (New York: Knopf, 1977), 269–79; Ziff, *Literary Democracy* (New York: Viking Press, 1981), 46.

6. EJ, 10, 227.

7. EPP, 105–8; EJ, 369.

8. EEL, 587.

9. EPP, 399.

10. Holmes, *Ralph Waldo Emerson* (Boston, 1885), 4; for William Emerson and the Antinomian crisis, see Joel Porte, *Representative Man* (New York: Oxford University Press, 1979), 99–104; Spranger, cited in Robert Wohl, *The Generation of 1914* (Cambridge: Harvard University Press, 1979), 70.

11. EJ, 61; More, cited in *The Generation of 1914*, 205.

12. EJ, 54; EPP, 27.

13. EJ, 66; JMN 7, 64.

14. *Feminization of American Culture*, 20; EPP, 279; see A. Bartlett Giamatti, *The University and the Public Interest* (New York: Atheneum, 1981), 172–77.

15. EPP, 283.

16. EJ, 324.

17. EJ, 337.

18. EJ, 422.

19. EJ, 420; *Poetical Works of James Russell Lowell* (Boston: Houghton, Mifflin, 1890), II, 49.

20. "Fortune of the Republic," in *Emerson's Complete Works, Riverside Edition* (Boston: Houghton, Mifflin, 1883), XI, 402, 404.

21. Ibid., 412–13.

22. Ibid., 424, 425.

23. *Letters of Herman Melville*, eds. Merrell R. Davis and William H. Gilman (New Haven: Yale University Press, 1960), 77–78.

24. Cf. EPP, 281.

25. *The Letters of William James*, II, 194.

FIVE EMERSON AS JOURNALIST

1. JMN 11, 173; EJ, 408.

2. Parker, cited in Henry Steele Commager, *Theodore Parker: Yankee Crusader* (Boston: Beacon Press, 1960), 132; JMN 11, 378.

3. WALDEN, 148; JMN 11, 192–93.

4. EJ, 268–69.

5. For the passage in "Lecture on the Times," see EEL, 156.

6. EPP, 417–19; *Ralph Waldo Emerson* (Boston, 1885), 148.

7. EJ, 352–53.

8. EJ, 424. It is worth reminding ourselves that Everett shared the platform with Lincoln at Gettysburg on November 19, 1863, and delivered an interminable address that few people remember today.

9. *Emerson Today* (Princeton: Princeton University Press, 1931), 43 ff.

10. EJ, 55–611.

11. EJ, 158.

SIX EMERSON AT HARVARD

1. Robert E. Spiller, *The American Literary Revolution* (New York: Anchor Books, 1967), 197, 204, 47–48.

2. EPP, 68; *American Literary Revolution*, 125.

3. LETTERS 4, 179.

4. LETTERS 1, 182.

5. LETTERS 1, 93–94.

6. LETTERS 1, 65; EPP, 62.

7. EJ, 240–41; WALDEN, 71; *Whitman: Poetry and Prose* (New York: Library of America, 1996), 45; EEL, 1316.

8. EPP, 196; LETTERS 1, 63.

SEVEN HOLMES'S EMERSON

1. Cf. the observations of Holmes's own biographer, John T. Morse, Jr., in *Life and Letters of Oliver Wendell Holmes* (Boston: Houghton, Mifflin, 1896; reprinted, New York: Chelsea House, 1980, 2, 55 ff.).

EIGHT EMERSON'S FRENCH CONNECTION

1. Howard Mumford Jones, *America and French Culture, 1750–1848* (Chapel Hill: University of North Carolina Press, 1927), 569.

2. Susan L. Roberson, *Emerson in His Sermons: A Man-Made Self* (Columbia: University of Missouri Press, 1995), 173. See also EPP, 14. Throughout Emerson's sermons, Fénelon is mentioned positively more than a dozen times; Robert D. Richardson, Jr., *Emerson: The Mind on Fire* (Berkeley: University of California Press, 1995), 21; cf. 89–90; LETTERS 1, 24.

3. "Remarks on the Character and Writings of Fenelon," in *The Works of William Ellery Channing, D.D.* (Boston: American Unitarian Association, 1841), 1, 167–215.

4. Ralph L. Rusk, *The Life of Ralph Waldo Emerson* (New York: Columbia University Press, 1957), 76; JMN 6, 128; in LETTERS 7, 517, Emerson includes Fénelon in a list of "all saints."

5. CW 4, 87–91. The standard scholarly treatment of Emerson and Montaigne is still Charles Lowell Young, *Emerson's Montaigne* (New York: Macmillan, 1941).

6. CW 4, 98.

7. CW 4, 85.

8. CW 4, 53–55.

9. See Patricia A. Ward, "Madame Guyon et l'influence quiétiste aux États Unis," in *Madame Guyon: Rencontres autours de la vie et l'oeuvre*, ed. Joseph Beaude et al. (Grenoble: Jérôme Millon, 1997), 132–43; Cf. Emerson's journal entry for April 19, 1841: "St Simon paints a Fenelon as he sees him from the army and the saloons of Versailles, so that his Fenelon is a St Simon in surplice, & no Fenelon at all." See JMN 7, 430; CW 4, 95.

10. Baroness Staël-Holstein, *Germany* (London: John Murray, 1813), 3 vols. For further discussion of Madame de Staël's influence on Emerson and his circle, see my *In Respect to Egotism* (New York: Cambridge University Press, 1991), 23–29; *Emerson: The Mind on Fire*, 54; EJ, 61.

11. *Germany*, 3,109–13; JMN 3, 261; JMN 3, 172; *Germany*, 3, 388.

12. *Germany*, 3, 316–24. Albertine Necker de Saussure's remark is cited in the variorum edition of *De L'Allemagne* edited by La Comtesse Jean de Pange (Paris: Librairie Hachette, 1960), 5, 98: "Pendant ses accès de chagrin, elle lisait souvent Fénelon, trouvant chez cet auteur une connaissance admirable des peines de l'âme" [Whenever her spirit was troubled, she frequently read Fénelon, finding in this author an admirable awareness of spiritual pain]. The library at Broglie contains an edition of Fénelon's work underlined throughout in Madame de Staël's hand.

13. JMN 4, 83–84.

14. See Paul Viallaneix in *Relire Lamartine Aujourd'hui*, eds. Simone Bernard-Griffiths and Christian Croisille (Paris: Librairie Nizet, 1993), 340–41: "The young Lamartine learned, while reading [Chateaubriand's] *The Genius of Christianity* and above all *Germany,* to identify the 'infinite' as what consciousness perceives to be the immediate datum of existence—that which rebels against the mathematical logic taught at school. 'The Germans, he explained to Virieu, will go much further than we have been able to go, because they ground everything

in a true and sublime principle: God is infinite.' Lamartine's faithful confidant immersed himself, in his turn, in a study of the final chapters of Madame de Staël's work, which deals with 'religion' and 'enthusiasm.' And Lamartine thanked him for reinforcing the lesson that he himself had already drawn from *Germany:* 'You have found the true word: the infinite. I had said the same to myself frequently without, however, nailing it down clearly. I had it in my spirit and you have brought it out: that's it; and one must take it to heart; everything is there. It is the entire soul of man and, consequently, everything that can and must act on the soul in all the arts should hold to this principle and proffer it constantly"; Lamartine's "Life of Fenelon," in *Adventures of Telemachus by Fenelon,* ed. O. W. Wight (Boston: Houghton, Mifflin, 1896), 78.

15. *Emerson: The Mind on Fire,* 53; *Germany,* 3, 419.

16. *America and French Culture,* 439; LETTERS 1, 156.

17. For more information on the Follens, see Patricia A. Ward, "Fénelon among the New England Abolitionists," in *Christianity and Literature* 50, 1 (Autumn 2000): 79–93; *Works of Channing,* 1, 175; *Adventures of Telemachus,* 57.

18. See Ward, "Madame Guyon," passim. *The Dial* for April 1843 concludes with a "Catalogue of Books" assembled by Bronson Alcott and Charles Lane. Thoreau, who edited the number in Emerson's absence, calls this list of "mystic and theosophic lore" a "remarkable fact in our literary history." The catalogue contains seven books by Madame Guyon and six by Fénelon. Cf. LETTERS 7, 517; *America and French Culture,* 440.

19. LETTERS 7, 235.

20. LETTERS 7, 410–11; LETTERS 5, 169.

21. *Later Lectures* (Athens: University of Georgia Press, 2001) 1, 308–32. Brief excerpts from the lecture, unreliably transcribed, were published by Lestrois Parish in a 1935 pamphlet, *Emerson's View of France and the French.* The only extended discussion of the lecture I have found is in Maurice Gonnaud, *An Uneasy Solitude: Individual and Society in the Work of Ralph Waldo Emerson* (Princeton: Princeton University Press, 1987), 416–18. Professor Gonnaud, who read the lecture in manuscript many years ago while working on *Individu et société dans l'oeuvre de Ralph Waldo Emerson* (1964), finds Emerson persistently negative toward France and the French.

22. CW 4, 93.

23. *Germany,* 3, 46–55.

24. On Emerson and Napoleon, see Perry Miller, "Emersonian Genius and the American Democracy," in *Nature's Nation* (Cambridge: Harvard University Press, 1967).

25. *America and French Culture*, 556.

26. *Works of Channing*, 1, 176.

27. For evidence of Edwards' interest in Fénelon see Ward, "Fénelon among the New England Abolitionists," 81. Cf. Austin Warren, *New England Saints* (Ann Arbor: University of Michigan Press, 1956), 64–65.

28. Cf. *An Uneasy Solitude*, 397.

29. EJ, 404, 427; CW 4, 130; EJ, 426; CW 4, 131, 147.

30. *Emerson: The Mind on Fire*, 89.

31. EJ, 115; JMN 4, 300–301.

32. *Life of Ralph Waldo Emerson*, 164; on Emerson and the Quakers, see also *Emerson in His Sermons*, 194–96. In his *Transcendentalism in New England*, O. B. Frothingham draws attention to chapter 16 of George Bancroft's *History of the United States*, wherein Bancroft compares William Penn to John Locke. The latter's philosophy of "sensation" comes off second-best when set next to Penn's belief in George Fox's "Inner Light": "Penn, like Plato and Fenelon, maintained the doctrine so terrible to despots, that God is to be loved for His own sake, and virtue to be practised for its intrinsic loveliness."; JMN 3, 207.

33. EL 2, 92; *Germany*, 3, 294.

34. EL 2, 93–94; cited in *The Cambridge History of English and American Literature* (1907–21), 8, "The Age of Dryden." In an early sermon, Emerson names Fénelon as a Catholic who believed that "God is in our souls as our soul is in our bodies," then directly quotes Leighton to similar effect. See CS 3, 88–89.

35. JMN 16, 195; JMN 13, 279; Staël-Holstein, *Choix de Lettres*, ed. Georges Solovieff (Paris: Editions Klincksieck, 1970), 513–14: "I do not need to tell you that liberty and religion are linked in my thought; religion clarified, just liberty: that is the goal, the true path. I believe that mysticism, which is to say the religion of Fénelon, that which has its sanctuary in the heart, and that joins love and good works, is a reformation of the *Reformation,* a development of Christianity that unites all that is good in Catholicism and Protestantism and that distances itself entirely from the religion that reflects the political influence of priests."

NINE   HENRY THOREAU AND THE REVEREND POLUPHLOISBOIOS THALASSA

1. EPP, 407; WALDEN, 17; J, 9, 121; CC, 95; PJ 1, 286, 284.

2. WEEK, 297; Gaston Bachelard, *The Poetics of Reverie*, trans. Daniel Russell (Boston: Beacon Press, 1971), 14, 18; WEEK, 297.

3. PJ 2, 173–74; Henry Thoreau, EXCURSIONS, 201; Marx, intro. to *Excursions* (New York: Corinth Books, 1962), xiii; EXCURSIONS, 161.

4. Henry Nash Smith, *Virgin Land: The American West as Symbol and Myth* (Cambridge: Harvard University Press, 1950). See also Edwin Fussell, *Frontier: American Literature and the American West* (Princeton: Princeton University Press, 1965), 181 ff.; Gaston Bachelard, *The Psychoanalysis of Fire*, trans. Alan C. M. Ross (Boston: Beacon Press, 1964), 109.

5. EXCURSIONS, 205, 162; WEEK, 70; EXCURSIONS, 185, 167, 188–90.

6. WALDEN, 98; *Frontier*, 177; Gaston Bachelard, *The Poetics of Space*, trans. Maria Jolas (Boston: Beacon Press, 1969), 8; EXCURSIONS, 207 (I have corrected a misprint in the original edition here).

7. PJ 5, 13; PJ 5, 188; PJ 6, 235–36; PJ 5, 188; PJ 6, 133; J 5, 39; PJ 8, 88; J 5, 255; WALDEN 87; PJ 6, 236.

8. *Excursions* (1962), xiii; *Frontier*, 181; William Ellery Channing, *Thoreau: The Poet-Naturalist* (Boston: C. E. Goodspeed, 1902), 341; a notable exception, however, is a thoughtful essay by Jonathan Bishop, "The Experience of the Sacred in Thoreau's *Week*," *ELH* 33.1 (1966): 66–91. See, more recently, Alan D. Hodder, *Thoreau's Ecstatic Vision* (New Haven: Yale University Press, 2001); WEEK 314. Cf. Sherman Paul, *The Shores of America: Thoreau's Inward Exploration* (Urbana: University of Illinois Press, 1958), 198: "To ascend the river to its fount was to get to the beginning or youth of time, to the summit where water was mist and mingled with light, and all was a golden age."

9. WEEK, 84, 128; Bachelard, *The Psychoanalysis of Fire*, 71; WEEK, 300; WALDEN, 249; WEEK, 235–36. Thoreau tells us not only that the water of the Merrimack is yellow but also that his boat is painted green below to correspond with the element in which it rides. Walden Pond is both yellowish and green.

10. Gaston Bachelard, *L'Eau et les Rêves: Essai sur l'imagination de la matière* (Paris: Corti, 1942) 5; my translation; *The Psychoanalysis of Fire*, 90.

11. CC 47, 81, 140; EXCURSIONS, 189–90; CC 25, 100, 148, 215, 99–100, 52, 149, 51.

12. CC 51; *Shores of America*, 381; *Thoreau: The Poet-Naturalist*, 77; *Poetics of Space*, 198; CC 51–52; Wallace Stevens, *Collected Poems* (New York: Knopf,

1957), 29, 30. Thoreau's tendency in the direction of a kind of language mysticism was undoubtedly reinforced by his acquaintance with the writings of Charles Kraitsir, a Hungarian émigré and protégé of Elizabeth Peabody, who was a sort of linguistic genius for the Transcendentalists. In his *Glossology . . . A Treatise on the Nature of Language and on the Language of Nature* (1852), from which Thoreau copied extracts into his Fact Book, Kraitsir elaborated concretely on the Emersonian notion that the harmony between man's spirit and nature is expressed directly through words. In his "apocalyptic phraseology," Kraitsir went so far as to assign colors, feelings, and shapes to vowels; and in a long chapter on "Germs and Roots," he cites Plato's *Cratylus* at great length concerning the "natural propriety" of Greek. Homer is used as Socrates' principal example of the God-given natural force of words. In fact, Thoreau's interest in *Poluphloisboios Thalassa* might have been stimulated by his reading here that Phi and Sigma "denote blowing," with Lambda "the tongue glides," Alpha is "great," and Omega "round." For a brief general treatment of the Transcendentalists' interest in linguistic theories, see John B. Wilson, "Grimm's Law and the Brahmins," *New England Quarterly* 38.2 (1965): 234–39. See also Philip Gura, *The Wisdom of Words: Language, Theology, and Literature in the American Renaissance* (Middletown, Conn.: Wesleyan University Press, 1981). Gaston Bachelard insists in *L'Eau et les Rêves* "that the voices of water are hardly metaphoric, that the language of waters is a direct poetic reality, that streams and rivers *give voice* to the silent landscape with a strange fidelity, that the noisy waters teach both birds and men to sing, to speak, to repeat, and that, to sum it up, there is continuity between the voice of water and human speech" (22).

13. Stevens, *Collected Poems,* 29, 30, 28; EPP, 309, 409; CC, 166; Stevens, *Collected Poems,* 24.

14. CC, 96; WALDEN, 98, 330. Thoreau copied into his Fact Book the following passage from M. F. Maury's *The Physical Geography of the Sea* (1855): "the greatest depths at which the bottom of the sea has been reached with the plummet are in the North Atlantic Ocean, and the places where it has been fathomed do not show it to be deeper than twenty-five thousand feet." (See *Thoreau's Fact Book,* annotated and indexed by Kenneth Walter Cameron [Hartford: Transcendental Books, 1966].) One wonders just what sort of consolation Thoreau found in learning that the North Atlantic was scarcely five miles deep when he himself had discovered that the "bottomless" Walden Pond had a "remarkable depth" of one hundred and seven feet! The alert reader of *Cape Cod,* by the way, will notice that the crucial question of *bottomlessness* is central also to

Thoreau's comparison between Christian theology and the preaching of the sea. Thoreau devotes a portion of "The Plains of Nauset" to a summary of the life and work of Nauset's first minister, the Rev. Samuel Treat. Thoreau openly admires the rigor and consistency of this "Calvinist of the strictest kind" who proclaimed "the doctrine of terror"; and we are offered an impressive sample of Reverend Treat's pulpit rhetoric from a discourse on Luke 16.23 beginning "Thou must ere long go to the bottomless pit" (CC, 37–40).

15. *Collected Poems,* 30. Cf. Sherman Paul *The Shores of America,* 201: "Like his experience on Ktaadn, his experience with the ocean gave him a terrifying sense of otherness, of a primordial nature apart from the interests of man, and not easily conquered by thought."

16. CC, 59–60.

17. It seems to me likely that Melville's animadversions on the failure of charity owe something to Thoreau, for this part of *Cape Cod* was first published in the August 1855 number of *Putnam's Monthly* magazine, which Melville undoubtedly noticed since it contained his own "The Bell-Tower." Melville began to write *The Confidence-Man* sometime in the late fall or early winter of 1855; *Paradise Lost* 2: 891–96. It is interesting to note that Thoreau, in describing another confrontation with unmediated wildness in "Ktaadn," alludes to this same "illimitable Ocean" passage from *Paradise Lost:* "This was that Earth of which we have heard, made out of Chaos and Old Night" (see MW, 70).

18. Bachelard, *The Poetics of Space,* 5, 32; WALDEN, 194. For fire, compare the poems by Thoreau and Ellen Sturgis Hooper in "House-Warming"; for the pond, compare "It is no dream of mine . . ." and Thoreau's statement in "The Ponds" that Walden is "earth's eye; looking into which the beholder measures the depth of his own nature." Bachelard cites this sentence in his chapter on "intimate immensity" in *The Poetics of Space,* 209–10.

19. See, e.g., Walter Harding, *The Days of Henry Thoreau* (New York: Alfred A. Knopf, 1965), 361.

20. George Santayana, *Winds of Doctrine* (New York: Harper & Brothers, 1957), 213–15.

21. WEEK, 297.

TEN SOCIETY AND SOLITUDE

1. WALDEN, 323.

2. Perry Miller, "The Responsibility of Mind in a Civilization of Machines," *The American Scholar,* 31, 1 (1961): 1–19.

3. *Democracy in America,* trans. Henry Reeve and ed. Francis Bowen and Phillips Bradley (New York: Random House, 1945), II, 104, 80–81.

4. *Leaves of Grass and Selected Prose,* ed. Sculley Bradley (New York: Rinehart & Co., 1949), 1, 23; *The Correspondence of Henry David Thoreau,* ed. Walter Harding and Carl Bode (New York: New York University Press, 1958), 445.

5. *Emerson and Thoreau: Transcendentalists in Conflict* (Middletown, Conn.: Wesleyan University Press, 1966), 150–51.

6. *Studies in Classic American Literature,* reprinted in *The Shock of Recognition,* ed. Edmund Wilson (New York: Modern Library, 1955), 910; *The Golden Day* (Boston: Beacon Press, 1957), xxi.

7. JMN 15, 16; RP, 89–90; WALDEN, 329–30.

8. JMN 8, 70.

9. Cf. Leo Stoller, "Thoreau's Doctrine of Simplicity," in *Thoreau: A Collection of Critical Essays,* ed. Sherman Paul (Englewood Cliffs, N.J.: Prentice-Hall, 1962), 37 ff. See also David Robinson, *Apostle of Culture* (Philadelphia: University of Pennsylvania Press, 1982), 11–29; 'The Art of Life,—The Scholar's Calling," in *The Dial,* I, 2 (October 1840): 175–82.

10. PJ 1, 121.

11. T. S. Eliot, *The Complete Poems and Plays* (New York: Harcourt, Brace, 1952), 127; Søren Kierkegaard, *The Sickness unto Death,* trans. Walter Lowrie (New York: Anchor Books, 1955), 147.

12. WALDEN, 131–32, 129.

13. WALDEN, 134; Benedict de Spinoza, *Ethics; Preceded by On the Improvement of the Understanding,* ed. James Gutmann (New York: Hafner Publishing Co., 1957), 6; see also 270–80.

14. WALDEN, 135; Ralph Waldo Emerson, *Society and Solitude* (Boston: Fields, Osgood & Co., 1870), 14. The following quotations are from 8–9, 12.

15. George Santayana, "Society and Solitude," in *Soliloquies in England and Later Soliloquies* (New York: Charles Scribner's Sons, 1922), 119–22.

16. WALDEN, 136.

ELEVEN "GOD HIMSELF CULMINATES IN THE PRESENT MOMENT":
THOUGHTS ON THOREAU'S FAITH

1. PJ 1, 51; PJ 1, 47.

2. EPP, 69; PJ 1, 54; PJ 1, 56; EPP, 75.

3. PJ 1, 55; EPP, 408.

4. WEEK, 65, 67.

5. WEEK, 67, 70.

6. WEEK, 71.

7. WALDEN, 324–25.

8. *Collected Poems of Wallace Stevens* (New York: Knopf, 1957), 481; WALDEN, 95.

9. EEL, 578.

10. WALDEN, 96; Rimbaud, cited in Edmund Wilson, *Axel's Castle* (New York: Scribner's, 1959), 270–72.

11. WEEK, 382.

12. WALDEN, 95–97.

13. WALDEN, 98.

14. *Collected Poems*, 475.

15. WALDEN, 188; WEEK, 379.

16. EPP, 426, 69; WEEK, 380; *Collected Poems*, 375.

TWELVE   "IN WILDNESS IS THE PRESERVATION OF THE WORLD":
THE NATURAL HISTORY OF HENRY DAVID THOREAU

1. EPP, 58.

2. PJ 5, 469; EXCURSIONS, 65, 72.

3. *The Poetry of Earth*, ed. E. D. H. Johnson (New York: Atheneum, 1966), viii, xiii; John Hildebidle, *Thoreau: A Naturalist's Liberty* (Cambridge: Harvard University Press, 1983), 61, 37.

4. Clarence King, *Mountaineering in the Sierra Nevada* (New York: Penguin Books, 1989), 153.

5. Laura Dassow Walls, *Seeing New Worlds: Henry David Thoreau and Nineteenth-Century Natural Science* (Madison: University of Wisconsin Press, 1995), 115–16. For an excellent discussion of Thoreau as a "scientist," especially vis-à-vis Louis Agassiz, see Robert D. Richardson's Introduction to *Faith in a Seed*, ed. Bradley P. Dean (Washington, D.C.: Island Press, 1993); EXCURSIONS, 72.

6. WALDEN, 312; PJ 6, 236.

7. Sherman Paul, *For Love of the World* (Iowa City: University of Iowa Press, 1992), 7.

8. Cited in Lawrence Buell, *The Environmental Imagination* (Cambridge: Harvard University Press, 1995), 358.

9. E. B. White, *Essays* (New York: Harper Perennial, 1992), 298; WALDEN, 215, 317–18.

10. For the "phallus impudicus" entry see J 9, 115–17.

11. WALDEN, 91; J 9, 117.

12. WALDEN, 282, 138, 221.

13. PJ 6, 302.

14. J 11, 204; J 9, 43.

15. WALDEN, 219, 210.

16. D. H. Lawrence, *Apocalypse* (New York: Viking Press, 1932), 43, 199–200; Morton Paley, *Energy and the Imagination* (Oxford: Clarendon Press, 1970), 1–29, 248.

17. WALDEN, 313.

18. Sherman Paul, *For Love of the World*, 5; WALDEN, 314–15.

19. WALDEN, 234; Stevens, *Collected Poems* (New York: Knopf, 1957), 474.

20. EXCURSIONS, 194.

21. EXCURSIONS, 218; WEEK, 174.

THIRTEEN   WRITING AND READING NEW ENGLANDLY

1. *The Renewal of Literature: Emersonian Reflections* (New York: Random House, 1987); *Poetry and Pragmatism* (Cambridge: Harvard University Press, 1992).

2. For the text of "Prudence," see EEL, 357–67.

3. For the text of "Heroism," see EEL, 371–81.

4. EEL, 476; ibid., 578; "Art and Criticism," in *Complete Works of Ralph Waldo Emerson*, ed. Edward Waldo Emerson (Boston: Houghton Mifflin, 1903), XII, 303.

5. WALDEN, 102.

6. *Poetry and Pragmatism*, 173; Paul de Man, *The Resistance to Theory* (Minneapolis: University of Minnesota Press, 1986), 21–26.

7. *Poetry and Pragmatism*, 178–79. I might note here that I myself studied with Brower in the graduate English program at Harvard though I never became part of his Hum 6 group. I admired Brower, but I found him overly fastidious and his method rather antiseptic, as if "ideas" or "values" were germs that had at all costs to be kept out of literary study. Poetic rhetoric that sounded as if it were making an actual claim on our belief systems was decidedly not congenial to him. For example, I concluded one of my papers for him by fearlessly quoting "Beauty is truth, truth beauty," and found, when I got it back, a terse marginal comment in his fine, small hand: "Bah!" Though I wasn't certain

whether Brower's scorn was directed at Keats or at my own naiveté, I understood the nature of my faux pas and never ventured to mention "truth" or "beauty" in future papers for him, though I retained the terms for other papers with different teachers (such as I. A. Richards, who was much less fussy about that sort of thing). Poirier seems to me still excessively under the influence of Brower's strictures about literary language that smacks of the religious or ethical, as when he notes (I assume with approval) that "Brower could never read aloud the ending [of *The Waste Land*], 'Shanti shanti shanti [sic],' without showing evident distaste." That is what I mean by Brower's fastidiousness. Merely as a form of calculation, Eliot's ending guaranteed that his poem would be noticed (who else, in English poetry, had ever dared do such a thing?). But it also represents a piece of cultural DNA, reminding the alert reader that Harvard had gone mad for Sanskrit literature, starting at least in the 1890s, and this desire to reach out from a provincial New England college to the great intellectual world beyond touched both Eliot and his sometime teacher, Santayana (as it had touched Emerson and Thoreau before them). Similarly, Poirier notes that the Hum 6 staff were "anxious to deny [themselves] the embarrassing Big Talk" of other Humanities courses like "Ideas of Good and Evil." But why be afraid of such things? Harvard freshmen, like students everywhere, loved to chew over these "resounding terms," and they were probably better off doing so under the controlled conditions of the classroom than in residential bull-sessions where the pseudodoxia always epidemic among undergraduates could flourish unchecked. See *Poetry and Pragmatism*, 171–93.

8. See William James, *Pragmatism* (New York: Longmans, Green, 1907), esp. 43–81; Stevens, *Collected Poems* (New York: Knopf, 1957), 203.

9. *Poetry and Pragmatism*, 133; *Works of George Santayana, Triton Edition* (New York; Scribner's, 1937), 7, 107; EPP, 37.

10. For Santayana's view of James see *Character and Opinion in the United States* (New York: Anchor Books, 1956), 39–60.

11. *Physical Order and Moral Liberty*, ed. John and Shirley Lachs (Nashville: Vanderbilt University Press, 1969), 232; Stevens, *Collected Poems*, 322, 320, 247.

12. Cavell, *In Quest of the Ordinary* (Chicago: University of Chicago Press, 1988), 40; *Poetry and Pragmatism*, 133.

13. Cavell's "The Politics of Interpretation" can be found in *Themes out of School* (San Francisco: North Point Press, 1984), 27–59.

14. As, for example, in this astounding remark in "The Resistance to Theory": "Literature is fiction not because it somehow refuses to acknowledge

'reality,' but because it is not *a priori* certain that language functions according to principles which are those, or which are *like* those, of the phenomenal world. It is therefore not *a priori* certain that literature is a reliable source of information about anything but its own language." I call this astounding not only because of its seeming disingenuousness but also because of its intellectual bad faith. Though it may not be "*a priori* certain" that language gives us access to "the phenomenal world" (is there any other?), it is certainly necessary that language ally itself with experience, otherwise we would be essentially without access to the world. Is it possible to care about a "literature" such as de Man appears to imagine—one that is securely isolated in its own linguistic cocoon? I believe that neither Emerson nor Cavell could be content with a language, "literary" or otherwise, that (to paraphrase Dickinson) refuses to "consent" to the world. See *The Resistance to Theory*, 11.

15. EEL, 1055.

BIBLIOGRAPHICAL NOTE

Previously published chapters first appeared as follows:

ONE: "Emerson, Thoreau, and the Double Consciousness," in *The New England Quarterly* (March 1968): 40–50.

TWO: "Transcendental Antics," in *Veins of Humor*, ed. Harry Levin, Harvard English Studies 3 (Cambridge: Harvard University Press, 1972), 167–83.

THREE: "The Problem of Emerson," in *Uses of Literature*, ed. Monroe Engel, Harvard English Studies 4 (Cambridge: Harvard University Press, 1973), 85–114.

FOUR: "Representing America," in *The Cambridge Companion to Ralph Waldo Emerson*, ed. Joel Porte and Saundra Morris (New York: Cambridge University Press, 1999), 1–12.

SEVEN: "Holmes's Emerson," preface to Oliver Wendell Holmes, *Ralph Waldo Emerson* (New York: Chelsea House, 1980), xvii–xxvii.

EIGHT: "Emerson's French Connection," in *Q/W/E/R/T/Y* 12 (October 2002): 175–86.

NINE: "Henry Thoreau and the Reverend Poluphloisboios Thalassa," in *The Chief Glory of Every People*, ed. Matthew J. Bruccoli (Carbondale: Southern Illinois University Press, 1973), 191–210.

TEN: "Society and Solitude," in *ESQ* 19.3 (3rd Quarter, 1973): 131–40.

ELEVEN: "God Himself Culminates in the Present Moment": Thoughts on Thoreau's Faith," in *Thoreau Society Bulletin* 144 (Summer 1978): 1–4.

THIRTEEN: "Writing and Reading New Englandly," in *The New England Quarterly* 66 (June 1993): 289–98.

INDEX